Data Mining Your Website

Data Mining Your Website

Jesus Mena

**Digital
Press**

Boston • Oxford • Auckland • Johannesburg • Melbourne • New Delhi

Butterworth–Heinemann supports the efforts of American Forests and the Global ReLeaf program in its campaign for the betterment of trees, forests, and our environment.

Library of Congress Cataloging-in-Publication Data

Mena, Jesus.
    Data mining your website / Jesus Mena.
        p.   cm.
    ISBN 1-55558-222-2 (alk. paper)
        1. Information technology—Management.   2. Data mining.
    3. Internet marketing.   4. Business enterprises—Computer networks.
    5. Web sites.   I. Title.
    HD30.2.M455   1999
    006.3—dc21   99-22694
                                        CIP

British Library Cataloguing-in-Publication Data
A catalogue record for this book is available from the British Library.

The publisher offers special discounts on bulk orders of this book.
For information, please contact:
Manager of Special Sales
Butterworth–Heinemann
225 Wildwood Avenue
Woburn, MA 01801-2041
Tel: 781-904-2500
Fax: 781-904-2620

For information on all Digital Press publications available, contact our World Wide Web home page at: http://www.bh.com/digitalpress

10 9 8 7 6 5 4 3 2 1

Printed in the United States of America

To Megs

Contents

CHAPTER 4   TEN STEPS TO MINING YOUR DATA   119

CHAPTER 5   THE TOOLS   155

CHAPTER 6   THE DATA COMPONENTS   193

CHAPTER 7   THE PROVIDERS   227

CHAPTER 8 E-RETAILING 267

mine2.com

The Web is like an organism made up of millions of cells that are all connected, intertwined, and communicating. It is a massive world-wide creature that is continuously evolving, spawning, and changing; since its birth, it has already mutated into a new type of species, where millions of computers and consumers connect to every company in the world and their product inventory databases. In this organic environment of constant ferment, the consumers drive product availability, features, and pricing. Electronic retailing, which is supported and nurtured in this environment itself, mimics the mechanisms of a single-cell organism—adapting to the needs, tastes, habits, and preferences of its customers. Billions of business transactions flow and evolve, subtly transforming consumers and retailers in this dynamic marketplace and the relationships between them.

This book is about biological-based business practices—processes and tools that mimic biological functions. The mining of website transactional data with artificial intelligence-based tools (programs designed to mimic human functions) is an attempt to recognize, anticipate, and learn the buying habits and preferences of customers in this new evolutionary business environment. It is of paramount importance that the retailer in a networked economy such as this be adaptive and receptive to the needs of its customers. In this expansive, competitive, and volatile environment, data mining will be a critical process impacting a retailer's long-term success, where failure to quickly react, adapt, and evolve can translate into customer attrition in the click of a mouse.

The Idle Portal

My decision to write this book stems in part from a series of e-mails I had with a marketing director from one of the major search engine companies. Like its competitors, this Internet company was expanding its services and products at a frantic pace. It was growing and moving at "Internet time," as they say, through a dizzying array of acquisitions, deals, partnerships, alliances, and redesigns. However, in its rush to expand its share of the marketplace and stay ahead of its competitors, it was failing to leverage one of its most important weapons—its knowledge about its visitors. As our e-mail exchange progressed, the magnitude of the problems facing most websites, and how data mining could assist companies on the Internet in coping with the millions of customer interactions they were accumulating on a daily basis, became clear to me.

This portal, like dozens of its rivals, was making an effort to personalize the content it provided to its visitors through its "myportal.com" feature (see Figure 1–1). In doing so it was soliciting important personal information from them via registration forms, which was by itself generating valuable databases for mining. More important, this same database could provide the foundation for obtaining additional demographic and household information for detailed profiles about visitor preferences, lifestyles, and consuming habits.

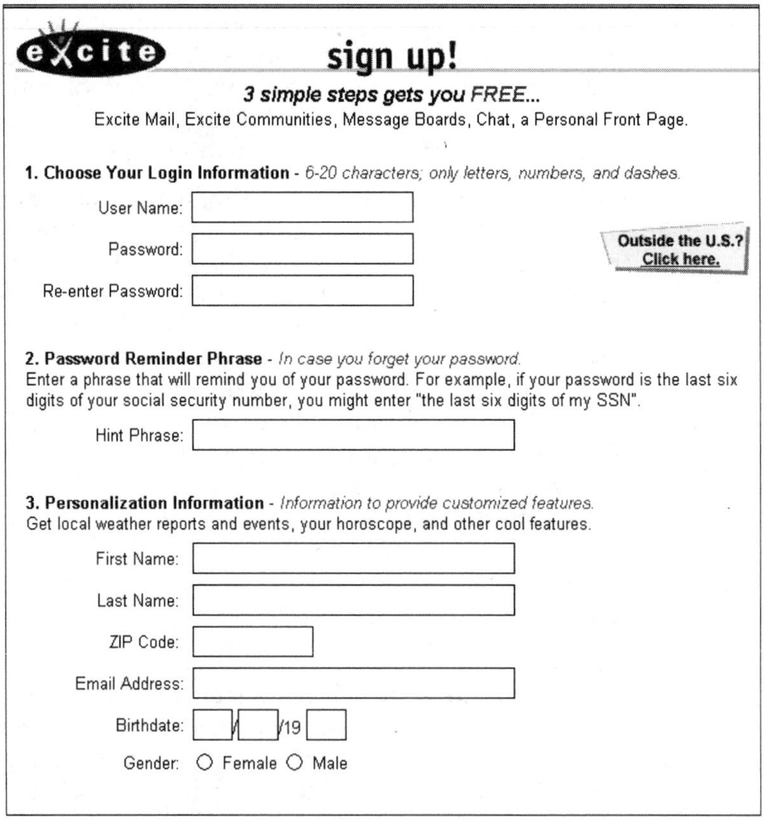

Figure 1–1A
The personaliza-tion of portals.

eXcite **sign up!**

3 simple steps gets you FREE...
Excite Mail, Excite Communities, Message Boards, Chat, a Personal Front Page.

1. Choose Your Login Information - *6-20 characters; only letters, numbers, and dashes.*

User Name:

Password:

Re-enter Password:

Outside the U.S.? Click here.

2. Password Reminder Phrase - *In case you forget your password.*
Enter a phrase that will remind you of your password. For example, if your password is the last six digits of your social security number, you might enter "the last six digits of my SSN".

Hint Phrase:

3. Personalization Information - *Information to provide customized features.*
Get local weather reports and events, your horoscope, and other cool features.

First Name:

Last Name:

ZIP Code:

Email Address:

Birthdate: / /19

Gender: ○ Female ○ Male

Figure 1–1B
The personalization of portals.

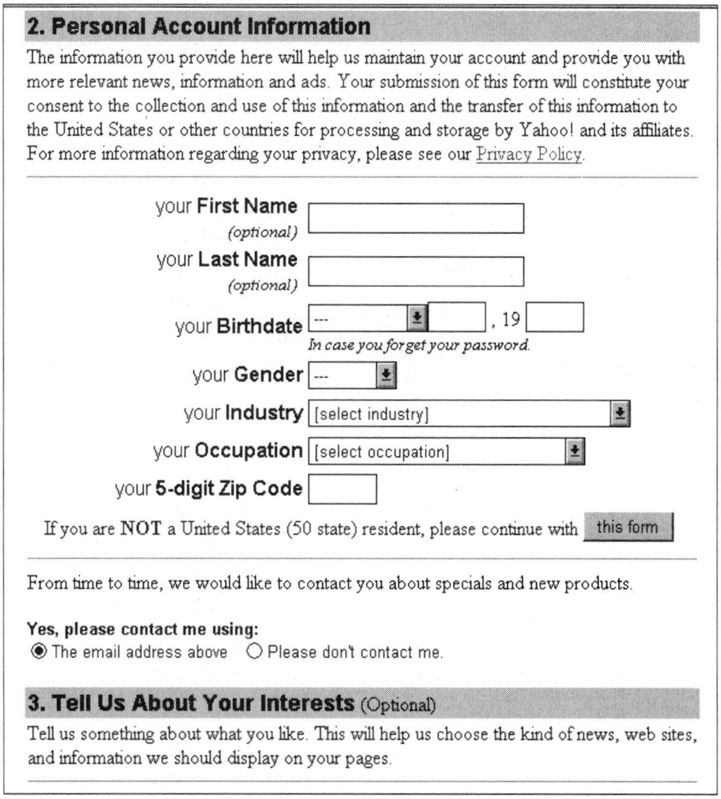

2. Personal Account Information
The information you provide here will help us maintain your account and provide you with more relevant news, information and ads. Your submission of this form will constitute your consent to the collection and use of this information and the transfer of this information to the United States or other countries for processing and storage by Yahoo! and its affiliates. For more information regarding your privacy, please see our Privacy Policy.
your First Name (optional)
your Last Name (optional)
your Birthdate --- , 19
In case you forget your password.
your Gender ---
your Industry [select industry]
your Occupation [select occupation]
your 5-digit Zip Code
If you are NOT a United States (50 state) resident, please continue with this form
From time to time, we would like to contact you about specials and new products.
Yes, please contact me using:
The email address above
Please don't contact me.
3. Tell Us About Your Interests (Optional)
Tell us something about what you like. This will help us choose the kind of news, web sites, and information we should display on your pages.

Figure 1–1C
The personalization of portals.

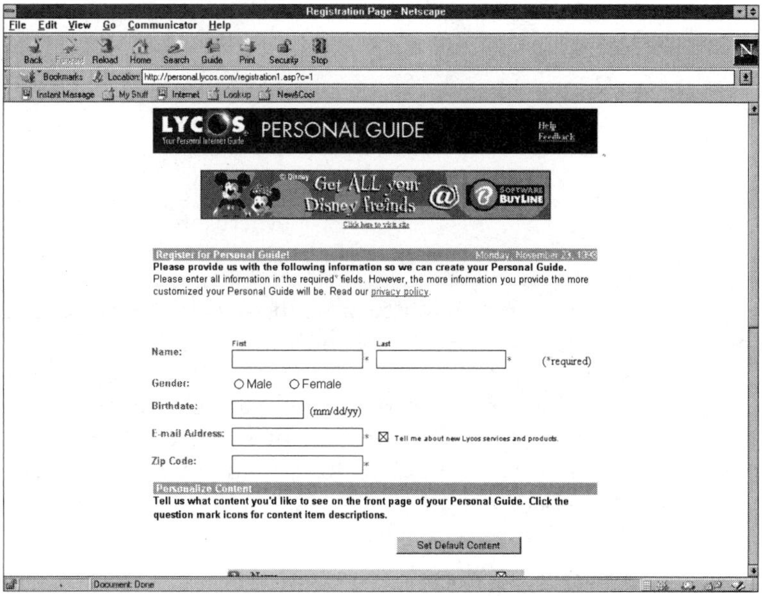

Registration Page - Netscape
File Edit View Go Communicator Help
Back Forward Reload Home Search Guide Print Security Stop
Bookmarks Location: http://personal.lycos.com/registration1.asp?c=1
Instant Message My Stuff Internet Lookup New&Cool
LYCOS PERSONAL GUIDE
Help
Feedback
Get ALL your Disney friends @ SOFTWARE BUYLINE
Register for Personal Guide!
Please provide us with the following information so we can create your Personal Guide.
Please enter all information in the required* fields. However, the more information you provide the more customized your Personal Guide will be. Read our privacy policy.
Name: First Last (*required)
Gender: Male Female
Birthdate: (mm/dd/yy)
E-mail Address: Tell me about new Lycos services and products.
Zip Code:
Personalize Content
Tell us what content you'd like to see on the front page of your Personal Guide. Click the question mark icons for content item descriptions.
Set Default Content
Document: Done

However, this search engine company really did not know who it was attracting or who was leaving its website. It did not know who its most valuable visitors were, or why. Like many major and small websites, this Internet company was discarding the valuable intelligence it was gathering every hour of every day—it was not mining the information it was accumulating from its millions of visitors. Although it was moving in the direction of data mining (due to pressure from advertisers), it did not know the characteristics and behavior of its visitors. It was placing ads in front of visitors based on the keywords they entered, rather than observed patterns modeled from data mining. It was a hardwired solution to an application ideally suited to modeling of observed human behavior.

Mining Data

Data mining, in a nutshell, is inductive data analysis. When data is too large and complex to be examined by humans, a summation in the form of a ratio or a formula can often reveal a pattern. The voluminous amounts of data generated from a website, for example, often hide patterns that reveal conditions when visitors are likely to make purchases or click on certain ads or banners.

IF	domain	AOL	
AND	keyword	broncos	
AND	gender	male	
AND	age	18–49	
THEN	ad	ESPN	68%
		AUTOTEL	18%
		Amazon	9%
		Microsoft	5%

Data mining software can reveal how the value of one field in a database is affected by the value of other fields. For example a field such as "total purchases" may be affected by other values or fields in your logs or forms database, such as the visitor's age, gender, referral engine, or keywords he or she used. In this example, "total purchases" is the field to be explained or predicted (that is, it is the *dependent variable* or *output* of your analysis) while the other fields are the inputs to your data mining model (the *conditions* or *independent variables*):

Value to Predict	Values or Conditions to Consider
Total Purchases (Output)	*Age, Gender, Engine, Keywords*
1	32, Female, Excite, children's software
2	43, Male, Yahoo, math software
3	53, Male, Infoseek, software

Data mining software enables us to relate the field to predict (in the above table, "total purchases") with the other fields in the database. The output from the data mining analysis can detail this relationship in the form of a decision tree diagram, IF/THEN rules, or a mathematical formula. The score obtained from this analysis can be used to grade new visitors based on their propensity to make purchases equal to the amount modeled via the data mining analysis.

Data mining, then, can be defined as the iterative process of detecting and extracting these patterns from large databases: it's *pattern-recognition.*

Data mining lets us identify "signatures" hidden in large databases, as well as learn from repeated examples. It lets us create models for the detection of, say, future potential customers likely to make a large number of total purchases. Data mining involves various solutions, techniques, and technologies, sometimes in combination, such as predictive modeling and customer profiling, arrived at via various techniques including association, classification, clustering, estimation, optimization, segmentation, sequencing, prediction, and visualization.

For the portal company, for example, data mining could be used to predict which visitors will click on what ads or banners by constructing a model based on observations of prior visitors who have behaved both positively and negatively to the advertisement banner. Another end product of data mining is an analysis of these clickthroughs that discovers and describes the factors (e.g., connect time) and the attributes of respondents (e.g., gender) who responded to an ad. This can provide you a profile of who is likely to respond to future ads and assist you in the design of future banners and campaigns.

Data mining is *not* query- or user-driven, nor is it a cumulative traffic report of hits to your site. Data mining is instead driven by the need to uncover the hidden undercurrents in the data, such as the "features" of the visitors generating the hits to your site. So far most analyses of websites data have involved "traffic reports," of which most are geared toward providing cumulative accounts of server TCP/IP-specific browser-to-server activity. Most server analysis packages lack the ability to provide any true business insight about customer demographics and online behavior, although some are moving in that direction as electronic commerce heats up.

Current traffic analysis tools, like Accrued, Andromedia, HitList, NetIntellect, NetTracker, and WebTrends, are geared at providing high-level predefined reports about domain names, IP addresses, browsers, cookies, and other machine-to-machine activity. These software packages originated from the need to report on the activity of the *server* and not on the behavior of its *visitors*. These server activity reports simply do not provide the type of bottom-line analysis that retailers, service providers, marketers, and advertisers in the business world have come to demand.

Data mining obviously requires the strategic use of a special type of software: one that is based on artificial intelligence technologies, such as self-organizing or back propagating neural networks or genetic and machine-learning algorithms. It may involve using the output from these tools with graphs and maps or incorporating code into production systems or automated e-mail generators. However, data mining is much more than its software tools; it is a *process* that involves a set of methodologies and procedures for extracting and preparing the data and then incorporating the solutions into your business and website. Data mining, for example, can involve the strategic capturing of visitor information via registration forms, merging of this online data with additional demographics, and then analyzing it with powerful pattern recognition software for the creation of predictive models. The formats of data mining are as varied and diverse as the multiple approaches and technologies. What you get out of data mining will to a large extent depend on what you require from it: it may be executable C code, SQL syntax, a 3D graph or map, a decision trees, or a set of rules. The end product of data mining, however, is *insight* about the identity and preferences of your online customers.

Most often, data mining is about providing business and marketing solutions using a combination of resources and techniques—a combination driven by not just the data mining tools you use, but also your IT resources, the analysts' skills, the quality of the data available for the analysis, and the support of the marketing and web team members. Data mining often requires developing some strategic techniques for preparing your server data and enhancing its value. Most of the data in today's systems, such as web servers, were designed for transaction processing, not for analysis. In the mining of website databases you will be involved in working with structured data, such as logs files and databases created from registration or purchase forms. You will most likely be working with either relational tables or flat text files, not with unstructured data like sound, video, paper, and digital feeds—the type of data with which the analysts in Langley, Virginia, must wrestle.

Nothing New

Today the goal for marketers is to know and serve every customer, one at a time, and to build long-term, mutually beneficial relationships. Data mining is the key to this customer knowledge and intimacy. For years marketers have been using databases to get a picture of their customers. Using data mining tools they can also compile a composite profile to predict which of their customers are most likely to buy a given product and service or respond to certain communication. Artificial intelligence (AI) technology in the form of data mining has been in use by:

- Cellular phone companies, to stop "churn" (customer attrition)
- Financial services firms, for portfolio and risk management
- Credit card companies, to detect fraud and set pricing
- Mail catalogers, to lift their response rates
- Retailers, for market basket analyses

These companies typically store their customer information in massive data warehouses where it is used for business intelligence, decision support, and relational marketing. To improve on the quality of their internal database, these firms have been merging their internal customer and transactional data with demographic and household information purchased from data resellers like Acxiom, Equifax, Metromail, Polk, and others. They do this in order to enhance their knowledge about their customers' lifestyles and to find out what kind of products and services they consume. Through the use of powerful pattern-recognition technologies incorporated in today's data mining suites, these firms have been attempting to anticipate their customers' behavior—will they respond, will they flee, will they pay, and (most often), will they *buy*, and if so, what, when, and where.

One of the world's largest data mining applications is that of Wal-Mart, which individually profiles every one of their 2,900 stores 52 weeks a year for product demands on over 700 million unique store/item combinations. Through data mining Wal-Mart is able to anticipate demand and thus reduce overhead, inventory costs, and stock. It is able to position the preferred type of mouthwash and dog food in front of the right consumers. This physical retailer uses NeoVista data mining software to be able to anticipate their customers' demands very accurately, similar to the way electronic retailers like Amazon are beginning to want to know how to position the right products online and manage their inventory in the back-end more effectively.

Depending on the type and detail of customer information a company has, such as ZIP code, date of birth, prefix, etc., additional information can be appended from data resellers and modeling vendors. For example, industry-specific scores can be purchased from such companies as Fair, Isaac, or Experian, which assign risk or value to individuals. Banks, insurance, and credit card companies commonly use these scores in determining what product offers to make to their clients or potential prospects. Coupled with enhanced customer information, these firms are using data mining technologies and techniques to drive their decisions and knowledge about their customers. Of course there are other data mining applications in use, such as quality control, monitoring production processes, and law enforcement, but the bulk of the applications (as with the mining of websites) are customer-centric, in which client behavior and knowledge of their preferences is the golden nugget being sought.

Mining Online

Websites today find themselves competing for customer loyalty and dollars in markets where it costs little for customers to switch to competitors. The electronic commerce landscape is evolving into a fast, competitive marketplace where millions of online transactions are being generated from log files and registration forms every hour of every day, and online shoppers browse by electronic retailing sites with their finger poised on their mouse, ready to buy or click on should they not find what they are looking for—that is, should the content, wording, incentive, promotion, product, or service of a website not meet their preferences. In other words, it is a market where browsers are attracted and retained based on how well the retailer remembers their needs and whims.

In such a hyper-competitive marketplace, the strategic use of customer information is critical to survival. As such, AI in the form of data mining has become a mainstay to doing business in fast-moving crowded markets. In accelerated markets the margins and profits go to the quick and responsive players who are able to leverage predictive models to anticipate customer behavior and preferences. Data mining of customer information is required in order to make decisions about which clients are the most profitable and desirable and what their characteristics are in order to find more customers just like them—the type of customer profiles and business knowledge electronic retailers and advertisers are beginning to expect from the Web after years of heavy investments and marginal ROIs (returns on investment).

The savviest retailers utilize sophisticated data mining software that is powered by genetic algorithm (GA) technology to optimize their inventory delivery systems based on consumer preferences and profiles. GAs are programs that replicate the process of evolution (selection, crossover, and mutation) in their search for an optimized solution from a given set of items. For example, GAs in combination with neural networks are being used by some retailers to not only control what inventory is placed in what store, but also design the stores themselves, leading to changes in everything from shelf heights to parking spaces. So if GAs can be used to optimize the design and layout of physical stores, such as a Wal-Mart or Sears, think what they could do to optimize the design of a large electronic retailing website like Amazon.

Several varied attempts are being made to personalize the browsing experience of website visitors, including collaborative filtering (Firefly) and the aggregate pooling of cookies through ad networks (DoubleClick). However, few companies involved in electronic retailing are looking at data mining technology for the analysis, modeling, and prediction of customer behavior. Some major portals are using software from Aptex, which is a spin-off from HNC, the world's largest neural network company, to position the appropriate banner and ad in front of "right" visitors based on Aptex's proprietary text and neural net technology. The cost and maintenance of this sophisticated type of software, however, is too steep for most commercial websites.

In the end, the mining and identification of your visitors' profiles can provide you an insight into what type of messages, banners, ads, offers, incentives, products, and services you want to place in front of them. Through the analysis of your website data—after it has been commingled with household and demographic information—your firm can begin to compile a profile of your potential future clients. The mining of your web data is also a strategic necessity for creating a lasting relation with your current customers and establishing a profitable online storefront. As previously mentioned, data mining often involves a combination of technologies that are able to provide assorted solutions and formats.

How Data Mining Answers Key Business Questions

Classification/Prediction

Who will buy, what will they buy, and how much will they buy? These types of business questions can be answered via data mining. They involve classification and prediction (which is a form of classification into the future) and can best be accomplished through the use of neural networks and genetic algorithms (see Figure 1–2). This type of inductive data analysis can be used to predict who will buy or how much they are likely to buy.

Neural and polynomial networks can be used to construct predictive models in order to anticipate your customers' behavior and their propensity to respond to ads, banners, and offers and (of course) their propensity to make online purchases. These predictive models are constructed out of observed behavior of current visitors and customers and are designed to predict the behavior of future visitors. As with fraud-detection models created with neural networks, a web-based model is trained with a sampling of positive (Sale) and negative (No Sale) customer accounts. A back-propagation neural network will recycle through thousands of samples until it learns to recognize the features and patterns made by the visitors to your web-

Figure 1–2
View of a network with multiple inputs designed to predict a response.

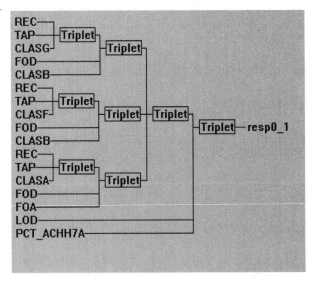

Figure 1–3
*Data mining
instrument
monitoring the
accuracy to a
model.*

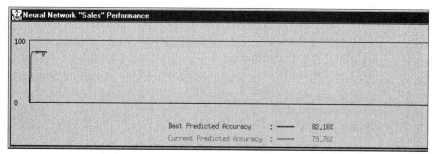

Figure 1–3
*Data mining
instrument
monitoring the
accuracy to a
model.*

site who made purchases or clicked through certain ads or banners. (See Figure 1–3.)

The end product of neural network analyses is usually C code, which can be used to target future visitors to your site via e-mail with product-specific offers. The C code itself is a set of weights, or a formula, that uses the inputs of the model to compute a projected output or score. This score is usually in the form of a binary output such as "0 = will not buy, or 1 = will buy." The output can also be a continuous value, such as the projected amount of purchases a visitor is likely to make. Here is an example of C code that can be extracted and used to predict propensity to purchase models:

```
double *purchase(double inarr[])
{
  /* visitor_age—Triplet */
  visitor_age  = 0 - 22.0566 - 40.4871*node5 - 18.3542*pow2(node5)
        + 0.174813*pow3(node5) - 68.848*node31
        - 156.303*node5*node31 - 83.2704*pow2(node5)*node31
        - 44.5781*pow2(node31) - 37.7005*node5*pow2(node31)
        - 0.0442751*pow3(node31) - 64.3699*node32
        - 54.3879*node5*node32 - 185.61*node31*node32
        - 156.467*node5*node31*node32 -
        - 0.109251*pow2(node32) - 0.272628*node31*pow2(node32)
        - 0.00897233*pow3(node32) ;
```

Segmentation

What are the different types of visitors to your website? Segmentation analysis using machine-learning algorithms can break down visitors to a website into unique groups with individual behavior. (See Figure 1–4.) These stratified groupings can then be used to make statistical projections, such as the potential amount of purchases they are likely to make.

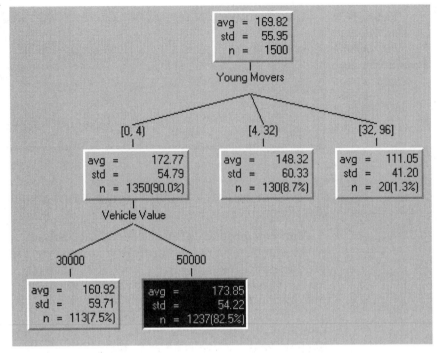

Figure 1–4
Segmentation of projected sales according to demographics of visitors.

Business rules can also be extracted directly from the web data during this type of segmentation analysis:

IF	search keyword is	*"math software"*
AND	age is	38–42
AND	gender	male
THEN	average projected sale amount is	$79.95

Segmentation analysis can take the form of a graphical decision tree (see Figure 1–5), where the average sales are lower to the left and higher to the right. The splits in the tree are determined by the transactional *conditions*, such as the connect time or domain, or by the visitors' demographics, such as their age or number of children, or on the basis of their consumer class according to their ZIP code.

The IF-THEN rules extracted from segmentation analysis can also be concise statements describing specific market segments:

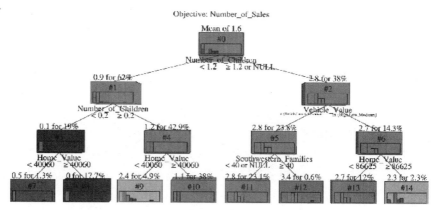

Figure 1–5
One common data mining format is a decision tree, which segments a database.

Condition	Attribute	
IF	Number of Children	>= 1.2
AND	Vehicle Value	Luxury
AND	Southwestern Families	>= 40%
THEN	Average Sale	3.4 (Node #12)

Or,

Condition	Attribute	
IF	Sub-Domain is	AOL
AND	Gender is	MALE
AND	Age is	37–42
AND	Is from ZIP Code	"High Rise Renter" 78–85%
THEN Will Purchase	Probability Score 81%	

Association

What relationships exist between your visitors and your products? Still another type of data mining analysis looks for hidden associations in your data, such as gender, age, domains, etc.

In the analysis shown in Figure 1–6, a relationship was found between the search keywords and product lines. Several data mining,

Figure 1–6
The stronger the association, the bolder the links.

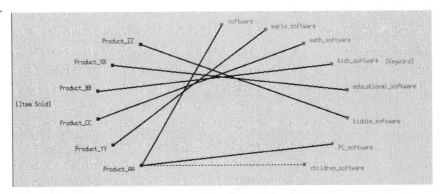

Figure 1–7
Summary report of links found at a website.

```
STRONG LINKS:
   Item Sold = Product_AA, Keyword = software (573)
   Item Sold = Product_YY, Keyword = mario_software (250)
   Item Sold = Product_CC, Keyword = math_software (211)
   Item Sold = Product_BB, Keyword = kids_software (187)
   Item Sold = Product_XX, Keyword = educational_software (181)
   Item Sold = Product_ZZ, Keyword = kiddie_software (74)
   Item Sold = Product_AA, Keyword = PC_software (53)

MEDIUM LINKS:

WEAK LINKS:
   Item Sold = Product_AA, Keyword = children_software (3)
```

visualization, and web analysis software programs provide this type of association output. In this instance we are using a data mining tool that not only provides a visual representation of the strong links between keywords and particular product lines, but it also generates a narrative summary report (Figure 1–7).

Association rules and graphs associate a particular conclusion (e.g., the purchase of a particular product) with a set of conditions, such as the purchase of several other products. Association rule algorithms automatically find the associations and present them via visualization techniques. The advantage of this type of association analysis over segmentation decision tree analysis is that association can exist between any of the attributes. A decision tree algorithm will only build rules with a single conclusion

Figure 1–8
Clustering of visitors based on the search engines they used to arrive at this website.

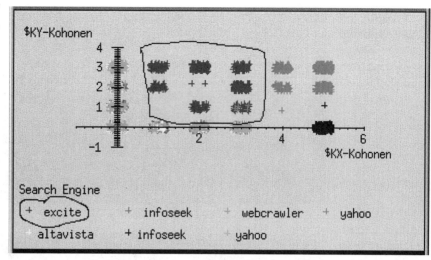

whereas association algortihms attempt to find rules that may have different conclusions.

Clustering

What are the groupings hidden in your data? Yet another format of data mining is that of *clustering,* which is commonly used to search for unique groupings within a data set. (See Figure 1–8.) A special type of neural network, known as a Kohonen network, or a Self-Organizing Map (SOM), is used to perform this type of analysis. An SOM is a form of "unsupervised learning" that organizes itself around distinct clusters in a data set without input from the analyst. SOMs are commonly used by retailers in market basket analysis to search for groupings between products that tend to sell in combination. SOMs can also be used to search for clusters in web data in order to find both the cross-selling patterns of products, as well as distinct clusters, such as the groupings of unique visitors' traits.

Visualization

What are the distributions and patterns in my website data? The human eye is critical in the mining of your data. Visualization can take many forms. For example, in Figures 1–9, 1–10, and 1–11, we have three increasingly narrowed geographical views of a website's visitors as seen from the ZIP codes as submitted in its registration form.

Figure 1–9
Most visitors to this website come from California and Texas.

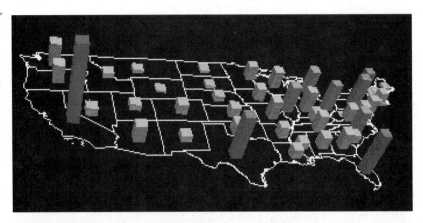

Figure 1–10
This data mining tool allows the user to drill down for further analysis.

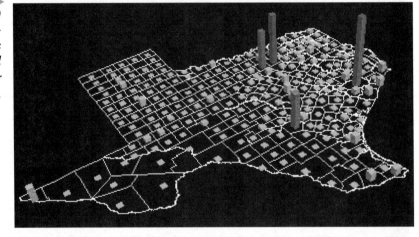

Figure 1–11
Color and height represent a higher than average amount of visitors.

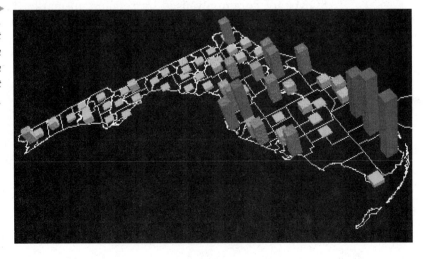

Optimization

How can you maximize your online presence and sales? Lastly, genetic algorithms (GAs) can be used to optimize your website presence and online sales. (See Figure 1–12.) As previously noted, GAs are optimization techniques and programs that use processes such as genetic selection, crossover, and mutation for the solution based on the concept of natural evolution. (See Figure 1–13.) For example, a GA in a data mining tool can be used to try thousands of settings and combinations of inputs in the fine-tuning of a neural network. Neural networks and genetic algorithms are also being used to design physical storefronts and can also be used to optimize websites, such as the arrangements of a site's products and services.

The use of a GA to fine-tune a neural network can be viewed as a form of data compression. For example, a GA can prune a very long file containing hundreds of variables down to only a few inputs for predicting sales. This process of optimization is a form of data reduction in which the software will try and reduce its own error rate, while at the same time compressing the number of inputs to a neural network.

A data mining analysis will likely involve the use of multiple techniques and technologies. (See Figure 1–14.) For example, it is a common practice to use a segmentation tool, such as a decision tree program or an association technique tool, to identify important variables in a database with a large number of fields, and then use a

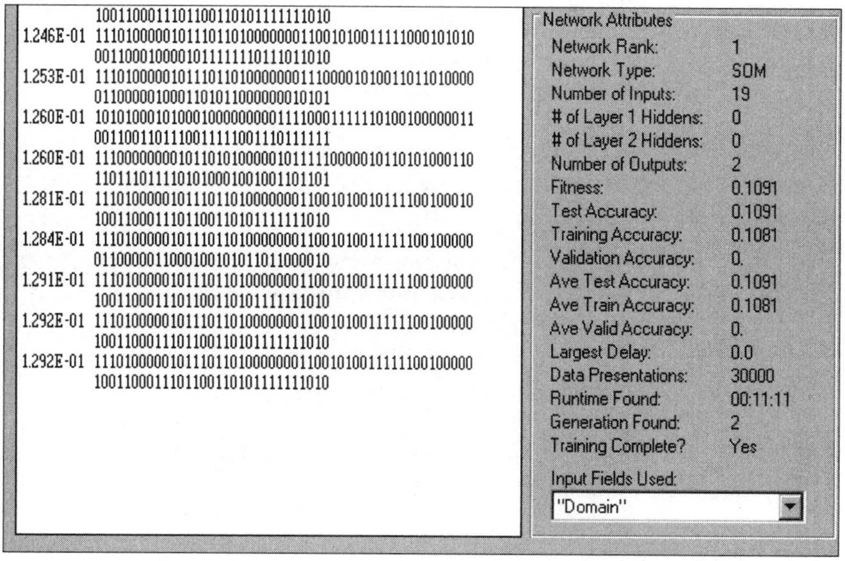

Figure 1–12
A GA can be used to optimize the performance of a neural network.

Network Attributes	
Network Rank:	1
Network Type:	SOM
Number of Inputs:	19
# of Layer 1 Hiddens:	0
# of Layer 2 Hiddens:	0
Number of Outputs:	2
Fitness:	0.1091
Test Accuracy:	0.1091
Training Accuracy:	0.1081
Validation Accuracy:	0.
Ave Test Accuracy:	0.1091
Ave Train Accuracy:	0.1081
Ave Valid Accuracy:	0.
Largest Delay:	0.0
Data Presentations:	30000
Runtime Found:	00:11:11
Generation Found:	2
Training Complete?	Yes

Input Fields Used:
"Domain"

Figure 1–13
GAs and neural networks can be used to predict online sales.

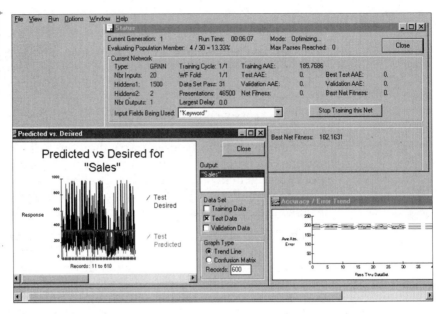

Figure 1–14
The identification of hidden patterns in your data often involves several steps.

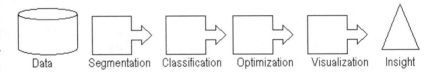

neural network to construct a model using those selected fields as inputs. Next, a genetic algorithm may be used to further try to optimize the neural network so that even fewer variables are used to predict such outcomes as total sales or the propensity to make purchases by new visitors to your website. Lastly, a visual tool may be employed to display the results and perhaps enhance the insight gained from the entire data mining process.

While all of these formats provide different types of inputs and results, they are not mutually exclusive; instead, they complement each other and should be considered and used in tandem. For example, the visualization of your data can be done both during your initial analysis (to get an overview of your data) as well as after you have performed your segmentation and classification processes. What data mining formats you obtain from your analysis and what sequence you select is really driven by your business needs. In fact, you may select to perform but one single process—it is your option.

The formats you obtain from your analysis will affect the steps that you go through in the mining of your website. There are ten general steps that are covered in more detail later in the book. Your data mining format will impact each of these steps, since it will influence your decisions on your objectives, the selection and preparation of your server data, the tools that you use, and how you integrate your findings.

Data Mining Drives Relational Marketing

While early adopters of data mining technology have tended to be from data warehouses in information-intensive and ultra-competitive industries such as financial services, telecommunications, and retailing, today virtually every company has a website generating massive amounts of customer information. Similar to data warehouses, large commercial websites involved in electronic retailing are today dealing with huge amounts of data that data mining tools are especially apt at dealing with. Indeed, with the advent of the Web and electronic commerce, nearly every company large or small is now in an "information-intensive and ultra-competitive" mode and thus likely to benefit greatly from data mining. The Web is an ideal marketing environment where every transaction can be captured, stored, and subsequently mined for a strategic advantage. The data mining of your website can allow you to:

- build unique market segments identifying the attributes of high-value prospects
- identify the key attributes of your web customers for each of your products
- select promotional strategies that best reach your web customer segments
- analyze your online sales to improve targeting of high-value customers
- test and determine which marketing activities have the greatest impact
- identify customers most likely to be interested in your new products
- reduce costs and improve the value of customer relationships
- improve your site's product cross-selling and up-selling
- leverage the knowledge about your online customers
- identify the best online prospects for your services
- understand the reasons for brand switching

- manage your web customer relationships
- improve your web ads and sales process
- maximize online ad throughputs

Mining your website data lets you focus your efforts on your most profitable customers and prospects. It allows you to design marketing strategies to reach your clients incrementally—from mass, to market segment, to individuals. As you begin to do electronic retailing you can also improve your relational marketing efforts by mining the data that you daily accumulate from your website. Relational marketing is about marketing in a continuously narrower and targeted range. Ideally it involves marketing to individuals based on observed behavior patterns rather than just demographics or on the basis of keywords you glean from log files.

Today, with ready access to increasingly larger amounts of website visitor information and data mining technology, a website can truly begin to offer individualized treatment to its online customer. Unlike mass marketing, with relational marketing, every customer is his or her own market segment. Relational marketing focuses a site on its true source of revenue and profits: *its customers*. In a dynamic and highly competitive environment such as the Web, electronic retailers must recognize that they can gain a competitive advantage by better understanding and caring for their most frequent visitors and best customers.

Web Privacy

At this point it is important to remind you of the importance of privacy and your need to explicitly tell your website customers how you plan to protect the information they provide you, because if you don't you will have no data to mine or business on the Web. It is important that you look at your website customers' personal information as your company's most valuable asset. You must be prepared to protect it and ensure it is not disclosed. The privacy of your website visitors must be guaranteed, period. Make no mistake, recent surveys indicate people on the Web are not willing to share personal or financial information that can be sold to third parties. In Europe, failure to protect this type of personal information is already illegal, so take care.

You must convince your website visitors and customers that whatever information they provide you will be used to save them time and money—in fact you need to prominently guarantee it in writing. The protection of your customer information is not only good business sense, but it is also the most valuable asset you have in terms of competitive intelligence. Think about it—what do you know about your online customers that your rival does not? If you are going to be data mining web-generated information for purposes of marketing and commerce, you need to create a trusting relationship with your visitors and customers. You need to adopt an explicit and prominent security and privacy policy in order to ensure an intimate dialog with your online clients. You need to state:

1. The information you need from them and why this will save them time and money.

2. The tangible benefits they will get in exchange for the information they disclose.

3. The actions you will take to protect and not disclose the information they provide.

4. The control they have over the information, such as their right to purge it or update it.

5. Your assurance that the personal information they provide you will solely be used to improve the service you provide them.

Benefits and Incentives

Website visitors and customers will provide information about themselves if they see some tangible benefits for doing so. For example, the Web continues to expand on a daily basis with the number of websites in the tens of millions and new ones going up every hour of every day. If you can assure your visitors that by completing a registration form you will be able to facilitate the location of important products or services they specifically want, then you are on your way to establishing a productive relationship with them. You need to assure them and prove to them that the more you know about them, the better you will get at serving them in a timely, accurate, and individualized manner. Personalized customer information must be mined with the full intent of improving your individual service to them.

The mining of this data will only ensure you are more efficient in how you respond to your customers' likes and preferences. Data mining is about leveraging pattern recognition technology toward a business objective, which in this case is customer service. This translates into knowing what your customers want before they know it themselves. Ultimately they will want to stay in the client relationship, since training another vendor or competitor will cost them time and effort.

One method of obtaining valuable customer information is by providing a free service in exchange (this is the business model used to provide free e-mail by HotMail). Another method of securing valuable information from your website visitors and customers is by providing them a special discount on your products and services. This may be in the form of a one-time offer, a coupon, a reduced rate, a free ticket, a free upgrade, technical analysis or support, a white paper, etc. Then there is the straightforward appeal. Phrase your requests in this manner: How can I best serve you? How can I provide you with local information, such as a weather report, if I don't have your ZIP code?

An established practice for your website should be that information collected for one purpose should not be used for another without your visitor's or customer's permission. For example, if your customer's e-mail address is being secured solely to contact them to rectify a billing error or to confirm an order, that should be made clear. Your website should be very straightforward about why you are asking for the information and how you plan to use it. Website visitors and customers should be given prior notice regarding the collection and usage of personal information or other type of tracking data. Finally, you should offer your customers the option to "opt in or out"—offer them various levels of privacy protection. The more information they provide you the more service they are likely to receive from you since you will be better able to deliver to them what they want, when they want it, in a manner unique to their needs.

Ten Steps to Mining Your Web Data

Before you start to mine your data you need to consider what your objective is and what kind of information you will need to capture to achieve your objective. For example, you may need to issue identification cookies during the completion of registration forms at your website. This will enable you to match the information captured from your forms, such as the visitor's ZIP code, with the transaction information generated from your cookies. It will also allow you to merge your cookie information, which will detail the locations where your visitors go to while in your website, with the specific attributes like age and gender from your forms. Additionally, a ZIP code or visitor address will allow you to match your cookie and form data with demographics and household information matched from third-party data resellers.

The data from your website will likely need to be scrubbed and prepared prior to any sort of data mining analysis. Log files, for example, can be fairly redundant since a single "hit" generates a record of not only that HTML but also of every graphic on that page.

However, once a template, script, or procedure has been developed for generating the proper recording of a single visit, the data can be input into a database format from which additional manipulations and refinements can take place. If you are using a site traffic analyzer tool, this data may already be format-ready for additional mining analysis. Keep in mind that several steps may be required prior to undertaking your analysis, including the following ones, which will be discussed in detail later in the book:

1. Identify your objective — *Profile your visitors?*
2. Select your data — *Form database?*
3. Prepare the data — *Append demographic information?*
4. Evaluate the data — *Visualization?*
5. Format the solution — *Segmentation, prediction?*
6. Select the tools — *Single or suite?*
7. Construct the models — *Train and test?*
8. Validate the findings — *Share with teams?*
9. Deliver the findings — *Provide report, code?*
10. Integrate the solutions — *Marketing campaign?*

Clearly not all of these steps are required, but you should consider them prior to starting any in-depth analysis. They certainly do not always follow this exact sequence, but personal experience bears out the fact that in most assignments these were the issues that needed to be resolved prior to completion of most data mining projects. Most of my prior data mining projects involved working with customer information files, datamarts, and data warehouses from retailers, banks, insurers, phone, and credit card companies, but they typically dealt with the same client-centered issues or questions, mainly: Who are the customers? What are their features? And how are they likely to behave? Electronic retailers face the same questions today.

Most likely you will need to do your data mining on a separate server dedicated to analysis. After your analysis you will need to validate your results through some sort of production system such as a marketing test e-mail campaign. Note that the costs involved with e-mail versus physical mail or phone calls allows for a very rapid assessment of your data mining and marketing efforts. It is certainly a very economical way to evaluate your data mining project: it only costs about five cents to e-mail a potential customer, compared with as much as five dollars for direct mail and eight to twelve dollars for a phone sales call. Planning and executing a traditional marketing campaign used to take months; today on the Web an e-mail campaign can take hours. The Web has precipitated the trend toward one-to-one marketing and the validation of data mining results by allowing the rapid evaluation of predictive models.

It is not difficult to assess the benefits of data mining and its return-on-investment (ROI). Simply consider the quantitative counts of clickthroughs of ads or banners prior and after your data mining analysis. Consider the percentage of sales or requests for product information, as well as the amounts of purchases made as a result of a data mining analysis. Consider the rates prior to your data mining efforts and afterwards. If you initiate a marketing e-mail campaign on the basis of your data mining analysis, consider the rate of responses by splitting your e-mails on those individuals targeted via your analysis and those excluded from the targeting. Measure the improved rate of responses and sales from those targeted via the data mining analysis and those without it.

The dynamics of your industry and marketplace will dictate how often you should mine your website data. The intervals for mining your data will depend on how often the attributes of your customers change. For example, a bank may have a cross-selling model for its call site that can be quite effective for months. The intervals in which the bank model are created may take place on a quarterly or monthly basis and still be relevant to the business questions they are trying to answer, such as cross-selling opportunities of their financial products like CDs, bankcards, loans, etc. For a portal, such as a search engine, models may need to be refreshed on a weekly basis, because the dynamics of the content, their visitors, and their features change more quickly than, say, with a bank's customers. The end products they are trying to predict are also subject to change more frequently, for a bank it is a loan, for a portal it is a banner or ad.

For an Internet company which exists completely on the Web, the data mining process represents a biofeedback system to its entire supply chain. Data mining can identify for electronic retailers key market segments, which can impact directly on its overall website design and inventory control systems. As with physical retailers, the leveraging of data mining pays off in the positioning of the right message, product, and service in front of the right customers at the right time in the right format.

Data mining is not an isolated process carried in a vacuum; it must be integrated into the entire electronic retailing and marketing processes. This is especially true with virtual storefronts because everything—selections, transactions, orders, customer communications—is accelerated to "Internet time." For a website entirely supported by advertising, data mining is even more critical since it can quickly discover and measure the effectiveness of a multitude of banners and ads on its continuous stream of visitors.

A Bookseller Example

Data mining can provide multiple solutions to website designers, marketers, and merchants, such as an online bookseller. For example, it can provide to a book site an insight about its electronic commerce activities and its clientele. Data mining analysis can help it resolve such questions as:

- What books are being sold to which visitors?
- Who and where are these visitors located?
- Which visitors are the most profitable?
- What factors impact its online sales?
- Who is likely to buy what books?

To answer these types of questions, the bookseller needs to start with an analysis of its customer information. The customer information can come from various sources, including of course the clients themselves, as captured by the registration forms located at its website. It may also be information maintained in its data warehouse or purchased externally from demographers or household data providers (see Figure 1–15).

On the basis of its visitors' ZIP code, ZIP+4, or full address, data resellers can provide the bookseller information about their incomes, the type of automobiles they drive, whether they own or rent, the presence of children and other lifestyle information. Once the book

Figure 1–15
A bookseller data set combines transactional and customer information.

Book Category	Income	State	Sales	Children	Gender	Age	LastSale	Top 1%	Wealthy Seaboard	Empty Nesters
Computers	51928	MA	366	0	M	55-50	19980215	0	0	0
Literature	25337	MA	272	2	M	40-44	19970829	0	0	0
Investing	25339	MA	153	1	M	40-44	19970829	0	0	0
Home	45575	MA	132	3	M	50-54	19970913	0	0	0
Internet	25340	MA	270	1	M	30-34	19970829	0	0	51
History	45576	MA	144	1	M	30-34	19970912	0	0	51
Horror	25342	MA	132	4	M	30-34	19970829	0	0	4
Garden	25343	MA	292	1	M	44-49	19970829	0	0	4
Home	25344	MA	144	2	M	40-44	19970829	0	0	4
History	25345	MA	226	2	M	50-54	19970829	0	0	0

site's data has been enhanced, several data mining techniques and technologies can be used to visualize, cluster, segment, classify, and profile its customers—including the modeling and prediction of their online behavior. For starters, this bookseller may want to:

1. *Visualize* the data to look for significant trends or hidden associations

2. *Split* the data to look for unique clusters or different groupings

3. *Model* the data to anticipate the behavior of its visitors

Look at the Data

This bookseller can graph and plot its customers' attributes in order to gain an overview of who they are. Such a visual inspection can reveal certain demographic features about who is buying and who is not, and provide the bookseller's website designers and marketers some direction on what type of campaigns, incentives, awards, and books to offer, and to whom. For example, at this book site (see Figure 1–16), fiction is the most popular category.

Relationships can also be discovered through visual data mining. Figure 1–17 depicts the links between book types and visitor age groups. The stronger the relationship the bolder the links appear on the web diagram. (See Figure 1–18.)

Figure 1–16
Most customers are male and buy fiction and Internet books.

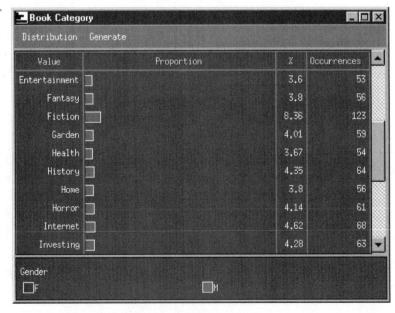

Figure 1–17
*Most of this
bookseller's
customers are
between 40 and
54 years old.*

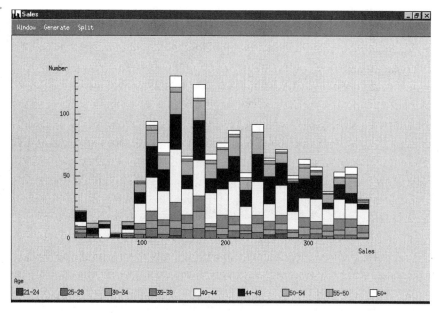

Figure 1–18
*Link analysis
showing the
associations
between book
categories and
age groups.*

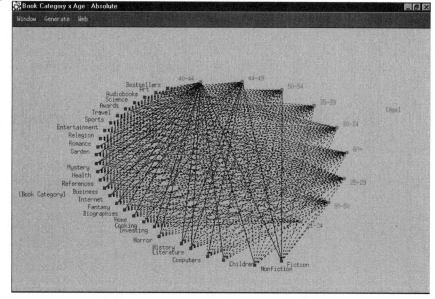

The associations in the diagram can also be summarized in tabular format with the actual counts of occurrences provided in a table, as in Figure 1–19.

The actual counts can be examined between products sold and customer features. Note that the benefits of data mining grow in importance as the size and complexity of the data increase. In this example, we are dealing with a very small sample size. An analysis of several hundred thousand transactions is quite common for large retailing websites.

Split the Data

A different type of visual analysis, and yet another way of splitting the data, is that of *clustering*.

Groups of clusters can be examined for additional information, as was the case with this analysis of region2 in the right side of Figure 1–20. Clustering offers the opportunity to find grouping in the data through a process known as *self-organization*—driven by the nature of data, rather than the intuition or hypothesis of the analyst. This sector can further be *"drilled"* by a data mining tool in order to discover some of its unique attributes. Rules can be extracted describing the features of the clusters in region2:

IF	Age	40–44
AND	State	NY
THEN	region2	Cluster for 56 visitors 98.2% Confidence

Or,

Figure 1–20
Clusters of data as grouped according to visitor age groups.

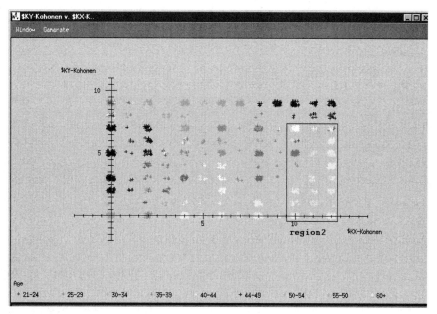

IF	Age	40–44
AND	Income	> $26,976
AND	State	NY
THEN	region2	Cluster for 37 visitors 97.3% Confidence

Segmentation analysis can discover important grouping in this bookseller's website data. The key difference between this and clustering analysis is that with the former you start with a clear objective, such as splitting the data according a specific value or output (i.e., "projected total sales"). In clustering, there is no predefined objective; it is a more exploratory type of analysis in which the data is allowed to organize itself. In segmentation, the bookseller starts the analysis by asking the questions, "who are my most profitable customers and how do I recognize them," which is in turn answered by the decision tree in Figure 1–21.

The results of segmentation analysis can also be interpreted as rules. For example, in Figure 1–21 the highest projected sales is $244.77, which is described in the following rule:

Figure 1–21
Segmentation analysis decision tree, in which avg = average sales, std = standard deviation, and n = number of observations.

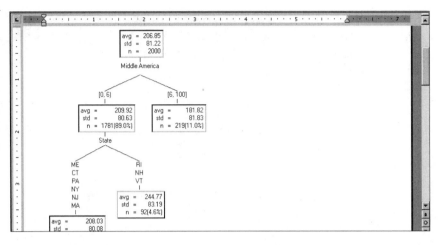

IF	Middle America Consumer Type ZIP code is greater than 0 but less than 6%
AND	visitor comes from Rhode Island, New Hampshire, or Vermont
THEN	projected online sales is $244.77, with a standard deviation of $83.19

NOTE: The average total customer sales for this site is $206.85.

Model the Data

One of the most important types of analysis a bookseller is likely to make is one involving the modeling of its website visitors' behavior. This type of analysis is known as *classification* or *prediction* and involves the discovery and learning of visitors' features and their online behavior. Like segmentation, classification involves examining visitors' features and their propensity to click through an ad or banner or make an online purchase. Modeling and predicting website visitor behavior can be accomplished using data mining tools incorporating neural networks. (See Figure 1–22.) A neural network is software designed to train itself on the patterns in large sets of samples, which in this case involve the online activity of its website visitors.

Modeling involves uncovering subtle customer and transactional nuances that can be coded in the form of "weights" in a formula for scoring the behavior of future new visitors. (See Figure 1–23.) On the basis of these scores, the bookseller can mount multiple targeted

Figure 1–22
*A network will
iterate through
thousands of
observations to
discover a
pattern.*

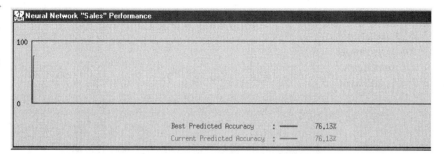

Figure 1–22
*A network will
iterate through
thousands of
observations to
discover a
pattern.*

Figure 1–23
*A network will
try several com-
binations of
inputs in an
effort to predict
an output.*

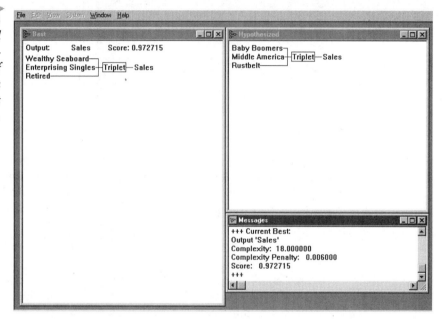

e-mail campaigns offering specific types of books only to those individuals likely to be interested and have a high propensity to want to
make a purchase. A recent study found that unique visitors to one
book site never go to another online bookseller. Once visitors learn
how to use one site and once that site learns their preferences and
buying habits, they're likely to remain with that bookseller.

Our bookseller, via data mining, can now offer enough value to
lock its customers into an electronic relationship to improve its
sales and to retain them as clients. A marketing law says it costs ten
times more to acquire a new customer than it does to sell to an
existing one. By using knowledge it already has about its clients, the

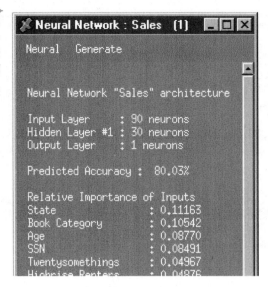

Figure 1–24
A sensitivity analysis report from a neural network.

bookseller can increase the efficiency of its marketing efforts. An additional value is that through this profiling effort it can now target potential new visitors armed with the knowledge of who its existing customers are. It can now furnish an image, lifestyle, and attitude to these potential new visitors who match the composite of its existing clients.

A *sensitivity report* from a neural network can tell the bookseller what factors are impacting his online sales, which in this analysis is the visitors' home state, book category, age, and so forth. In Figure 1–24, the sensitivity report coincides with the findings of the visual, association, and segmentation analyses, which found that customers who purchase fiction and Internet books (Books Category), live in Rhode Island, New Hampshire, and Vermont (State), and are between 40 and 44 (Age), to be the most profitable and possess the greatest loyalty. The visitor's gender was excluded as an input from the neural network model, since we already knew that males are a dominant characteristic.

Integrate the Solution

Data mining should not be considered as an isolated independent, one-time process. It should instead be an integrated process of analysis impacting every aspect of a retailing site. On the basis of data mining analyses, a retailer can project and anticipate the allocation of shipping resources, which can affect the speed by which it is able to deliver the goods, purchased at its website. Shipping on the Web involves not only the physical transportation of goods, but includes the electronic delivery of information. On the basis of this analysis, seasonal and product-specific trends can be discovered and monitored. Patterns can be uncovered that can alert the retailer on what resources it may need to ensure prompt deliveries of its products and services.

Through the mining of its sales data, an electronic retailer can formulate the marketing strategy to deploy at its site. Analysis of its visitors' demographics and the products being purchased by them can impart valuable insight. Product-specific patterns may be uncovered, which can be used to evaluate marketing campaigns. Mining can reveal what domains, keywords, gender, age, income levels, and other visitor attributes are associated with each sale at a retailing site. As such, marketing strategies can be keyed to specific products, involving targeted ads and e-mail promotions.

The analysis of retail sales data, as with physical stores, can directly impact a website's everyday operations, including that of its inventory controls. Through the analysis of its retailing data a website can adequately plan and anticipate product demand. The benefits of such analysis may take the form of reduced overhead and the prompt delivery of its products and services. Seasonal trends can be anticipated and incorporated into how a site stocks its inventory, whether it be books, CDs, or software. Analysis of the demographics of its customers can provide the retailer vital clues about who is buying what, when, and why.

Because of the rapid nature of electronic commerce, retailers must be prepared to move quickly to meet the needs of its online customers. The flexibility of online retailing allows merchants to monitor sales and quickly adjust pricing and availability of products and services. Data mining of retail information, whether in the form of bar code data or server databases, can reveal important trends and patterns that can affect all aspects of production including shipping, marketing, inventory, and sales.

Compiling an Identity

The key to knowing who will buy, what is selling, and how to sell resides in the transactional and customer data generated from a retailing site, and the key to compiling and capturing this shopper information starts with the establishment of a unique identifier: a visitor ID number, or *key*. This key is needed to associate all of these components into a single record for each visitor. Once linked, this single record string can be used to link to additional customer information from your data warehouse, or appended with external household and demographic information from commercial data reseller. As this visitor profile is built multiple analyses can be performed.

A proven strategy for assigning keys to your visitors is to have them register initially at your site by providing them a special service or incentive or by offering access to a special section in your site. Another strategy is to hold periodic contests or door prizes for which you ask visitors to "register to win." When they register, you may set a cookie that can be used as the unique ID number. From that point on, the unique key can enable you to track every interaction with that visitor. The key will also allow you to link the information from your server log files, cookies, and forms with your data warehouse and other demographic and household information.

Server log files provide domains, time of access, keywords, search engine used:

        13:04.9, "furby", excite, id344,384 etc.

id344,384

Cookies dispensed from the server track browser visits and pages viewed:

        id344,384, visit_3, prod22.htm, etc.

id344,384

Forms capture important visitor personal information, such as gender, age, or ZIP code:

        id344,384, male, 35, 94551, etc.

id344,384

Demographic and household data can be appended, such as total sales or annual income:

id344,384, excite, prod22.htm, male, 35, 94551, total_sales_$350, $75k_income, SUV, 2_children, etc.

id344,384

The above string can take the form of an Oracle table or a flat-file, comma-delimited text file, which can be linked or imported into your data mining tool of choice.

The Architecture for Analysis

The analysis you perform can serve as a feedback system to your retailing site, which can impact your site design, sales, inventory, and marketing teams. Data mining of your customer information can address such issues as:

- *Who is buying:* Customer profiles, who purchases what items and at what rates.
- *What is selling:* Adjust inventory, plan your orders, shipping, and inventory.
- *How to sell:* What incentives, offers, and ads work, and what site design and style are most successful.

Data mining reports take various formats, including the delivery of reports, statistical models, graphics, maps, SQL syntax, and/or C code containing the weights for prediction of online visitor behavior. These analyses will be iterative in nature due in part to the dynamic nature of the website and the traffic patterns it is designed to model.

Access to data for analysis can be made either in the format of a flat ASCII file or by invoking ODBC drivers. Depending on the type of tool you are using, data can be extracted directly from existing tables on your server (or servers). Most high-end data mining tools support access to databases such as Informix, Ingress, Oracle, and Sybase. If a flat-file format is chosen, a fixed-length or a delimited character file must be specified. Comma-delimited files are the most compact and should be used when space is a concern. Most tools will convert the data they import into a proprietary structure of their own, which is then used for the actual views and analyses. In most instances, your data mining analysis will need to be performed in a dedicated server or data mart.

Personalized Future

Today you can personalize every major "portal" you use to access the Web. This means that "the Web" is now "my Web," allowing you to tailor all types of information streams into your own customized news, weather, market, and stock reports. However, in exchange for your own unique view of the world, most of these portals (such as major search engines, online directories, and large content providers) require some personal information from you. They typically require you to complete a short form—which in turn provides some useful data to the portal that can be mined, allowing for a more targeted and proactive dialog between the website and you. This information, coupled with the topics you select and the "keywords" that you use over time, can be mined for purposes of creating a *profile* of you. This profile can be used, among other things, to suggest new sites; provide timely recommendations on products and services; and favorably position certain ads, banners, and buttons that are more likely to get a response from you. Gradually, users are becoming accustomed to getting timely and accurate product recommendations based on their preferences and personalized features—features that can quickly be discovered by mining the data from these portal registration forms.

The Web provides an extensive and prevalent choice of options, which has spawned an audience of very savvy and knowledgeable customers. Today, it is easy to accumulate a vast amount of product information and comparative data. In a customer-centric environment such as the Web, the customer is not only always right, she is also very well informed. To stay competitive in such an environment your website must establish a relationship with your customers. The data that you gather from them must not only be protected, it must be strategically used. Even inactive data must be converted into actionable intelligence via data mining.

The increased availability of choice has also eroded brand loyalty. For example, if a portal does not provide a user with the type of content that interests him, he will, with a click of the mouse, switch to a competitor who will. To succeed in such an environment you need to personalize your site, and in doing so you can benefit from better customer loyalty, lower marketing costs, and a competitive advantage. The advantage comes through the relationships established between your site and your online customers.

You must attend to your web customers' needs by making it convenient for them to gain a substantial benefit for doing business with you by customizing your products and services to meet their unique

Figure 1–25
Data mining can involve many different enterprise professionals, processes, and sources.

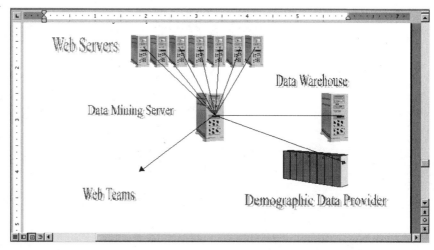

needs. When a customer takes the time to complete a form about them, they have just invested time and effort into building a business relation with your website. To gain the most benefit from that customer information you must mine the data.

As previously discussed, one way of maximizing the benefit of that information is by the integration of your website with your data warehouse of other customer information file. (See Figure 1–25.) This allows you to mine interactions on an individual basis and to construct customer profiles. Your website and its various components, such as forums, chat, and e-mail, allow you to learn from your customers and to engage in an interactive dialog, which in turn leads to the personalization of your site.

The personalization of your customers' websites requires that you gather information from your customers and store it in a database for mining. This increases your chances of becoming indispensable to your clients, and it also encourages customer retention with each transaction. Personalization requires that your website customers and visitors have the ability to create, modify, control, and delete their profiles. The benefits of this interaction, however, is that over time (1) it will cost you less to market to these web customers, and (2) their purchases will surpass the initial expenses of personalizing your website. You will be able to calculate their value based on the duration of their relationship with your site and the amount of money they spend with you or the number of transactions they have with you.

Personalization empowers web visitors and customers to dictate what information they want and in what format and at what intervals.

It allows them to construct their own profiles and to control the duration of their relation with your company. The Web has accelerated the marketplace by increasing the availability of options to the consumer. To deliver personalized services at your website you need to mine your data to discover customer segments and then specific individual profiles. To what extent you personalize your site via data mining is really dependent on your budget and resources.

General	Segmented	Relational
Mass Communication	Demographic	One-to-One E-mail
No Targeting	Content Targeting	Specific Targeting
No Date Mining	Mining by Decision Tree	Mining by Neural Network
No Web Data Analysis	Log and Form Analysis	Cookie and Profiling Analysis

Nonintrusive, yet responsive personalized service is or will become the norm on the Web. Customers will appreciate being able to search and find the products, service, and information they want when they need it at the lowest possible price. Commercial websites will have to integrate themselves with their company inventory databases in order to come up with the proper product requests unique to that customer's profile. This integration will also allow for additional cross-selling recommendations based on data mining analysis. For example, if a data mining analysis using a clustering network discovers a propensity for certain individuals with matching demographics to like a specific product, you may want to make a product recommendation to that customer based on that match.

Analysis of customer transactions and personal information should be scheduled and performed on a regular basis. Keep in mind that personal customer information is cumulative and should not be requested all in one session. It should be requested when you are going to use it to personalize your service. For example, don't ask for an e-mail address unless you plan to use it immediately for some sort of notification. Gradually, as the customer returns to your site to make more purchases, you should collect more data regarding each transaction so that your interactions are more targeted and based on accumulated data you have mined from prior visits. Personalization is about using information accumulated through your relationship with customers and mining the data in order to deliver a better shopping experience for them.

The current explosion in web databases has resulted in a growing glut of customer data. Your company's ability to strategically deal with these terabytes of web data will depend on your effective use of data mining technology, which can offer new insights and improve your firm's ability to deal with the personalization of the Web. To stay competitive, you need to actively monitor your online transactional trends within your web data in order to target and nurture your most loyal and profitable customers. If you are successful in obtaining customer information you need to immediately put it to use in order for them to return to your website again and again. After all, the mining of your website is simply about being able to see, talk, and relate with your online customers.

Why Bother?

Data mining, whether in the physical or virtual marketplace, has always been much more than the mere use of software tools. It is a business *process* designed to extract actionable intelligence for product and financial analysis sales, marketing support, and customer segmentation. It is about knowledge discovery for a strategic, tangible, competitive business advantage. Now more than ever this actionable insight comes from the highly dynamic data a firm daily gathers from its online customer information file: its website.

Through the mining of its website data and the discovery of the distinguishing features of its visitors, a company can provide them with the type of information, product, and services they are most likely to want. The mining of website data can also assist in the overall design and direction that site will evolve into over time. The process of mining, modification, marketing, and evolution of a website as it changes to meet the demands of its visitors and customers is almost *organic* in nature. As with some of the data mining tools rooted in the evolutionary concepts of computing, the purpose for data mining your website data is to recognize and learn from your visitors, so that you may serve them better than your competitors.

As websites increasingly become the first point of contact between a company and its current and future customers, the mining of website data is becoming a critical method by which to attract and retain visitors. This is especially true in a marketplace with millions of websites—all competing for the attentions and dollars of millions of browsers and shoppers. As with the physical retailers, telcos, banks, and credit card companies, the mining of web server data is driven by the competition in the marketplace and the need to know or predict the behavior of consumers. More than anything the Web has precipitated the trend of one-to-one marketing of which data mining is an important component.

At around the time I was having my e-mail dialog with the search engine company, I had also been involved in preliminary discussions with an insurance company about the mining of their call site data. It occurred to me then that as more and more individuals had started to use the Web on a daily basis, their interactions with this insurance firm, like that with that of other retailers and service providers, were changing from phoning their call site to directly interacting with their website. The transactional data that I commonly mine for these companies is today rapidly migrating to their websites, where it is often faster to place or check on the status of an order, make a reservation, or get the information a customer traditionally deals with through intermediates, whether independent agents or their call site employees.

Clearly the future of electronic retailing pivots around positioning the "right" web content, products, and services to attract and retain customers; an electronic commerce future in which the number of businesses conducting online transactions is expected to exceed hundreds of thousands; a marketplace where the number of consumers buying over the Web will exceed 100 million and the projected number of sales will go from a few to hundreds of billions; where in the ebb and flow of these online transactions gradual patterns will evolve from which electronic retailers will be able to mine and discover their customer tendencies, preferences, features, and behavior. The future of electronic retailing hinges on the strategic use of data mining technology for providing prompt personalized services and products—where the sales clerk will likely be an AI.

2

What Is Data Mining?

It's about Predators and Patterns

Data mining is a "hot" new technology about one of the oldest processes of human endeavor: *pattern recognition*. Our hairy ancestors relied on their ability to recognize the patterns of predators, paths, prey, and the seasons to survive. Today, companies inundated with data that is daily generated with every customer transaction, web hit, bar scan, credit card swipe, and phone call are faced with the same challenge of recognizing the patterns of opportunity and threat to their survival. Throw in the real-time, hyper-competitive, networked business environment that is the Web, and you will see why the ability to decipher these patterns is fast becoming a critical factor to a company.

For example, let's say you are a retailer of hot pepper sauces on the Web. A data mining tool can discover the following rule—which .is actually an important ratio—or insight about your customers' identity and purchasing patterns:

IF	Visitor Sub-Domain is AOL
AND	Visitor Gender is MALE
AND	Visitor Age is 37–42
AND	Visitor is from ZIP Code "High Rise Renter" 78–85%
THEN	Visitor Will Purchase Score = 81%

You can benefit from data mining even if you don't sell habaneros online. Whether you provide a service or a product, data mining can assist you in discovering previously unknown patterns or features about your website visitor, your online customers, and your relationship with them. By recognizing who your customers are you can begin to establish a stronger relationship with them, which in the long run will enhance your chances of retaining them over their consumer life.

Data mining differs from other data analysis methods in a fundamental way: it discovers hidden structures, ratios, patterns, and signatures. Data mining is uniquely dynamic in that you don't need to prepare queries or set out to resolve a particular problem before you mine. Data mining retrieves relationships and enables "drill-up" analysis based on them. For example, your discovery in the hot sauce sample may lead you to do subsequent queries for website visitors with the same consumer class "High Rise Renters" or age bracket.

Just as a forensic investigator is able to approximate the weight and height of a perpetrator from a single footprint on a beach, so can your company calibrate the value and unique features of your most loyal and profitable website visitors and customers. How? Through a careful analysis of the clues in the patterns evolving from your daily website interactions. Customer profiles and prospect composites are provided to you every day with every visit to your site. The clues to identifying profitable visitors and potential new clients are contained in the data generated from your log, cookie, and registration forms. The tools and techniques for uncovering them are in data mining technology.

A Definition

Data mining is the process of discovering actionable and meaningful patterns, profiles, and trends by sifting through your (website's) data using pattern recognition technologies such as neural networks and machine-learning and genetic algorithms. It is an iterative process of extracting patterns from online business transactions—everything from clickthroughs of your banner ad to requests for e-mail information and form registrations—for purposes of improving your website company's bottom line. Data mining is the automatic discovery of usable knowledge from your stored server data and leveraging pattern recognition technology toward answering such business questions as:

- Who are my most profitable online customers?
- How do I increase my online market share?
- How do I optimize my online inventory?
- Who are my website visitors?

Drowning in Data

Data storage is getting cheaper while at the same time the amount of data is exploding. The United Nations 1996 Population Report estimated the world population growth to be about 3.1 percent per year. In contrast, the estimated disk storage is growing at about 130 percent per year, as reported by the information technology research group the International Data Corporation (IDC). All of these figures and projections are of course exclusive of the Web and the new data it is generating every second of the day with thousands of new websites going online.

Information flows into your company's website every day—information about your visitors and potential future customers. So much information is coming in that the average business uses only about 7 percent of the data they keep. Still another marketing research firm, the Gartner Group, estimates that only 2 percent of the existing online data is currently being analyzed, a percentage which is rapidly falling toward zero as storage more than doubles each year. Meanwhile the growth of the Internet, websites, and electronic commerce is also expected to continue its growth over the next few years. Further, Figure 2–1 shows Emerging Technologies Research Group estimates that Internet usage from all types of methods of access will continue to increase into the next century. Forrester Research, Inc. estimates e-commerce will reach $3.2 trillion in 2003.

Figure 2–1
The growth of the Web continues to increase. Courtesy of Emerging Technologies Research Group.

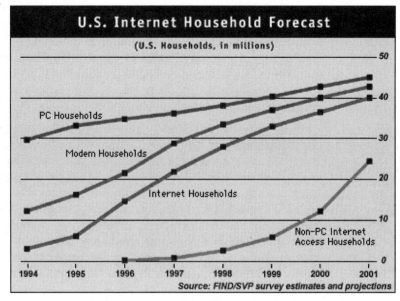

Figure 2–2
*Projected
growth for EC.
Courtesy of
International
Data
Corporation.*

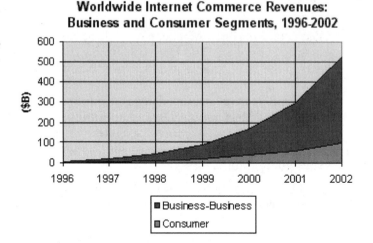

This growth is expected to be even more dramatic as electronic commerce increases in business-to-business transactions. (See Figure 2–2.) Given such a scenario, the only way to address this gross under-utilization of stored data is through advanced methods of analysis and pattern recognition. These new approaches are the foundation of the technologies incorporated in today's data mining tools.

During the last decade, the capabilities to both generate and collect data have grown enormously. For example, a retailer such as Wal-Mart needs to make daily updates of over a million transactions to its data warehouse for inventory analysis. With the advent of the Web, millions of new transactions are now occurring around the clock worldwide. One search engine is looking at analyzing between 25 and 75 million transactions every *day!* (Some of the first applications of data mining technology, such as Autoclass, originated with NASA. Why? Consider having to perform pattern recognition analysis on their Earth Observing System, which generates over 50 gigabytes of data per hour.)

Today the current rates of transactions, due in part to low storage costs, have flooded both forms databases and website servers and generated an urgent need for new tools that can intelligently assist in the analysis of this expanding ocean of data. For a company, data mining offers a solution to this problem by automating the search for relevant website visitors and online customer attributes. More importantly, data mining has the advantage of being totally unbiased and nonlinear in its approach to developing predictive models. Manual methods of data analysis, such as those of query tools, statistical programs, or website traffic reports, simply cannot keep pace with the explosive growth of online data. Hypothesis-based methods of data analyses are very time-consuming, while current website analysis tools are very limited in discovering the features of site visitors and customers.

The Complexity of Loyalty

The most valuable assets a website has are its customers—especially loyal customers, who return again and again over a period of time. The value of customers can be measured according to their lifetime value (LTV), i.e., the duration of their relationship with a site and the amount of money they spend during that time. As electronic retailing has evolved, sites have begun to find it profitable to group their clients into LTV classes with unique marketing needs. The retailer can then tailor its marketing activities according to different customer objectives and their potential worth to their site. The more loyal, and profitable, a client is, the more perks and incentives he/she is provided.

Distilling the value of customers involves in-depth market research and analysis. In a forms database with thousands of records and hundreds of attributes, how do you determine the demographic and psychographic attributes that distinguish valuable visitors from less profitable ones? At what point do you differentiate between "high" and "premium" customers? How do you find hidden groups of new users, brand switchers, dormants, upgraders, recent winbacks, and all the other clusters of customer classes? In short, how do you measure loyalty? The answer is in data mining.

A company's customer database can have hundreds of fields recording different types of interactions both offline and online culled from various contact points including a firm's website:

Data Field	Customer Attribute
Field 1	Account start date
Field 2	Number of purchases
Field 3	ZIP code
Field 798	Total number of visits
Field 799	Average length of visits
Field 800	Monthly access rate

In order to construct a customer loyalty model, you must discover two key items in the data: the significant *attributes* and *intervals*, which identify a pattern or signature of customers who have been retained by the company. This can involve combining attributes of existing customers and new website visitors who have recently signed on with a website. Through this process a "signature" of potentially highly loyal and profitable new clients can be discovered. These new customers may be targeted for high incentives and special offers.

The first goal of this analysis is to discover the attributes that are the most important signals in identifying those clients likely to be the most profitable: Is it the ZIP code they reside in, or maybe their establishment account date? Is it their monthly access rate, or their age or gender? Or is it a combination of factors, and if it is, which attributes?

The second question that needs to be answered from the data is that of ranges or intervals. For example, after what establishment account date is a customer likely to not defect? Or what range of ZIP codes? Or what website access rate signals a "highly loyal" or profitable customer? Now, theoretically you could go about discovering these attributes and ranges manually; however, it would take you weeks of trial and error, rather than hours to discover the answers that can be achieved using a data mining tool incorporating a machine-learning algorithm or a neural network. Again, as the numbers of data attributes increase, so does the complexity of the problem, making data mining the clear alternative to fast and effective analysis for an electronic retailer.

Measuring loyalty, however, is difficult, especially on the Web, where the complexity of data analysis is compounded by the dynamic of time. If you are in a market where it costs little for a customer to switch products or services, such as financial services, telecommunications, or retail, then you know you are in a hyper-competitive market. Likewise it is so on the Internet, where it costs little for a visitor or customer to click away from your website and over to your competitor. Data mining provides an electronic retailer many benefits in such a competitive online environment. Firms in highly saturated markets like retailing and financial services are dependent on using their data to drive their business decisions. They depend on their data to retain their customers, expand their market share, and to differentiate themselves from their rivals. Likewise this is so on the Web, where competition is fierce and loyalty is ephemeral.

Traditional Data Mining Applications

A recent META Group survey revealed that Fortune 500 firms were using data mining for three general purposes: 64 percent for strategic planning, 49 percent for competitive intelligence, and 46 percent to increase their market share. A study by this research group entitled *Data Mining: Trends, Technology, and Implementation Imperatives* (1998) forecasted a growth in the area of data mining driven by database marketing. It cites such applications as customer retention and churn management; cross-selling and up-selling; campaign management; market, channel and pricing analysis; and customer segmentation analysis. The study warns, "The competitive advantage enjoyed by the technology elite that deployed data mining early on is certain to dissipate through the Year 2000. Driven by the need for customer-centric marketing, data mining technology is rapidly becoming mainstream. Information technology and marketing departments that don't stay on top of this trend will wake up to discover that their competitors have beaten them to the punch." The report goes on to state that data mining "provides companies extremely valuable insight that has, to date, been closely guarded as corporate stealth technology to protect competitive advantage." So far, the following have been the traditional applications of data mining technology by industry sectors:

Retailers	Database marketing, advertising effectiveness, inventory and category management.
Banking and Insurance	Financial modeling, fraud detection, market and industry profiling, database marketing, customer segmentation.
Brokerage/Stock Exchange	Financial modeling, fraud detection.
Telecommunication	Call detail record analysis, optimal use of capital equipment, targeted marketing.
Government	Collections, workload selection, fraud detection, logistics, and intelligence gathering.
Manufacturing	Production quality control, supply-chain and inventory control.

The study fails to examine the potential growth of data mining in the area of electronic retailing. Customer-centric marketing requires sophisticated data mining applications because it seeks to better understand customers in their totality, including their buying patterns, demographic, and psychographic trends, and other types of customer knowledge. Such marketing will clearly accelerate with the advent of electronic commerce and the dynamic and explosive growth of Internet-generated databases.

New Data Mining Applications

In a web-centric networked environment, data mining is able to deliver new decision-support applications in two areas. First, data mining can be used to perform analysis on Internet-generated data from a website, which is what this book is about. And second, the technology can be used to monitor and detect the signature of network anomalies and potential problems before they happen.

One way of defining what data mining is about is to contrast it with more traditional methods of data analysis, such as statistics, Online Analytical Processing (OLAP), visualization, and web traffic analysis tools. We will now examine these various methods of data analysis and show that they are not exclusive of each other but are instead complementary, each contributing to the insight of your website visitors and customers and the effectiveness of your online presence.

Statistics

For centuries, man has been looking at the world and gathering data in an attempt to explain natural phenomena. People have been manually analyzing data in their search for explanations and patterns. The science of statistics originated as a way of making sense out of these observations. *Traditional statistics* have developed over time to help scientists, engineers, psychologists, and business analysts make sense of the data they generate and collect. *Descriptive statistics,* for example, provide general information about these observations, such as the average and median values, the observed errors, and the distribution of values. Another form of statistics is *regression analysis,* which is a technique used to interpolate and extrapolate these observations in an effort to make some intelligent predictions about the future.

Insurance and financial services companies were some of the first to try and predict customer behavior and to do risk analysis. Banks and insurers have typically used regression models to rank their customers' overall value or risk, all of which are attempts to fit a line to an observed phenomenon. SAS has built an empire by providing a host of enterprise-wide statistical applications to the financial services market sector. Fair Isaac, a modeling company, provides a wide assortment of services using statistics in the areas of behavior and their FICO credit scoring for financial services firms and other companies that do not do in-house analysis. Claritas provides demographic data to financial service firms designed to help them estimate sales potential of customers and segment markets by age, income, etc.; it sells its P$YCLE demographic data to financial companies, which allows them to differentiate households in terms of expected financial behavior.

This kind of statistical data analysis involves analysts who formulate a theory about a possible relation in a database and then convert this hypothesis into a query; it is a manual, user-driven, top-down approach to data analysis. In statistics, you usually begin the process of data analysis with a hypothesis about the relation in the data, which is the reverse of how data mining works. Some of the most popular statistical tools include the following:

Data Desk uses animation to help you see patterns you might miss in a static display. For example, you can easily link a sliding control to any part of an equation and see the effects of sliding the value as display update. Data Desk automatically makes sliders to help you find optimal transformations of variables, to learn about the sensitivity of analyses to small shifts in variables, and to assess the sensitivity of nonlinear regressions. You can easily build your own animations.

MATLAB is a powerful integrated technical computing environment that combines numeric computation, advanced graphics and visualization, and a high-level programming language.

SAS is a modular, integrated, hardware-independent statistical and visualization system of software for enterprise-wide information delivery. SAS recently recognized the benefits of data mining and is now offering *Enterprise Miner* a data mining add-on module to its base system.

S-Plus is the commercial version of "S," an interactive, object-oriented programming language for data analysis developed by AT&T Bell Labs. It is supported and marketed by MathSoft. *S/S-Plus* has proved to be a useful platform for both general-purpose data analysis including clustering, classification, summarization, visualization, regression, and CART.

SPSS is a powerful, easy-to-use, easy-to-learn statistical package for business or research. It features most of the standard statistics, along with high-resolution graphics with reporting and distributing capabilities. SPSS also recognized the importance of data mining when it purchased Clementine, a data mining tool from ISL (Integrated Solutions Limited).

STATlab is an exploratory data analysis software for drilling down into data and performing a multitude of analyses. STATlab can import data from common formats such as relational databases, ASCII files, popular spreadsheets, and most of the popular statistical data systems.

Data Mining vs. Statistics

The deciding distinction between statistics and data mining is the direction of the query: In data mining, the interrogation of the data is done by the machine-learning algorithm or neural network, rather than by the statistician or business analyst. In other words, data mining is data-driven, rather than user-driven or verification-driven, as it is with most statistical analyses. Statistical manual factorial and multivariate analyses of variance may be performed in order to identify the relationships of factors influencing the outcome of product sales using such tools as SPSS or SAS. Pearson's correlation may be generated for every field in a database to measure the strength and direction of their relationship to some dependent variable, like total sales.

A skilled SAS statistician conversant with that system's PROC syntax can perform that type of analysis rather quickly. However, one of the problems with this approach, aside from the fact that it is very resource-intensive, is that the techniques tend to focus on tasks in which all the attributes have continuous or ordinal values. Many of them are also parametric; for instance, a linear classifier assumes that class can be expressed as a linear combination of the attribute values. Statistical methodology assumes a bell-shaped normal distribution of data—which in the real world of business and Internet databases simply is nonexistent and too costly to accommodate. However, these statistical tool vendors are well aware of these shortcomings; as both SPSS and SAS are now making available new data mining modules and add-ons to their main products.

Data mining also has major advantages over statistics when the scale of databases increase in size, simply because manual approaches to data analysis are rendered impractical. For example, suppose there are 100 attributes in a database to choose from, of which you don't know which are significant. With even this small problem there are $100 \times 99 = 9,900$ combinations of attributes to consider. If there are three classes, such as high, medium, and low, there are now $100 \times 99 \times 98 = 970,200$ possible combinations. If there are 800 attributes, such as in our large website bookseller customer database ... well, you get the picture. Consider analyzing millions of transactions on a daily basis, as is the case with a large electronic retailing site, and it quickly becomes apparent that the manual approach to pattern-recognition simply does not scale to the task. Data mining, rather than hindering the traditional statistical approach to data analysis and knowledge discovery, extends it by allowing the automated examination of large numbers of hypotheses and the segmentation of very large databases.

Online Analytical Processing

OLAP tools are descendants of query generation packages, which are in turn descendants of mainframe batch report programs. They, like their ancestors, are designed to answer top-down queries from the data or draw "what if" scenarios for business analysts. Recently, OLAP tools have grown very popular as the primary methods of accessing company database, datamarts, and data warehouses.

OLAP tools were designed to get data analysts out of the custom-report-writing business and into the "cube construction" business. The OLAP data structure is similar to a Rubik's Cube of data that an analyst can twist and twirl in different ways to work through multiple reports and "what-would-happen" scenarios. OLAP tools primarily provide multidimensional data analysis—that is, they allow data to be broken down and summarized by product line and marketing region. The basic difference between OLAP and data mining is that OLAP is about aggregates, while data mining is about ratios. OLAP is addition while data mining is division.

OLAP deals with facts or *dimensions* typically containing transactional data relating to a firm's products, locations, and times. Each dimension also can contain some hierarchy. For example, the time dimension may drill down from year, to quarter, to month, and even to weeks and days. A geographical dimension may drill up from city, to state, to region, to country, and even to hemisphere, if necessary. For example, Widget A, by Western Region, by Month of November, which can be further "drilled" by Blue Widgets A, by San Jose, by November 10, and so on. The data in these dimensions, called *measures,* is generally aggregated (for example, total or average sales in dollars or units, or budget dollars or sales-forecast numbers).

Many organizations have been in existence for some time and have accumulated considerable quantities of data that could be useful for business planning. Historical trends and future projections could be used to analyze business alternatives and make more informed decisions that could gain or maintain a competitive advantage. During the last decade, data warehouses have become common in large corporations, many of which use OLAP tools for reports and decision support. These OLAP applications span a variety of organizational functions. Finance departments use OLAP for applications such as budgeting, activity-based costing (allocations), financial performance analysis, and financial modeling. Sales analysis and forecasting are two of the OLAP applications found in sales departments. Among other applications, marketing departments use OLAP for market research analysis, sales forecasting, promotion analysis, customer analysis, and market/customer segmentation. Typical manufacturing OLAP applications include production planning and defect analysis. The following are some of the current OLAP tools in the market:

Current OLAP Tools

ActiveOLAP, Analyzer, Aperio, Acuity/ES, Acumate ES, Advance for Windows, amis, Arbor Essbase Analysis Server, BrioQuery, Business Objects, Commander OLAP, Decision, Prism, Control, CrossTarget, Crystal Info for Essbase, Cube-It, FICS Group, datadriller, OpenAir Software, Inc., Dataman, DataTracker, dbProbe, DecisionSuite, DecisionView, Delta Solutions ALEA, Demon for Windows, DSS Agent, DynamicCube.OCX, EKS/Empower, Essbase/400, Express Server, Objects Fiscal, Fusion, FYI Planner, Gentia, Harry Cube, Helm, Holos, Hyperion OLAP, InfoBeacon, Informer, inSight, Intelligent Decision Server, IQ/Vision, Khalix, Lightship, Matryx, Media, Metacube, MIK-Solution, MineShare, MIT/400, MUSE, NetCube, NGS-IQ, OpenOLAP, Pablo, ParaScope, PowerPlay, Rapid OLAP, Sagent Datamart Solution, SAS System, SpaceOLAP, StarTrieve The Ant Colony, TM/1, Toto for Excel, Track Objects, Visualizer Plans for OS/2, VSFLEX

Data Mining vs. OLAP

With the proliferation of data warehouses, new data mining tools are flooding the market offering to discover hidden gold in your data. Many traditional report and query tools and statistical analysis systems are using the term "data mining" in their product descriptions. In the midst of this marketing activity it is sometimes difficult to know what a data mining tool is and how it works. Perhaps a definition would help in clearing the confusion.

The methodology of data mining involves the extraction of hidden predictive information from large databases. However, with such a broad definition as this, an online analytical processing OLAP product could be said to qualify as a data mining tool. That is where the technology comes in, because for true knowledge discovery to take place, a data mining tool should arrive at this hidden information *automatically*.

Still another difference between OLAP and data mining is how they *operate* on the data. Similar to the direction of statistics, OLAP is a top-down approach to data analysis. OLAP tools are powerful and fast tools for *reporting* on data, in contrast to data mining tools that focus on *finding patterns* in data. For example, OLAP involves the summation of multiple databases into highly complex tables; OLAP tools deal with aggregates and are basically concerned with addition and the summation of numeric values, such as dollar amounts or cash. Manual OLAP may be based on need-to-know facts, such as regional sales reports stratified by type of businesses, while automatic data mining is based on the need to *discover* what factors are influencing these sales.

An OLAP tool is not a data mining tool since the query originates with the user. Neural networks, machine-learning, and genetic algorithms, on the other hand, do qualify as true automatic data mining tools because they autonomously interrogate the data for patterns. This is known as *supervised learning,* while another less common form of data mining is called "clustering" or *unsupervised learning.* In both instances, however, the bottom-up approach to data analysis distinguishes data mining from OLAP.

The current crop of OLAP tools have tremendous capabilities for performing sophisticated user-driven queries, but they are limited in their capability to discover hidden trends and patterns in a database. Statistical tools can provide excellent features for describing and visualizing large chunks of data, as well as performing verification-driven data analysis. Autonomous data mining tools, however, based on artificial intelligence (AI) technologies, are the only tools designed to automate the process of knowledge discovery—and to optimize this with their "built-for-business" features:

- Robustness for handling any kind of data: noisy, missing, mixed
- Exportable solutions in the form of practical business rules
- Easy to understand results via graphical decision trees
- Accurate results, especially with real-world data sets

Data mining by this definition is thus data-driven, not user-driven or verification-driven.

Traditionally, the goal of identifying and utilizing information hidden in data has been achieved through the use of query generators and data interpretation systems. This involves a user forming a theory about a possible relation in a database and converting this hypothesis into a query. For example, a user might have a hypothesis about the relationship between the sales of color printers to business customers. A query would be generated against the user's data warehouse or website inventory database and segmented into a report by client accounts using Standard Industry Codes and quarterly sales.

Certainly the information generated will provide a good overview on the relationship, if any, between types of businesses and sales of printers. However, this verification type of data mining is limited in several ways. First, it is based on a hunch—that there is a relationship between the industry a company is in and the number of printers it buys or leases. Second, the quality of the extracted information is based on the user's interpretation of the results and is thus subject to error.

In another example, an OLAP tool can tell a bookseller about the total number of books it sold for a region during a quarter. Data mining, on the other hand, can tell it about *the factors influencing* the sales of the books. A typical OLAP report is an aggregate count from several tables:

Category	Amount	Percentage Variance from Budget
Product Sales		
Fiction	1,847,743.00	2.13%
Nonfiction	606,735.00	2.03%
Periodicals	807,987.00	0.19%
Accessories	532,585.00	1.77%
Total Sales	3,262,465.00	1.76%
Margin	2,189,687.00	1.64%
Total Expenses	1,262,312.00	2.04%
Profit	927,375.00	1.07%

Thus, OLAP can tell you about the total number of books sold for this region during this quarter. Data mining can tell you about the patterns of book sales, while statistics can provide another dimension about these sales. Online analytical processing and statistics provide top-down, query-driven analysis, while data mining provides bottom-up, discovery-driven analysis. Data mining requires no assumptions. Rather, it identifies facts or conclusions based on patterns discovered.

Website Analysis Tools

With a firm's website increasingly becoming the first point of contact between a potential client and that company, its importance has increased. Today websites demand full-time design and maintenance teams and multimillion-dollar budgets. Management must know who's visiting and, more important, who is buying. In addition, companies that place ads on a site want to gauge their effectiveness. Websites today must earn their keep as business investments and, just like any other marketing effort, they must justify themselves. That's where some of the current website analysis tools come in.

Every time you visit a site, the web server enters a valuable record of that transaction in a log file. Every time you visit an electronic commerce site, a cookie is issued to you for tracking what your interests are and what products or services you are purchasing; every time you complete a form at a site, that information is written to a file.

Although these server log files and form-generated databases are rich in information, the data is itself usually abbreviated and cryptic in plain text format with comma delimiters, making it difficult and time-consuming to mine them. The volume of information is also overwhelming: A one-megabyte log file typically contains 4,000 to 5,000 page requests. Website analysis tools typically import the log-file data into a built-in database, which in turn transforms the data into aggregate reports or graphs.

This information can be fine-tuned to meet the needs of different individuals in your firm. For example, a web administrator may want to know about the clicks leading to documents and images, files, scripts, and applets. A designer will want to know how visitors navigate the site and whether there are paths or points from which many visitors jump to another site. The marketing team will want to know the effectiveness of certain promotions. Advertisers and partners may be interested in the number of clickthroughs your website has generated to their sites. Most website analysis tools provide answers to such questions as:

- What are the most common paths to the most important pages on your site?
- What keywords bring the most traffic to your site from search engines?
- How long does it take visitors from Texas to view your homepage?
- How many pages do visitors typically view on your website?
- How may visitors are you getting from Europe or Asia?
- How much time do visitors spend in your website?
- How many new users visit your site every month?

Most tools provide graphical views of your website traffic via different criteria and, like statistical and OLAP tools, provide the same type of aggregate views of web-generated data. Figure 2–3 is a report showing how many visits on a website by the hour in a day. A "visit" is a series of clicks by the same user. Figure 2–4 is a website traffic report showing the organizations or search engines that sent visitors to this site most frequently. There must be referral information in the log files for this report to be generated.

Obviously the more you know about how many people are visiting your site, who they are, and what parts of your site they are using, the better off your site will be. Using this information to improve your site and relating it to other traditional marketing programs will help you refine your overall website design. The average businesses today spends anywhere from $25,000 a year for a standard intranet site to $1.25 million for a full-featured website that supports electronic commerce, according to recent estimates from International

Figure 2–3
A graphical report of website daily "hits."

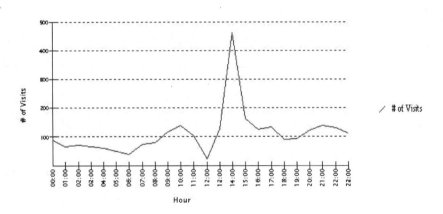

Figure 2–4
A graphical report of referring websites and search engines.

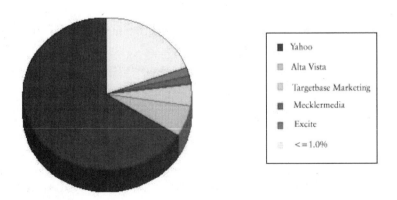

Data Corporation. With costs such as these it is common for a justification of these expenditures to be made. One way of protecting these huge investments is through the monitoring of web traffic.

The best—and sometimes only—way to glean that information in a usable format is with traffic analysis and monitoring software. The software runs the gamut in functionality and price, as tools range from free to upward of $100,000. On the low end, basic packages and downloadable utilities provide entry-level analysis for small- to medium-volume sites and intranets. These packages can tell you such information as how many visitors came to the site, the most- and least-requested pages, where visitors entered and exited, and other notable path analysis and historical trend data. High-volume websites involved in electronic retailing most likely will opt for more sophisticated high-dollar software that provides comprehensive analysis of traffic flow as well as detailed information about each visitor and their trek through the site. Knowing who enters—and who buys your product—can be critical to the success or failure of your electronic business.

"Log file analyzers" do as their name suggests—they take information recorded by your server and summarize the data in an intelligible format. Most analyzers compile data into a database from which they can run reports; their speed is measured in terms of both loading data into the database and compiling the report. Certain programs load in real time by "sniffing" every packet and stuffing the database. Others load the log file into the database at off-peak times specified by the administrator. Complex commerce sites may also require analysis tools with the capabilities to conduct qualitative and quantitative analysis of marketing and advertising data. If a company runs an ad on three different websites, a tool should be able to compare how many people were referred from each site, or which links were most commonly selected.

Lastly, for sites with search capabilities, some web analysis tools can report on which keywords visitors used, which sites have links to you and provide the majority of users, and which search engines provided the most valuable visitors. All of this information is readily available from log files. Since the first action for most visitors to a website is a search, it is sometimes very important to know what they're looking for. If you know that information along with where they're coming from, where they're going, and how long they will linger, then your site can truly become an effective marketing engine. The following is a partial listing of some of these web analysis tools, along with a discussion of some of their features and limitations:

Figure 2–5
This is a three-dimensional view of website traffic for a single month.

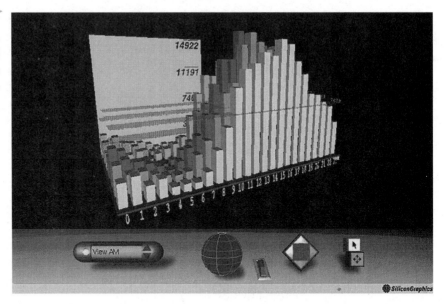

3Dstats is an Access Statistics Generator. It analyzes web server log files and creates a Virtual Reality Markup Language (VRML) model with the average loads by day and hour. With a VRML viewer like CosmoPlayer, the user can "walk" through the statistical "scene" and examine the bar chart from different points of view for daily, weekly, or monthly reports. See Figure 2–5.

Accrue Insight analyzes packets of information in real time (also known as *packet sniffing*). Insight gauges performance according to how fast a server responds to requests. It can collect and store data on more than a million hits per hour, and the resulting data is stored in the most granular form possible to allow for the widest variety of sorting, analysis, and report-generation possibilities. The product is especially good at tracking click streams through a large commercial multi-server site.

Aquas Bazaar Analyzer is based entirely on Java, which means reports can be viewed with any browser. With this analyzer, the log file needn't be transferred to the viewer's machine to be massaged. Reports are generated in your browser window, with graphs appearing as customizable Java applets.

Aria uses agents to analyze real-time traffic right on the server and generates real-time reports with plenty of information. The Aria architecture consists of three parts: the monitor, the recorder, and the reporter. The monitor takes the form of server agents that intercept traffic from the web server; the recorder receives

Figure 2–6
Mercury Interactive's Astra SiteManger dynamically link maps your web-site activity.

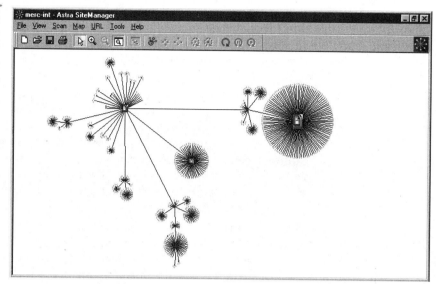

and processes the data; and the reporter presents the information in charts. The monitor module records information about the activity between the web client and server, including request data, form-field posted data, server-response data, cookie data, and user-profile data. It stores the information in an object-oriented database that comes with the software. No other database is needed.

Astra checks and validates all of your site's links and shows you any access problems you may be having. Your site is turned into a visual tree-diagram map, complete with links to CGI scripts and Java applets. Bad links are displayed as red points on the map for quick access and repairs. You can use Astra SiteManager as a log analysis tool: It reads your server's log file and superimposes usage patterns directly over your site map, showing you exactly which pages are getting the most clicks. (See Figure 2–6.) Astra SiteManager scans your entire site, highlighting functional areas with color-coded links and URLs to give you a complete visual map of your website.

Hit List Standard and *Hit List Pro* from Marketwave offers a wide variety of 27 preconfigured reports that help you track your web traffic. Hit List creates its own relational database of your server logs instead of working directly from the logs themselves. All reports can be redesigned through the design feature. Hit List Standard tracks user paths to and through a site and tallies download attempts. Hit List Pro can tell you the average number of pages that users coming from a certain site tend to view, and it can parse search strings from other sites, such as Yahoo!, to determine exactly why and how a user comes to your site. It also offers extensive querying capabilities for clickthrough rates of specific online advertisements.

Interse offers tracking software with several standard report types detailing hits, visitors, browser types, and traffic patterns. This tool creates its reports from log files off-line, which is good if your provider does not want your software on its network and if monthly reporting is all you need. You can cross-reference data from multiple websites or expand your usage analysis by integrating data from additional sources such as demographic and psychographic registration forms.

net.Analysis Pro, by net.Genesis, offers marketing and technical reports. It provides extensive path analysis and entry and exit page reports, as well as some demographic information. net.Analysis Pro not only reports top domains accessing the site and the most popular geographical areas, but it correlates them into a single report. This information is limited in value by large Internet service providers (ISPs), like EarthLink and FlashNet, that serve users throughout the country.

NetIntellect is another log-file analysis tool. Through compression, the NetIntellect database is as much as 95 percent smaller than your original server logs. Compression is essential for reports spanning weeks, months, or even years, because without it the combined files get too large for processing. NetIntellect lets you process more than one log file at a time, and it provides a feature for comparing log files as well.

NetStats Pro has a query builder with which you can construct your own customized log reports. You can filter whatever fields you wish either into or out of the report (complete with multiple Boolean expressions and time/date ranges). The program can analyze local log files or download files from your server machine through FTP. The standard report includes details on the top three domain extensions from which your visitors come, the files they access, and the activity across the day and the week.

NetTracker is another Java-written analyzer. Users do not need to download log files to their machines, nor do they need to run any software besides their browsers.

PressVu is an log analysis tool for small peer websites running over dedicated dial-up connections using Microsoft PWS on Windows 95 or NT Workstation. PressVu Desktop imports plain text source logs into an xBase file format database. The PressVu main interface supports easy access to the InterNIC WHOIS database and DNS hostname lookup.

SurfReport is a unique web traffic analysis tool in that it can generate reports via e-mail or your browser. SurfReport runs on virtually any platform and any operating system and is completely server-based, allowing the generation of reports from anywhere on the Web.

Webtrends lets you scan your server statistics almost immediately, working in the background to compile the information it needs. It doesn't require lengthy initial importing of log files into its database format, but instead creates its first reports on the fly as the log files are being read in. WebTrends works primarily on server log files, but it also allows you to capture cookie information, referring sites, browser identity, and user details.

Website Analysis Tools vs. Data Mining Tools

Modern web analysis tools provide the same type of views of data as statistical and OLAP tools. They emphasize aggregate counts and spatial views of website traffic over time, which like statistical and OLAP tools, are not easily able to discover hidden patterns without extensive interactive queries.

Because of the massive amount of data that even the simplest log file contains, the process of pattern recognition can be extremely difficult if not impossible with this generation of tools. As with statistical and OLAP tools, web analysis tools are verification-driven. They operate from the top down rather than self-organize themselves around the data via the use of a machine-learning algorithm or a neural network. Like OLAP tools, web analysis tools are good at generating aggregate reports via several dimensions, which are important to management, web administrators, and designers, who are limited to measuring browser, not shopper activity.

Daily Totals for http://www.webminer.com/

Date	Clients	Hits	Pages
Mon Oct 28 1999	196	1291	407
Tue Oct 29 1999	165	1092	330

Period Totals for http://www.webminer.com/

Individual Clients	Total Hits	Page Hits
353	2383	737

Daily Averages for http://www.webminer.com/

Clients	Hits	Page Hits
181	1192	369

However, almost all web analysis tools lack the capability to identify important market segments from web-generated data. With the exception of Aptex, which is really a text-analysis software product incorporating neural network and proprietary modeling technology, no web analysis tool does pattern recognition. (Aptex is developing neural network predictive models to do "intelligent advertising" in such sites as Netscape, Excite, and InfoSeek.)

Almost all of the current web analysis tools do very good and innovative data reporting via tables, charts, graphs, and 3D VRML. Several vendors, like Astra, are beginning to explore advanced forms of visualization such as link analysis. Some, like NetTracker and SurfReport, are taking advantage of the Web to deliver their results via thin client browser by writing their reports tools in Java. Still other firms are offering network services by which your website traffic data is transferred to their servers, like I/PRO's *NetLine* for third party analysis and auditing.

Today's advertising-funded websites rely on usage statistics like TV networks rely on Nielsen rating points. Hit traffic counts, the traditional measure of a website's effectiveness, is all but useless to advertisers. Instead of counting the number of times a page is viewed, they are more interested in tabulating every inline graphic, Common Gateway Interface (CGI) script, and Java class resulted in a click-through or sale. Advertisers need to know not only how many pages are viewed, but also how many people visit their website. These marketers need to know the demographics of their visitors, so they can sell ads. For starters they want to know who is accessing the website and where these visitors are coming from. Some of this information is available from log files, like referral information, but some is not. It is at this juncture that data mining tools and techniques can assist the web marketer and electronic retailer.

A data mining tool does not replace a web analysis tool, but it does give the web administrator a lot of additional possibilities for answering some of the marketing and business questions. For example, imagine trying to formulate answers to questions such as:

What is an optimal segmentation of my website visitors?

Who is likely to purchase my new online products and services?

What are the most important trends in my website visitors' behavior?

What are the characteristics or features of my most loyal online clients?

Theoretically, these questions could be answered with a web analysis tool. For example, a web administrator could try to define criteria for a customer profile and query the data to see whether they work or not. In a process of trial and error, a marketer could gradually develop enough intuitions about the distinguishing features of its predominant website customers, such as their gender, age, location, income levels, etc. However, in a dynamic environment such as the Web this type of analysis is very time-consuming and subject to bias and error.

Manual processing in this fashion could take days or months to find the optimal customer profile for this dynamic market segment from a large retailing site. On the other hand, a data mining tool (such as a decision tree generator) that incorporates machine-learning technology could find a better answer automatically, in a much shorter time—typically within minutes. More importantly, this type of autonomous segmentation is unbiased and driven by the data, not the analyst's intuition.

For example, using a data mining tool, a log file can be segmented into statistically significant clusters very quickly. The decision tree in Figure 2–7 was generated by a data mining tool incorporating several symbolic classifiers, including ID3 (Interactive Dichotomizer, a machine-learning algorithm) and two statistical algorithms, CHAID (CHI-squared Automatic Interaction Detection) and CART (Classification and Regression Tree). A unique feature of the tool is that it runs CART and CHAID concurrently, which means both continuous and discrete dependent and independent variables can be modeled without preprocessing or scaling. The tool generates Multivariate Decision Trees, IF-THEN rules, and SQL syntax.

In Figure 2–8 a data mining tool was able to generate a decision tree identifying two important features about its website visitors. It identified key *attributes,* the type of computer products being sold by this website and *intervals,* the income dollar

Figure 2–7
*Data mining a
website can
reveal hidden
ratios for online
sales.*

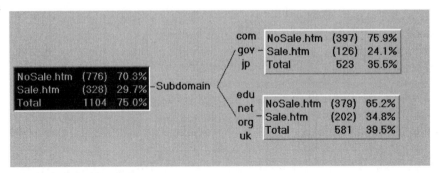

Figure 2–8
*The leaves of a
decision tree
represent market
segments of
online
customers.*

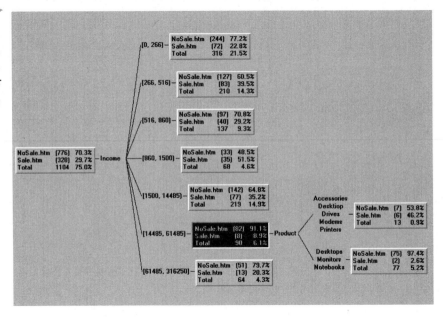

ranges—differentiating between customers who made online purchases and those who did not.

What is important to note is that these clusters, which represent market segments, were discovered by a machine-learning algorithm in a matter of minutes rather than by a web administrator's manual analysis of the reports. Data mining does not replace data analysis; it simply automates it. Equally important to note is that while a data mining tool may discover a cluster or a potentially profitable market segment, a web analysis tool can provide the needed analysis to perform the projected profits from each of these market segments. A web analysis statistical tool can provide the charts to visually represent the findings to management about the significance of these newly discovered market segments. In conclusion, you should use all of the tools available to you. As in the construction of a building, several types of tools are required, each designed for specific tasks and yet each contributing to the completion of the total project.

Visual Data Mining

An optional method by which to perform data mining is through the use of visualization tools. The value of these tools is gained when used in conjunction with other tools such as neural networks and machine-learning algorithms. Some of the features of these tools are being incorporated in current web analysis tools such as Mercury Interactive's Astra SiteManager, which uses a form of link analysis.

The sections that follow list several of these systems and discuss their unique capabilities, including features, functions, user interfaces, volume of information, customization, integration issues, and typical uses. Of interest is of course how they can be used to supplement your insight about your website patterns in conjunction with other data mining tools. These visualization systems fall into three general classes: visualization packages, link analysis systems, and quantitative displays.

Visualization Packages

Information visualization uses abstract representations in interactive, immersive, 3D, virtual environments to display large quantities of data. It is one of the best methods for proactively exposing trends within a data warehouse (and website data), which is usually accomplished by navigating data landscapes and visually orienting the data to reveal hidden biases. Information visualization systems are also geared toward support of real-time applications, since parametric values can be displayed as an animated or simulated dimension of data. The following tools are representative of these visualization packages: *SpotFire*, *Visual-ID (Lucent Technologies)*, *Visible Decisions* (VDI), and *Metaphor Mixer* (Maxus Corporation).

Figure 2–9 is a view of customers of a department store that utilizes a visualization tool to design a direct mailing campaign based on several client features, such as ZIP code, gender, and age. A tool such as this can be used to examine the demographics of your website visitors in order to explore possible pockets of geographic interest by ZIP codes or other criteria. This tool provides an interactive feature that allows the user to move the sliders on the right and view the

Figure 2–9
*Variables, like
gender, can be
moved on the
right and viewed
on the chart
and map.*

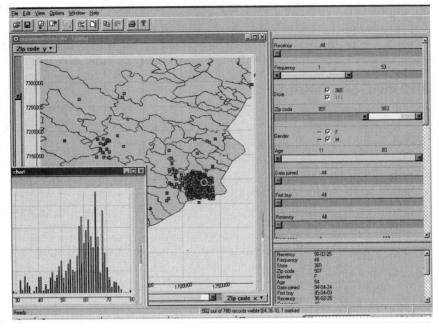

changes between multiple variables, such as frequency of purchase and receipt average, both on the map and on the chart on the left.

Link Analysis Systems

Link analysis is based on a branch of mathematics called *graph theory,* and uses a combination of binary relationships established between object representations to generate networks of interactions and associations from defined data sets. Link analysis is not applicable to all types of data nor can it solve all types of problems. The aggregate number of data records presented using link analysis is somewhat limited and the analyses tend to focus on verifying sets of related information. Different layouts, filter assessments, and presentation formats provide link analysis systems with the candid ability to quickly identify patterns that occur from unusual relationships, emerging groups, and important connections.

Some of the areas where link analysis has yielded good results are in analyzing telephone call patterns and combining leads of information sources. A cellular phone company may use a link system in order to analyze call patterns for purposes of discovering how customers differ. The FBI is using a link analysis system to combine information from disparate sources to help the bureau in solving crimes. Link analysis is able to capitalize on relationships and derive

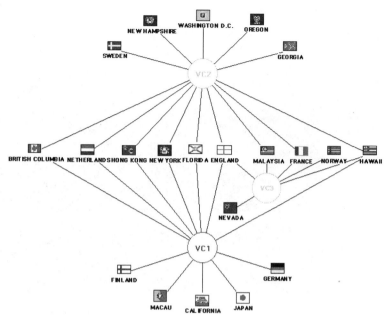

Figure 2–10
A link analysis tool discovered the behavior and relationships in a fraudulent scheme.

characteristics that normally may be missed by traditional methods of analysis.

A link analysis tool can be used to identify relationships between certain products or web pages in your site. It can also provide a visual insight into other hidden relationships based on the demographics of your website visitors. (See Figure 2–10.) However, one major drawback to link systems is their inefficient performance in relational databases. The following tools are representative of link analysis type systems: *NETMAP* (ALTA Analytics), *IMAGIX-4D* (Imagix Corporation), *Analyst Notebook* (I2), *WATSON* (Harlequin), and *GVA* (United Information Systems).

Quantitative Display

Quantitative diagrams can handle extremely large volumes of data, typically containing numerical representations. These diagrams tend to have a traditional statistical look and feel to them for clustering, summarization, and range comparisons. Recent implementations have pushed the limits of these diagrams to perform hyper-dimensional analyses, which make them ideal candidates for identifying *linear* or exponential trends occurring within data sets. (See Figure 2–11.) The following tools represent quantitative display systems: *DIAMONDS* (IBM/SPSS), *CrossGraphs* (Belmont Research), and *Temple-MVV* (Mihalisin).

Figure 2–11
*In a 3D environ-
ment, layers of
noisy data can
be removed to
find clusters
of hidden
knowledge.*

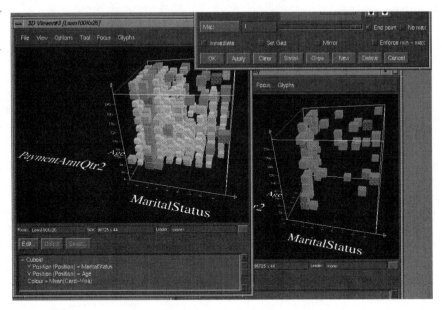

Data Mining Solutions

Data mining can confirm marketing and management observations about your website and its visitors. Through data mining you can quantify these observations so that you know at what point in time sales are likely to occur, or what dollar ranges exist between profitable and unprofitable web sessions. Data mining can lead to subtle improvements in efficiency as well as breakthrough findings in the design and structure of your website. Through the mining of your website you may find that, yes, your best customers are between age 36 and 42, or you may discover to your surprise that your products and services do best with women and not men, as you originally thought! The information that you gather from your registration forms and the mining of the content in your database can tell you this and much more, such as what products to associate for increase cross-selling opportunities, or what information links or advertising to provide your visitors based on their gender, age, demographics, and lifestyle interests. Local sources can also be associated based on ZIP code culled from these registration forms.

As previously stated, data mining is more than the use of software tools, it is a business *process* designed to extract actionable intelligence for product and financial analysis, sales, marketing support, and customer segmentation gathered from your dynamic customer information file. Data mining is about knowledge discovery for

Figure 2–12
One common data mining solution is a decision tree, which segments a database.

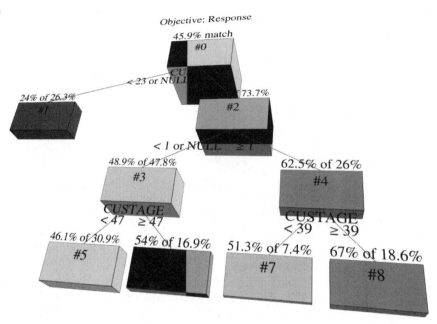

strategic advantage. The format of a data mining analysis or data mining tools may vary. For example, it may be in the form of visualization, such the graphical decision tree shown in Figure 2–12.

The results of data mining can also be in the form of IF-THEN rules, which are usually market segments extracted from your website data:

IF	website customer age is less than 47
THEN	response to offer is 46.1%
IF	website customer age is greater than or equal to 47
THEN	response to offer is 54%
IF	website customer age is less than 39
THEN	response to offer is 51.3%
IF	website customer age is greater than or equal to 39
THEN	response to offer is 67%

Still another possible solution available from the data mining process is C code, which usually is representative of a set of weights, or formulas. These weights are usually extracted from a data mining tool incorporating a neural or polynomial network as its core technology:

```
**************/
double *webminer(double inarr[])
{
/* node5—Successful_Suburbanites */
    node5  = -1.19493 + 0.032543*LIMIT(Successful_Suburbanites,0,82.9);
    /* node31—Young_Frequent_Movers */ node31  = -0.22708 +
    0.0943097*LIMIT(Young_Frequent_Movers,0,100);
    /* node32—Rural_Industrial_Workers */
    node32  = -0.367938 + 0.0455085*LIMIT(Rural_Industrial_Workers,0,100);
    /* node51—Triplet */
    node51  = 0 - 22.0566 - 40.4871*node5 - 18.3542*pow2(node5)
        + 0.174813*pow3(node5) - 68.848*node31
        - 156.303*node5*node31 - 83.2704*pow2(node5)*node31
        - 44.5781*pow2(node31) - 37.7005*node5*pow2(node31)
        - 0.0442751*pow3(node31) - 64.3699*node32
        - 54.3879*node5*node32 - 185.61*node31*node32
        - 156.467*node5*node31*node32 - 0.270547*pow2(node31)*node32
        - 0.109251*pow2(node32) - 0.272628*node31*pow2(node32)
        - 0.00897233*pow3(node32) ;
```

Some data mining tools are also able to generate SQL syntax, which can be exported from the analysis and used in a production system to extract a set of records in your databases, which meet the parameters of the query:

```
/* SQL 1 */
select * from table
where
    (
        High Rise Renters = 0 or
        High Rise Renters = 0.1 or
        High Rise Renters = 0.6
    );
/* SQL 2 */
select * from table
where
    (
        High Rise Renters = 1.7
    );
/* SQL 3 */
select * from table
where
    (
        High Rise Renters = 11.7 or
        High Rise Renters = 28.4
    );
/* SQL 4 */
select * from table
where
    (
        High Rise Renters = 51.3 or
        High Rise Renters = 83 or
        High Rise Renters = 91
    );
```

Keep in mind that the data mining process and the multiple formats of its solutions all have one single goal: insight into the behavior of your online visitors and customers.

Why and Who, Not What

Data mining is about *why,* not *what.* Data mining is about discovering *why* the total sales in your website are up for a particular product or service, or *why* certain website visitors have purchased from your online catalog certain items from certain ZIP codes and age ranges, while others have not. It is about *why* certain website visitors are likely to continuously purchase your product and services, while others will not. Data mining is about discovering *why* the sales figures in your website traffic activity reports are as they are, and as such, it is a much more powerful technology than simple aggregate domain counts.

Data mining is also about *who.* Who visits your website and buys your products and services, who your most loyal and profitable online customers are. Data mining is about ratios, rules, attributes, features, patterns, signatures, and influences hidden in your website data. It is about discovering the reasons or relations behind the numbers in your website traffic activity reports. It is also about uncovering the core differences between your website visitors, online customers, services, products, and sales. Data mining is about *why* and *who,* not *how many.* It can be used to answer such questions as:

- What makes a website visitor profitable or unprofitable?
- What kinds of website visitors respond to your advertising?
- What traits do profitable visitors have in common?
- Why did this online product sell with this visitor?
- What will these website visitors buy next week?

Data mining is about using autonomous pattern recognition technology for achieving specific business objectives, such as increasing your website sales. It is about *perception, learning,* and *evolving*—all human functions that can assist your company in recognizing the fast-changing electronic commerce environment. For example, data mining is about increasing your market share by recognizing who your most valuable online customers are—understanding their features and using that knowledge to identify new website visitors through targeted marketing and advertising.

The Online Corner Store

With detailed information about the customer's habits at the point-of-contact, a website can provide individualized interaction, much like the neighborhood store. For example, a bookseller website can display titles matching an individual consumer's preferences. With growing personalized attention during every transaction, a website customer will perceive added value in their relation with that bookseller. The focus of this type of individualized marketing is on owning a greater market share of an individual customer over time. A clear advantage to relational marketing is that during the process of increasing the share of each customer, the company is both building a long-term relationship and learning about that customer with every transaction. This has an additional benefit since it is cheaper to increase sales to existing customers than to acquire new customers.

The website can track customers, it can enable interactive dialog, and it can allow mass customization of products and services created and presented to an individual's unique needs and requirements. The key is to know about as much as possible about each of your website customers. Dialog is the most important aspect of relational marketing. You need to facilitate website visitor communications—act on their feedback and reciprocate by making suggestions and recommendations—in order to build trusting and loyal relationships, which in turn will translate into more online sales and profits.

The use of lifestyle data, or "psychographics," became prevalent in the 1980s, and in the 1990s Regis McKenna introduced the concept of relationship marketing. McKenna suggested moving away from marketing to everybody and instead concentrating on knowing your customers and developing a relationship with them. McKenna's marketing concepts are about developing products and services to serve a specific market, by defining the standards in that market and developing a deep relationship with those customers. More important, relational marketing is a concept ideal for the Web and electronic retailing. The rapid decline of computer prices, coupled with their increased performance and storage capacity, has made the practice of using databases in marketing almost commonplace during the last decade.

A more recent concept further narrows the marketing from segment to that of individuals. Marketing visionaries Peppers and Rogers in their book *The One-to-One Future* actually saw the marketing environment a full year before the Web burst into the scene. In their book they introduced the concept of marketing to an individual on a one-to-one basis over an extended period of time and in the process learning as much about them as possible. Today, like the little corner store, the web merchant can remember what products you like, stock for your convenience, then e-mail you product-specific offers.

Selling as a Service

The goal of selling on the Web is to increase repeat purchases by focusing on brand recognition and customer profitability over their lifetime. Selling on the Web is an opportunity to build loyalty, which will reduce customer attrition and build a higher rate of profit per customer. Because each transaction requires less cost than the initial one, loyal clients are the most profitable, as they tend to spend more over time. Loyalty is fostered by feedback, which should be facilitated either via CGI forms and e-mail so that your clients can tell you who they are and what they want from your website.

In the process of interacting with your website customers, it is important that you assure them of the confidentiality of the information they are disclosing. Keep in mind that customer information is your competitive arsenal and should not be shared or provided to another firm without your clients' approval. On your registration forms, ensure you don't ask for all of the information at once and that you give your website customers an option over what information they provide you. Lastly, give them something in exchange for the information they do disclose to you, such as a special shopping area or a discounted pricing rate.

Data mining performs many functions: it can assist you in assessing the performance of your website and in the integration of your website visitor profiles; it can help you in segmenting your website customers by profitability, loyalty value, overall usage, and number of visits; it can also assist you in the construction of predictive models for targeting future clients.

There is a continuum in this process of data acquisition. For example, the targeting of your products and services is first of all driven by your website's content. A customer will go to an auto site because she wants information on that new sport utility model, or to a sport site because she wants details on that game last night. This is the first level. The second level of the continuum involves some server and browser specifics, and at this point the data is contained in log files, such as access time and day, referring engine, sub-domain and HTMLs requested and viewed. At the third level, the data involves registration and demographic information gleaned from ZIP codes. At this point you are dealing at a market segment level, which can be mined by such data mining tools as a decision trees generator. At the fourth and final level, the data involves individual customer behavior, including page views, clickthroughs, queries, ad impressions, and transactions. At this narrow one-to-one level a neural network tool is required for scoring individuals by propensity to purchase specific products or services.

Web Marketing

Because the Web can track visitors at the granular level, ads can be targeted to those potential customers most likely to respond based on confidential user profiles and their mined behavior. Data mining typically involves a process know as "supervised learning" in which a pattern or a signature is discovered for a particular group of consumers. These are customers with specific tendencies and attributes, which when identified can be used to target new potential prospects with similar profiles. The benefit of relational marketing via data mining is that it gives your visitors and customers the opportunity to teach you what they truly want and desire.

Before you can mine your website data you must plan and design the processes by which you can capture the attributes of your visitors and customers. For starters, your website data has the capacity of targeting ads, products, and services at several levels, the first of which begins with your server log files:

- geographic location
- prior purchases
- browser type
- time of day
- past clicks
- IP address

If you are using forms for purchases, registration, games, guest books, contests, or other types of promotions, you have a second level by which you can begin to capture actual visitor and customer profile information, such as:

- occupation
- profession
- ZIP code
- gender
- age

At the third level you have the actual behavior of your customers, whose actions you can mine in order to identify specific patterns or signatures. At this level, an additional data component from cookie files can begin to be assembled and mined in order to discover propensities for clickthroughs and actual online sales. Data from the prior two other levels can also be merged in order to construct models and profiles identifying the attributes of these customers.

When this information is assembled, data mining techniques can be used to infer customer composites about lifestyle similarities, attributes, and characteristics. With these insights you can begin to fine tune your advertising and marketing campaigns. Through the careful design and integration of your forms you can begin to learn from your visitors and customers what they like and don't like about your products and services and those of your competitors. Through this process you can increase your revenue stream from each customer and begin to gain a competitive advantage. In the process of retaining customers, the cost of attracting new ones is reduced, since it costs less to keep them than to acquire new ones. Tracking, capturing, and mining data from advertising and your website promotional efforts are important, especially if you are gathering useful demographic data relevant to your business objective: *online sales.*

The more targeted your ads and online promotions are, the more qualified the leads you're likely to get and the higher a response you are likely to see. Website visitors and customers behave differently and have unique needs for using the Internet, which means you should be aware of their idiosyncrasies. With the data mining of your website you will gradually "learn" to deal with your customers in subtle but effective ways—with different cues, offers, and content—targeted much narrower than traditional media.

Your website has the ability to provide individualized products and services when it captures enough data for mining from assorted log and cookie files and personal information captured from your site's forms. There are additional technologies, techniques, and services unique to the Web which you can use to generate the data for mining, including products and services from BroadVision's Relational, ADSmart, Engage Technologies, and GuestTrack. However, before this can succeed, security and privacy concerns need to be addressed. You need to respond to concerns over silent tracking techniques via cookies, collaborative agents, ad servers, etc., and explicitly inform your visitors and customers how you plan to use the data you are capturing to personalize their experience while they are in your website. Your primary reason for data mining should be to create such a high level of customer service that your clients will not want to defect to your competitors.

Online Coupons

Online coupons are a very cost-effective vehicle for conducting market research over the Web and collecting very accurate consumer product information. To collect online coupons, shoppers choose savings offers from a special selection in a retailer's website. After clicking on their personal choices, shoppers receive securely printed, copy-resistant coupons through the mail, redeemable at any of the retailer's physical locations.

Blending traditional market research and web ad tracking, electronic and physical retailers are beginning to use online coupons to efficiently and cost effectively learn more about their customers. (See Figure 2–13.) Visitors to retailer websites can complete forms in order to obtain coupons, and as they do so they are asked about their gender, the number of people in their household, whether they have a pet, and so forth, in order for the coupons to be tailor-made to their consuming specifications. Online coupons have a high response rate—in some cases, over 20 percent on a variety of national branded

Figure 2–13
Online coupons can gather important consumer information.

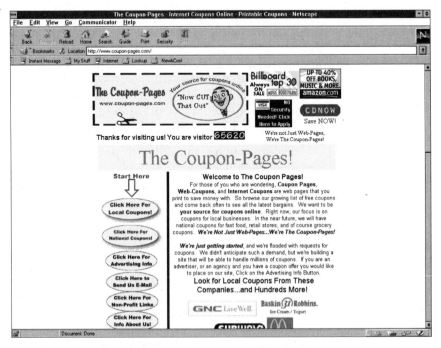

products from leading consumer-packaged goods manufacturers. Traditional coupons average less than 2 percent redemption.

Mining Customer Value

Most of today's data mining tools are based in part on statistical algorithms such as CHAID (CHI-squared Automatic Interaction Detection) or CART (Classification and Regression Trees) and in part on several artificial intelligence technologies designed to emulate human perception, such as neural networks and machine-learning. Some of these data mining tools search for patterns in data and then organize their solutions as conjunctions or business rules. Data mining analyzers can deliver their solutions in useable business statements that are easy to grasp and implement by a web or marketing teams in an electronic commerce environment:

IF	Total Number of Visits Made =	7 through 9
AND	Category of Book Purchased =	Database Management
THEN	Total Projected Sales for Year =	$90

Unlike website tracking software, data mining technologies are designed to sort through hundreds and even thousands of data fields to find the few significant ones for profiling online customers by potential profit groups or market clusters. The core technology of most of today's data mining tools can split and evaluate hundreds of thousands of records and data fields in a web-generated database in order to arrive at those attributes that are influencing important business factors such as total sales.

The underlying mathematics of most data mining tools is manifested in how they compute the amount of "information gain" in a record relating to its class membership. *Gain criterion* is actually a measurement of information, or the amount of information conveyed in a message. Data mining tools (at least those incorporating symbolic classifier algorithms) actually compute this measurement as they process the records in a database in their search for patterns; they "interrogate" the database via a sequential process of small decisions, with each decision conceptually a yes/no classification based on properties of each customer record. The following is an example of how a data mining analysis may partition a single transaction in a website doing business-to-business retailing:

	Low LTV	High LTV
ZIP Code	94501	94502
Customer Since	1994	1996
Catalog Code	V78	B49
Last Purchase	96/04	98/04
Revolving Limit	$7,500	$51,000
Credit/Debit Ratio	45%	34%
Sub-domain	ORG	COM
# of Employees	32	12
SIC	896	456

Here, the transactions are split between Low and High LTV (lifetime value, i.e., the duration of their relationship with a site and the amount of money they spend during that time) on the basis of the data, rather than a hypothesis, hunch, or intuition of the web or marketing analyst, thus automating the process of stratification. Most data mining tools perform somewhat the same process on a database: they split it into classes that differ as much as possible in their relation to a selected output, such as total sales. In other words, a web database is split into subsets according to the results of statistical tests conducted on an output by the data mining algorithm and not a statistician, web, or marketing analyst.

One way to see this process is as a game of "20 Questions," where one player asks questions to determine the kind of object another player has in mind. Presented with a large web-generated customer database with varying "total sales," a data mining tool asks a series of questions about the LTV of each record, with a goal of classifying each sample into a class or group. LTV classes are thus determined by the properties of records in a database and generalized into predictive models from specific examples in that data set.

Another way of viewing data mining technology is as a simplifier. It enables the "pruning of noise" so that the web marketer or electronic retailer can identify the specific customer attributes, such as *establishment date* or *sub-domain*, which have the most effect on predicting online customer LTV. In addition to facilitating and improving web marketing efforts for its most profitable online customers, LTV analysis can indicate which Low LTV customers might warrant additional attention, enabling you to convert them to High LTV, or identifying those that do not warrant additional marketing since they are not profitable.

Data mining analysis can also assist marketing in the search for new online prospects, which "fit" the High LTV profile of your current customers. The following website database reflects an average customer sale amount of $200, but a data mining analysis uncovered three clusters of customers with varying LTVs and some insightful features. The three groups of LTV customers reflect total sales ranging from a low of $70 to a high of $900.

The Occasional Web Customer: Low LTV

IF	Sub-domain	=	AOL
AND	Connection Time	=	4 Through 6 Minutes
AND	Gender	=	Female
THEN	Total Sales	=	$70

The Average Web Customer: Medium LTV

IF	Transactions	=	3–4
AND	Age	=	40–49
AND	Gender	=	Male
THEN	Total Sale	=	$200

The Premier Web Customer: High LTV

IF	Age	=	25–39
AND	Sub-domain	=	NET
AND	Gender	=	Female
THEN	Total Sales	=	$900

With this analysis an electronic retailer may concentrate its banners, ads, and other marketing campaigns on retaining all *female* customers between 25 and 39 with sub-domains *.net*, since they represent the highest LTV for this company. At the same time, this website may want to construct a marketing campaign to introduce the Occasional Customers to the additional products they may not be aware of through banners designed to "educate" them, with an effort toward increasing sales. Through this process of segmentation a retailer can begin to construct marketing campaigns on the basis of what each market segment represents to their business. What's important in this example is that the data mining process discovered the unique features and intervals in the data signaling a unique "signature" of High LTV web customers vs. Low and Medium LTV buyers.

A key distinction between manual methods of web data analysis and data mining is that the process used to discover the key customer *attributes*, such as sub-domain and gender, or the *intervals*, the number of transactions 3 to 4, or age ranges 25 to 39 in the data set. The key difference in using data mining tools in the analysis of web data is that the algorithms and not the user discovered the customer attributes and value ranges. The data mining process can also discover the key intervals indicating when a web customer may be expected to go from a Low LTV to a High LTV. The iterative analysis of your web data can also point out such customer profiles as a "brand-switcher" or a "win-back" for a specific product or service, based on historical online trends and web transaction patterns.

Once a LTV profile has been identified by the mining of web-based data, additional enhancements can be made through "appends" from demographic and household external databases. Internal web customer databases can be improved through a "merge and purge" methodology, that is, by merging an internal web customer database with external lifestyle and demographic information. Through this process new features about online customers may be discovered. Next, through the use of data mining, irrelevant attributes can be purged from the database for determining LTV. For example, a website marketer may discover that High LTV web customers have unique attributes regarding specific income levels, or other lifestyle traits. Once the data mining tools have "learned" the dominant features of each LTV group, it can rank them in order of statistical importance:

Name	Ranges	Rank
Zip Code	1211 to 98776	13
# of Employees	03 to 89	49
SIC	000 to 999	03
Customer Since	1996 to 1998	04
Revolving Limit	0 to 90000	01
Credit/Debit Ratio	0 to 100	06

Using this type of rank table, a web marketer can purge those customer attributes in a database that have little or no use in identifying High LTV clients. For example, in the above data mining analysis of a business-to-business web retailer, *Revolving Limit* is the most important attribute in the data, while *Number of Employees* was of no importance and may be excluded from subsequent analysis. The merge-purge process can be viewed as a method of "condensing" a very large database, enabling the electronic retailer and marketer to focus on only those factors relevant to the grouping of high revenue producing online customers.

Networks and Algorithms

They're about Learning and Evolving

In the preceding chapters we discussed some of the electronic retailing applications of data mining and how the technology differs from traditional methods of data analysis. Now we will discuss in more detail how each of the technologies operates on a data set and what insight they can provide about your website. How do neural networks learn from data? How do machine-learning and statistical algorithms segment a database? How do genetic algorithms optimize the entire learning process into a method of evolutionary computing? In short, what are the underlying pattern recognition processes of today's data mining tools and toolboxes?

In order to understand and fully benefit from the process of pattern recognition, we need to know how this technology came about. We will take a short historical trek through several branches of artificial intelligence and some key events leading to the developments and acceptance of neural networks, machine-learning, and genetic algorithms, with maybe a couple of short excursions into the area of fuzzy logic and an introduction to the statistical algorithms CART (Classification and Regression Trees) and CHAID (CHI-squared Automatic Interaction Detection). These technologies are at the core of most of the current data mining tools, so knowing something about them will help you know how to use them to your advantage and in conjunction with each other to optimize your mining efforts.

Although we will not go into the gory details or math of back-propagation and Kohonen networks or the Interactive Dichotomizer and C5.0 algorithms, we will instead concentrate on explaining these concepts and the difference between what each network and algorithm does, specifically how each of them operates on the data and what you can expect from each in terms of business solutions. The scope of this chapter is to assist you in knowing how to leverage these technologies to improve your marketing presence and effectiveness on the Web, that is, to use the networks and algorithms effectively to improve your online bottom line.

Data mining is rooted in artificial intelligence. However, AI is a diverse field involving everything from natural language to expert systems. Most of the current data mining tools are based specifically on neural networks and genetic- and machine-learning algorithms—three branches of AI that continue to evolve today, but that experienced some important breakthroughs during the last decade. As such, they are relatively mature technologies that have migrated to commercial software in the form of both data mining tools for the desktop and high-end multiple-paradigm toolboxes for parallel processing servers.

AI has traditionally sought to emulate human processes. Its applications have basically involved attempts to get machines to do what humans do best. From robotics in manufacturing to agents on the Web, both are technologies designed to assist their creators. Likewise, neural networks and machine-learning and genetic algorithms are similar efforts to do through code what humans have been doing for millennia—to learn to recognize patterns. AI seeks to emulate human memory, learning, and evolution. However, not too long ago, the techniques for how to best do this were a matter of controversy and conflict. Two major forces of AI battled with each other not only in their approach on how to best replicate human functions, but also over government funding and corporate attention.

The AI War

Basically, there are two main schools of thought on how machines should learn: *inductive* and *deductive* analysis. (See Figure 3–1.) The deductive approach involves the construction of rules obtained from domain experts through interviews by knowledge engineers. These knowledge engineers go on to construct "expert system" programs containing sets of rules designed to "fire" when certain conditions are encountered by users. The inductive approach, on the other hand, involves the generation of rules directly from the data, rather than from domain experts.

The Top-Down Approach

The deductive approach was the dominant AI branch, receiving the most hype and attention during the 1970s and 1980s. Ten years ago when AI was the "hot" new technology expert systems received the

Figure 3–1
The roots of data mining are based on the inductive approach to knowledge discovery.

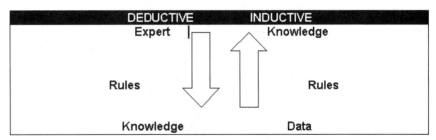

DEDUCTIVE	INDUCTIVE
Expert	Knowledge
Rules	Rules
Knowledge	Data

majority of support from both the government and venture funding. Expert systems used special languages, such as LISP and Prolog, and in some instances special workstations. For example, at one time American Express used an expert system to assist them in approving credit, while the Internal Revenue Service tried to use an expert system in the selection of tax returns for audits. A soup company attempted to construct an expert system by codifying the processes of its master cook.

The success of these expert systems, however, was short lived, as the programs suffered from significant shortcomings: they were brittle and expensive to maintain. Some expert systems required hundreds of rules that had to be manually maintained and updated to stay in tune to a rapidly changing business environment. Expert systems eventually proved to be too fragile and rigid to keep pace with the rapidly evolving conditions of everyday transactions. However, it was during this period that two researchers from the Massachusetts Institute of Technology, Seymour Papert and Marvin Minsky, vying for funding for expert system technology, wrote about the deficiencies of neural networks and thus stymied the development of the inductive approach to AI for several years.

The Bottom-Up Approach

The alternate approach to AI is inductive data analysis, which extracts patterns from data and learns from examples. The inductive approach to AI involves generating the rules for a system from thousands of cases, in contrast to extracting the rules from experts via interviews. It was an approach to rule generation that did not take off until the 1980s with the work of several researchers from diverse fields of mathematics, statistics, and computational science. John Hopfield advanced the concept of a feedback neural network. J. Ross Quinlan, a mathematician, developed the Interative Dichotomiser ID3 machine-learning algorithm, and John Holland discovered genetic algorithms.

Working independent of one another, these three researchers have had a vast impact on data mining, for it is from their work that almost all of the current data mining tools are derived—decision trees, neural networks, rule generators, evolutionary programs, etc. Through the process of a feedback network, Hopfield demonstrated how a neural network could adjust and eventually learn a pattern from repeated exposure to case samples. Quinland's work on ID3 was one of the first learning systems capable of generating rules in the form of a decision tree. Holland's work at the University of Michigan led to the theory of schema, which provided the groundwork for genetic algorithms and demonstrated how programs can work toward the optimization of solutions. Holland and his colleagues mapped the future of evolutionary computing, which will have a long-term impact on the future of data mining and electronic retailing on the Web.

Neural Networks

Neural networks are so named due to their overall design, which is based on the structure of the brain: both have many highly interconnected neurons. Like the brain, a neural network is a massively parallel, dynamic system of highly interconnected interacting parts. It is able to construct nonlinear predictive models that learn through training and resemble biological neural units in structure. The ability to learn is one of the features of neural networks; they are not programmed as much as trained.

At the core of the network are the hidden connections that contain layers of "weights," which are the formulae to pattern recognition. That is, they work even when given incomplete information. Most neural networks have some sort of "training" rule whereby the weights of connections are adjusted on the basis of presented patterns, and they "learn" from examples. A neural network consists of layers of neurons, which are connected to each other. Some of the neurons will be used to input data into the network and send it to the inner layers of neurons. The output neurons provide the network's response or output. Neurons are connected and combined to generate an output, as Figure 3–2 shows.

In other words, a neural network is a system of software programs and data structures that approximates the operation of the brain. They usually involve a large number of processors operating in parallel, each with its own small sphere of knowledge and access to data in its local memory. Typically, a neural network is initially "trained" or fed large amounts of data and rules about data relationships (e.g., "AOL sub-domains purchase printers but not scanners"). Neural net-

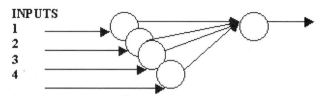

Figure 3–2
This one output network is the equivalent of logistic regression.

works are basically computing memories where the operations are association and similarity. They can learn when sets of events go together, such as when one product is sold, another is likely to sell as well, based on patterns they have observed over time.

In a neural network, after a pattern is learned, such as when a website visitor selects a series of pages, the network examines the possibilities and makes an immediate match, such as a specific ad, offer, price, or link. This is the type of problem for which a web marketer may make a decision based on personal observations. However, what if the problem is not for just one page, but hundreds, and what if the options are not just two or three but 20 or 30? This is where a neural network can be trained to recognize subtle and small differences. It can learn a pattern of interaction and activity over that website and split the information up across its many neurons. It is trained using hundreds or thousands of sessions so that very quickly it learns what path which type of visitors should be offered.

From Slugs to VISA

In 1982, John Hopfield, of Caltech, presented to the National Academy of Sciences the first paper on neural computing presented to any distinguished body since the 1960s. The paper described Hopfield's neural computing system, called the "Hopfield Model" or "cross-bar associative network." Using research based on the olfactory system of a garden slug, Hopfield presented a neural computing system consisting of interconnected processing elements that seek an energy minimum. Hopfield's model represented neuron operation as a thresholding operation and illustrated memory as information stored in the interconnections between neuron units. He also illustrated and modeled the brain's ability to call up responses from many locations in response to a stimulus; he thus modeled how a neural system "associates" information from multiple storage sites for a given input.

Hopfield's enthusiasm, reputation, and clarity of presentation was well received and prompted researchers to become interested again in the fascinating field of neural computing. The increasing attention in the field also opened many sources of funding necessary for the pursuit of neural computing research and the inductive approach to AI. His work led to an explosion in neural networks papers, conferences, and software companies, which continues to this day. Today, neural networks are successful in applications requiring prediction, data classification, and pattern matching. Examples of successful applications include mortgage risk evaluation, production control, handwriting recognition, and credit card fraud. The credit card you carry is being monitored every hour of every day by a neural network for potential patterns of irregularity; the system being used is most likely from HNC, a neural network company from San Diego, which monitors over 150 million credit cards.

Back-Propagation Networks

Neural networks were not seriously considered until Paul Werbo's groundbreaking 1974 Harvard doctorate thesis, *Beyond Regression*, which laid the statistical foundation to the work on back-propagation by several researchers from varied fields. In 1985 the back-propagation neural network architecture was simultaneously discovered by three groups of researchers: D. E. Rumelhart, G. E. Hinton, and R. J. Williams; Y. Le Cun; and D. Parker.

A back-propagation neural network consists of several input nodes, some hidden nodes, and one or more output nodes. Data cycles through the nodes as the net trains and adjusts (Figure 3–3). Back propagation is a learning method where an error signal from an output node is fed back through the network altering weights as it goes, to prevent the same error from happening again. The process involves, as with the other types of networks, a gradual process of training with incremental improvement over time, until a network learns a pattern. This pattern can be anything, including the behavior of website visitors and customers. The back propagation architecture is the most dominant of all neural networks, and it is the most popular in the current crop of data mining tools involved in supervised learning.

To demonstrate how a back-propagation network works we can try it by solving the exclusive-or (XOR) function whose output is logically true (or has the value "1") when the two inputs are opposite (Figure 3–4). The numbers between the neurons are the strengths of the connections between them, or the weights. The weight values will be modified as the network is trained. For training, the network is started with a random set of weights (Figure 3–5).

We start with the assumption of the threshold for the neurons to be .01. This means that if the sum of the inputs is greater than .01,

Figure 3–3
*This network
with a hidden
layer allows it
to recognize
patterns.*

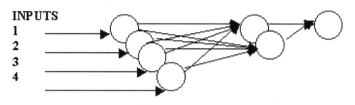

INPUTS
1
2
3
4

Figure 3–4
*The Simple XOR
Function.*

LOGIC TRUTH TABLE

INPUTS		OUTPUTS
1	1	0
0	0	0
1	0	1

Figure 3–5
*XOR function
using linear
threshold units
in a back-
propagation
network.*

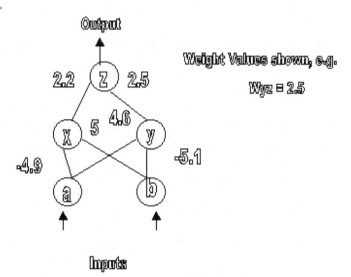

the neuron will output a 0, and if the sum of the inputs is less than
.01, then the output will be 1. After applying a training pattern of 1
on each of the two inputs, the neurons' outputs are computed and
adjusted, as Figure 3–6 shows.

Each of the neuron's output is noted for each node along with the
sum of the neuron's internal signals. Neurons *a* and *b* are both sending
1's to the next layer. Neuron *x* gets two signals, one from neuron *a* and
one from neuron *b*. The weight from neurons *a* to neuron *x* is W*xa*,
and its value is −4.9. We multiply the signal times its weight and get
−4.9. The input to neuron *x* from neuron *b* has a weight W*xb* that is

Figure 3–6
XOR function back-propagation network input calculations.

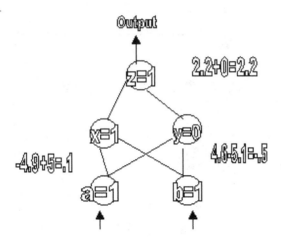

equal to 5. The signal from b is 1. This contributes 5 to neuron x. We next add -4.9 and 5 to get a total internal signal of .1 at neuron x. This is greater than the threshold of .01 so neuron x outputs a 1. In the same way the outputs of y and z can be computed. With the training pattern of the network, the final output should have been a 0, but it was a 1. The network determines an error factor by adjusting the weights from the last layer to the first layer, one layer at a time. The error at neuron z, Ez, is the desired output minus the actual output $Ez = 0 - 1 = -1$.

The weight adjustment is computed by multiplying the error at the neuron times the output of the neuron that the weight is associated with, so that $Wzx = -1 + 2.2 = 1.2$. This is added to the current value of Wzx with the new $Wzx = -1 + 2.2 = 1.2$. This new weight is now the error at z times the signal from y, added to the current value of Wzy. The new Wzy is $= (-1 * 0) = 2.5 = 2.5$. Wzy is unchanged. We next compute the error at the neurons in the next layer back. For neuron x, it is equal to the error at z times the weight of the connection from x to z: $Ex = -1 * 2.2 = -2.2$. To compute the new Wxv, we multiply the error at x by the signal from a, then add the current Wxa, so that the new $Wxa = (-2.2 * 1) - 4.9 = -7.1$. After all the weights are adjusted, a new input pattern is applied and if there is an error, the sequence of back-error propagation is repeated. When all four pairs of input patterns produce the correct outputs, the process stops.

Supervised Learning

This is basically how most neural networks learn: by example in a supervised mode. Supervised models, like back-propagation networks, are trained with pairs of examples: positive and negative. A given input pattern is matched with a desired output pattern. Training a supervised network is a process of providing a set of inputs and outputs, one at a time. The network trains by taking in each input pattern, producing an output pattern, and then comparing its output to the desired output. If the network output is different from the desired output, the network adjusts its internal connection strengths (weights) in order to reduce the difference between the actual output and the desired output. If, however, its output matches the desired output, then the network has learned the pattern and no correction is made.

This process continues until the network gets the patterns of inputs/outputs correct or until an acceptable error rate is attained. However, because the network may get one set of patterns correct and another wrong, the adjustments that it makes are continuous. For this reason, training of a network is an iterative process where input/output patterns are presented over and over until the network "gets" the patterns correct.

In your website, the data (inputs or target patterns) may be in the form of continuous value variables or a set or ranges. For example, the connection time of online sessions could be represented by the actual number of minutes (a continuous valued variable) or one of four states (ranges of time): –30 seconds, –90 seconds, –300 seconds, and +300 seconds. In the latter case, four neurons, each with bipolar values, would be appropriate; in the former case a single neuron would be used.

In general, it is easier for a neural network to learn a set of distinct responses than a continuous valued response. However, breaking up a continuous valued variable into artificial distinct categories can make it more difficult for the data mining tool to learn examples that occur on, or near, the boundaries of the groups. For this reason, continuous valued input variables should be carefully used to represent distinct quantities such as connected time from log files, or visitors' age from registration forms.

Training a Network

In most instances you will be using a back-propagation neural network involving supervised learning. This means that the training set you use consists of records whose prediction or classification values are already known. It is imperative that you train your network with good, current data. Selecting the data for the training of a neural network is probably the most important step in data mining you will take. Selecting the wrong type of data will doom your efforts no matter how good or expensive a data mining tool you use.

The most important factor in the selection of your data is to ensure you include all the ranges of values for all the variables that the network is subject to encounter. In your website, this means including the least and most expensive items and the lowest and highest amounts of sales, session times, units sold, etc. As a rule, you should have several examples in the training set for each value of a categorical attribute and for a range of value for ordered discrete and continuous valued features.

A trained network has the ability to generalize on unseen data, that is, the ability to correctly assess samples that were not on the training data set. Once you train a network the next step is to test it. Expose the network to samples it has not seen before and observe the network's output. A common methodology is to split your data, training on a portion of your data and testing on the rest. One way to determine the patterns your network is finding difficult to learn is to observe closely the errors it is making. To correct them you can retrain your neural network by giving it more samples of the errors it is having difficulty learning.

Preparing Your Data

Real-world data, including that from your website, may be spotty, dirty, or skewed. That is, it may be distributed in an uneven way, making it difficult for a neural network to converge into a good model. A skewed distribution can prevent a network from effectively using an important attribute in your data.

A common way to deal with this problem is to "discrete" an attribute. Rather than having a single input for dollar sale amount, you might break it down to several ranges. Here is an example. Let's say your website sells software products that range in price from very low to very high:

$10–$19	very low	=	00001	=> Input 1
$20–$50	low	=	00010	=> Input 2
$51–$100	average	=	00100	=> Input 3
$101–$199	high	=	01000	=> Input 4
$200–$999	very high	=	10000	=> Input 5

Most of today's modern data mining tools are able to shift the data into these discrete ranges, but you will need to do some of these transformations yourself should the tools you use fail to have this

Figure 3-7
*Common fea-
tures captured
and transformed
during a web
session.*

Attributes	Range of Values	Value	Conversion
Time(seconds)	1-1254	210	.4646
Age	5-57	9	.3333
Gender	M-F	F	.0000
Sub-Domain Type	com,net,edu	com	.1000
ZIP Code	01254-95432	94125	.0010
Registered User	Y-N	Y	.1000
Referred From	Engine-Other	Engine	.1000
Sale Price(dollars)	2-567	120	.5263

functionality. Another technique for dealing with skewed and categorical data is to use their logarithmic or square root value, as well as doing "1-of-N" conversions, as the above sample demonstrates.

During the initial phase of using a neural network tool, you will need to train it using examples of website sessions in which actual sales took place. The samples need to reflect as many features as you can possibly capture, such as when the sale was made and who made it (Figure 3-7). However, since a neural network works best when all inputs and outputs are between 0 and 1, certain conversions need to be made from the web-generated data. Both continuous and categorical values need to be converted—a process which good data mining tools are able to do relatively easy.

Webbing Your Features

Date and time fields can be inputted into your website's neural network in one of two ways. Any date can be represented as is and left as a single number for a specific day in a month. A variable such as a length of connection in seconds or minutes can also be represented as a fixed point in time. Because you are looking at patterns of transactions in your website, you may want to do some conversions of dates, in order to detect trends in ads, marketing campaigns, seasonal or network cycles, etc. For example, you may want to extract a date and deal with it as an additional input into your network:

Access Date	Day of the Week	Additional Input
030299	Monday	00001
030399	Tuesday	00010
030499	Wednesday	00100
030599	Thursday	01000
030699	Friday	10000

Address fields on the Web present another problem. For example, the ZIP code 94502 is not greater than 94501 by one, or larger by 93269 than the ZIP 01233. It is instead another *class*. A ZIP code is a category, not a continuous value number. One of the best ways of dealing with this type of categorical variable is to use another tool or network for clustering. The time needed to train a neural network is directly related to the number of input features used by the network, which means the more features you input, the longer it takes for a net to converge.

A good way of dealing with these types of inputs is to use a machine-learning algorithm tool to create clusters of similar ZIP codes, which can then be transformed into 1-of-N values for inputting into your neural network. Using another data mining tool to prioritize the inputs into a neural network is a good way of determining which features are the most important for training and constructing your model. Another technique for "data compression" is to do statistical correlation, such as Pearson's. Some of the more advanced neural network tools include features for pruning variables, prior to training on data sets.

Purchasing Propensity

The output of a neural network is in the format of a continuous value. As such it can be difficult to interpret for categorical results, such as "will buy vs. will not buy." However, there is a method by which you can take a normal neural network output and create categorical results, which involves creating multiple outputs, as Figure 3–8 shows.

In these situations, you may want to have multiple outputs with each category being a propensity to purchase unique products or services. You may opt to position certain ads or offers on the basis of how a neural network score corresponds with the maximum possible value, or the top three values, or if it exceeds a certain threshold value.

Figure 3–8
A multiple output network for predicting propensity to purchase different products.

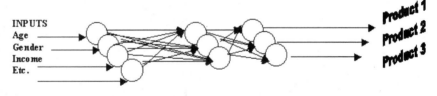

Training Cycle

Your main task is ensuring you are capturing the relevant and important features from your website, which can be used for prediction and classification. As such, your objectives when using a neural network tool are to ensure you:

1. Identify the input variables—this is *very* important!
2. Convert the variables into usable ranges—pick a tool which will do this.
3. Decide on the format of the output—continuous or categorical?
4. Decide on the training data set sample and a training schedule.
5. Test the model and apply it to your website objectives.

Setting up a schedule for the training of a neural network is important because your model will deteriorate gradually over time. One of the downfalls of any model, especially one designed to predict web behavior, is that it will eventually go stale. The model you create with a neural network will age and atrophy as your website traffic evolves beyond the data used to train your net. As you introduce new products and services, or as you make changes and improvements to your website, changes occur in your traffic and transaction patterns. As such you will need to train your network with fresh data.

Self-Organizing Maps (SOM)

Neural networks perform best in situations whose outputs are non-linear and with complex problems that do not require a solution of absolute accuracy. They also are ideal in situations where a large amount of historical data is available for training and where a "black box" solution will do and no explanation is required. Most of today's data mining tools incorporate two main types of neural networks, back-propagation and SOMs, also known as Kohonen networks, after its inventor.

In 1981 Tuevo Kohonen proposed and demonstrated a completely different network architecture. An SOM network resembles a collection of neurons, as in the human brain, each connected to its neighbor. As an SOM is exposed to samples, it begins to create self-organizing clusters, like cellophane spreading itself over chunks of data. Gradually, a Kohonen network will organize clusters and can thus be used for situations where no output or dependent variable is known. SOMs have been used to discover associations for such purposes as market basket analysis in retailing.

The key difference between back-propagation nets and Kohonen nets is that the former is used for supervised learning where a training sample is needed to construct a classification model. For example, with a back-propagation neural network, training is usually done with a balanced sample of website visitors who made a purchase versus those who did not. Also unlike the back-propagation networks which usually have a single output, an SOM network can have multiple outputs competing with each other. SOMs involve unsupervised learning, a training sample for which no output is known, and is commonly used to discover relations in a data set. This by the way does not preclude using both paradigms—first the SOM to discover a sub-class within the data, then a back-propagation network for classification of that class. The same can be said for using neural networks in combination with genetic and machine-learning algorithms.

SOMs are probably second only to back-propagation architecture in terms of the number of applications and tools for which it is being used. The most significant difference between the back-propagation and the self-organization models is the fact that the SOM is trained without supervision. The SOM network is more biologically oriented than the back-propagation models in that it bears more resemblance to the way humans learn and the brain is organized. If you don't really know what you are attempting to classify (such as the website patterns you are looking for), or if you feel there may be more than one way to categorize your visitors or customers, you may want to start with an SOM.

Calibrating Clusters

Using an SOM to discover clusters in your data can often lead to a problem in trying to extrapolate a meaning for each of the groupings. There are two ways of dealing with this problem. The first involves obtaining the average value for each of the features in the data. For example, if the number of children or customer age is one of the input features, then what you need to obtain is the average value for each of these features in each of the clusters the SOM discovered. The other method involves passing each of the clusters through a machine-learning algorithm in order to generate a set of rules describing the features of that grouping. This second option requires the ability to link the output from an SOM to the inputs of a machine-learning algorithm tool like C4.5, CHAID, or CART, which is possible with some of the new data mining suites, or toolboxes like Clementine.

Keep in mind that neural networks are basically memories: they do not compute solutions as much as remember answers. As such, the data samples that are used to train a network are critical in determining the accuracy of the network model. If the memory is organized in the proper way, then the look-up table of that network and its core weights, which is really what networks are all about, will generalize in a manner which will be very accurate. Despite the rap networks take for being black-box wonders from which no explanation to their solutions is forthcoming (which, ironically, may be said for regression), they are very good tools. Neural networks are good data mining tools for classification and prediction and work best when used in conjunction with machine-learning and genetic algorithms.

Neural Network Tools

Most of the work involved in the use of neural networks is in the preparation of the data. Luckily, most of today's data mining tools are sophisticated enough to handle the dirty work involved in such tasks as balancing the data. (*Balancing* is using an equal sample of positive and negative cases (Buyers vs. Non-Buyers) to train a network.) Another task involves the scaling of the data; converting all inputs to a range from 0 to 1 and back in the output. This may also involve using functions for dealing with skewed data sets, such as taking the logarithm or the square root of their values prior to passing the data through a network. Still another task involves converting categorical inputs into either 1-of-N values or thermometer values:

If Number of Children is:	1-of-N Value	Thermometer Value
0	00001	0.5000
1	00010	0.7500
2	00100	0.8750
3	01000	0.9375
4	10000	1.0000

The following data mining tools incorporate back propagation and, in some instances, SOM networks for classification. Most of these tools are mature, third- or fourth-generation versions of their software, which provide some functions for data preparation and balancing of inputs prior to training and model creation. Care must still be taken in their use, since they do require some adjustments, such as the selection of their topography and the setting of learning rates. The next generation of these tools is also beginning to incorporate genetic algorithms to optimize their settings and improve their results. These groups of tools include: 4Thought, BrainMaker, INSPECT, MATLAB NN Toolbox, ModelQuest, NGO, NeuralWorks Predict, NeuralWorks Professional II/PLUS, Proforma, PRW, SPSS Neural Connection, and Trajecta.

A common sense rule for determining when to use a data mining tool based on a neural network involves the following considerations:

- Are you dealing with a complex problem involving much input and which does not require a true model or a clear-cut solution with absolute accuracy?
- Will being close be good enough?
- Are you trying to solve nonlinear problems, that is to say, is there a clear-cut relation between your inputs and outputs?
- Are you dealing with very large amounts of historical data?
- Do you need a solution quickly, and does that solution require an explanation (will a "black box" model do)?

If in your opinion your problem meets these requirements, then the use of a neural network tool will work for you. However, a neural network solution should be avoided in situations where a problem requires a robust model. A neural network should also be avoided in situations where a clear understanding or an insight into the pattern you are trying to discover is required. Some neural network tools provide sensitivity reports, which enable you to see some of the relationships between the inputs and your desired output.

Machine-Learning Algorithms

Machine-learning algorithms are commonly used to segment a database, with their output being either in the form of a decision tree or a series of IF/THEN rules. They commonly work in supervised learning situations where they attempt to find a test for splitting a database among the most desired categories, such as "website visitor will buy vs. will not buy." In both instances these algorithms seek to duplicate the protocol that a skilled statistician would follow in analyzing a data set: to identify important data clusters of features within a database.

Data mining tools incorporating machine-learning algorithms such as CART (classification and regression trees), CHAID (chi-squared automatic integration detection), ID3 (Interactive Dichotomizer), or C4.5 or C5.0 will segment a data set into statistically significant clusters of classes based on a desired output. As noted, some of these tools generate "decision trees" that provide a graphical breakdown of a data set (a sort of map of significant clusters), while others produce IF/THEN rules, which segment a data set into classes that can point out important *ranges* and *features*. Such a rule has two parts, a condition (IF) and a result (THEN), and is represented as a statement:

If Customer code *is* <u>03</u>
And Number of purchases made this year *is* 06
And ZIP Code *is* 79905
Then PROSPECT *will purchase Product X*
Rule's probability: .88
The rule exists in 13000 *records.*
Significance level: Error probability < 0.13

A Measure of Information

Most of these types of data mining tools evolve from two lines of research and development. The first is from the area of statistical decision trees and the other in machine learning, such as the ID3. Mathematician J. Ross Quinlan, in his ID3 system, introduced and popularized the concept of today's data mining decision tree tools. There are two main types of decision trees: binary and multiple branches. A binary decision tree splits from a node in two directions with each node representing a yes-or-no question. ID3 is a program that can build trees automatically from given positive and negative instances. Each leaf of a decision tree asserts a positive or negative concept.

To classify a particular input we start at the top and follow assertions down until we reach an answer. For example, in the ID3 algorithm, the sequence of fields that are selected as predictors is determined by a measure of entropy. This information measure is best for the attribute whose value, when known, minimizes the departure of your guess, or prediction, from the actual value of the dependent variable. Other fields are then examined for their ability to further differentiate values in the decedent nodes of the resulting tree. The

ID3 algorithm works by computing the entropy associated with each attribute. The calculation is made as follows:

$$H(C) = -\sum_{i=1}^{N} p(c_i) \log_2 p(c_i)$$

Rather than work you through the math, suffice to say that ID3 performs a measurement of entropy or noise in order to measure the amount of data an attribute contains. The overall entropy of the classification is the expected amount of information that will be gained when the class is specified. For example, let's say you are trying to determine which attribute contains the most information in the classification of fruit:

"What is it, a banana, an apple or an orange?"		
Data	*Attribute*	*Information Gain*
It's 7.8 oz.	Weight	Little
It's round.	Shape	Some
It's red.	Color	Most

Figure 3–9 is an example of an ID3 decision tree. Notice that ID3 forms a branch for unique clusters with similar income categories. ID3 is the precursor to C4.5 and C5.0, which were developed also by Quinlan and use a criterion known as *information gain* to compare and generate potential splits within a data set. C5.0, the newest and latest algorithm, uses the ratio of the total information gain due to a proposed split to the information gain attributable solely to the number of subsets created, as the criterion for evaluating proposed splits. The ID3 and C4.5 algorithms are based on concept learning, where the number of branches equals number of categories for predictor outputs.

The Rules

Machine algorithms, which are the core technology of most decision tree and rule-generating data mining tools, take a "divide and conquer" approach. In any given data set, such as your log files or forms database, the algorithms look at the attributes (domain,

Figure 3–9
*A decision tree
can segment
your website
customers based
on different
attributes, such
as their income,
age, gender,
domains, or
location.*

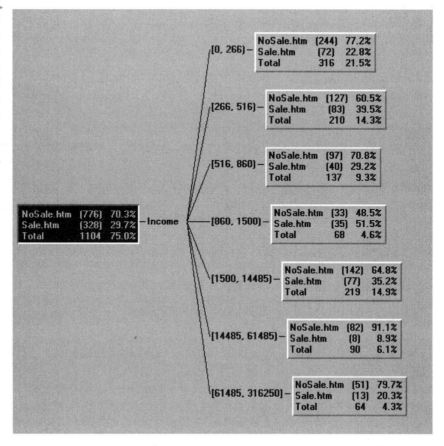

Figure 3–9
A decision tree can segment your website customers based on different attributes, such as their income, age, gender, domains, or location.

referred engine, age, gender) and perform a test at a node of a tree or a rule in order to generate a number of possible branches or IF/THEN statements. If the attribute that is tested at a node is a nominal one, the number of branches in the decision tree are usually the number of possible values of the attribute (for example, for gender, it will be Male, Female, or Unknown). If the attribute is numeric, the nodes in a decision tree usually test whether its value is less than a predetermined constant, giving a two-way split. (Missing values in a data set are treated as an attribute value in their own right. Consideration is given to the fact that a missing value may be of some significance.)

Some data mining tools are able to generate decision rules directly from a database and offer a popular alternative to decision trees. It is also possible to read a set of rules directly off a decision tree, with one rule being generated from each leaf.

Figure 3–10
*Rules can be
generated from a
decision tree.*

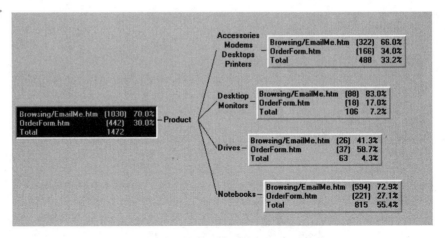

IF	Product = Accessories, Modems, Desktops, or Printers	
THEN	HTM = Browsing/E-mailMe.htm	66.0%
	HTM = OrderForm.htm	34.0%
IF	Product = Desktop or Monitors	
THEN	HTM = Browsing/E-mailMe.htm	83.0%
	HTM = OrderForm.htm	17.0%
IF	Product = Drives	
THEN	HTM = Browsing/E-mailMe.htm	41.3%
	HTM = OrderForm.htm	58.7%
IF	Product = Notebooks	
THEN	HTM = Browsing/E-mailMe.htm	72.9%
	HTM = OrderForm.htm	27.1%

Note that these rules are the same as those displayed in Figure 3–10 and can be generated by the software.

The Trees

There are many algorithms for generating decision trees. The CART algorithm generates binary trees (2 splits) it rates high on statistical prediction. It generates two branches from each nonterminal node and uses cross-validation and pruning to determine the size of the tree. Its output or response variable can be quantitative or nominal.

CART splits a data set on the basis of diversity, and it looks at all the variables in a database to determine which ones make the best separators or splinters. The best separators are those data fields that do the best job splitting a database into groups where a single class is dominant. Its inputs or independent predictor variables can be nominal or ordinal, with continuous predictors also being supported.

Then there is the AID family of algorithms: AID, THAID, CHAID, MAID, XAID, FIRM, TREEDISC, etc. These algorithms, the most popular being CHAID, are based on the concept of detecting complex statistical relationships. They generate decision trees where the number of branches varies from two to the number of categories of predictor. A key difference between CHAID and CART or C4.5 is that CHAID is highly conservative; it stops growing trees in an effort to avoid overfitting. CHAID also only works on categorical variables. All of these algorithms segment data sets on the basis of statistical significance tests, which they also use to determine the size of their tree. AID, MAID, and XAID were designed for quantitative responses, while THAID, CHAID, and TREEDISC are for nominal responses. Some data mining tools combine two or more algorithms, such as KnowledgSEEKER, which uses CART, CHAID, and ID3, or Clementine, which uses ID3 and C5.0. The algorithm C5.0 is available from Quinland's own company, Rulequest.

The Trees vs. The Rules

Decision trees are popular in many areas of marketing and can also be used to analyze web-based data. The advantages of decision trees are found in their ability to generate understandable business rules in a decision-support environment and the ability to model nonlinear relationships with logical rules. ID3, and its successors C4.5, C5.0, CART, CHAID, and other variations of machine-learning algorithms, perform somewhat the same process on a database: *they split it into classes that differ as much as possible in their relation to a selected output.* In other words, a database is split into subsets according to the results of statistical tests conducted on an output by the *algorithm*—not the user. CART, developed by L. Briemen in 1984, builds binary trees that allow the classification on the basis of the attributes, which are the best splitters and separators. CHAID, which was developed nearly a decade before by J. S. Hartigan in 1975, was designed for purposes of detecting statistical relationships in data and is restricted to categorical variables.

In general, rules are more complex than necessary, and rules derived from trees are usually pruned to remove redundant tests.

Rules are not notably more compact than a tree, though, and in fact they are just what you would get by reading rules *from* a tree. In some situations, however, rules are considerably more compact than trees—particularly if it is possible to have a default rule that covers cases not specified by the other rules. One reason why rules are popular is that each rule seems to represent an independent insight into database. New rules can be added to an existing rule set without disturbing ones already there, whereas making an addition to a tree structure reshapes the whole tree. Most rules can often achieve surprisingly high accuracy, perhaps because the structure many real-world data sets exhibit is quite rudimentary, and interactions between the attributes can be safely ignored.

Automatic Segmentation

The process of stratification or classification is automated by machine-learning algorithms on the basis of the data—rather than the hypothesis, or hunch, of the user. Attributes are chosen to split the set, and a tree is build for each subset, until all members of the subsets belong to the same class. Which algorithm is best for you is dependent on the nature of your data mining problem.

Keep in mind what each of the algorithms were designed to do and how they operate on the data. CHAID was designed to detect statistical relationships between variables and is restricted to analysis of categorical variables, such as low, medium, and high. CART is designed to measure the degree of diversity of variables in making its splits—it looks to see which variable is the best splitter or separator in a database (in other words, which website customer attribute is the best "splitter" between your buyers and browsers). ID3 and C4.5 use the concept of "information gain" to make these splitting decisions: which online customer attributes tell you the most about buyers and nonbuyers in your website. The information gained depends on its probability as measured in bits as minus the logarithm to base 2 of that probability. The CART procedures induce strictly binary trees while ID3 partitions by attribute values. CART also uses a statistical resampling technique for both error estimation and cost complexity pruning. Lastly, keep in mind that the output for each of the algorithms differs somewhat—almost all generate some type of decision tree with most also generating IF/THEN rules in varying degrees of numbers. Remember that CART and ID3 can only generate binary trees, whereas CHAID, C4.5, and C5.0 produce multiple branch trees.

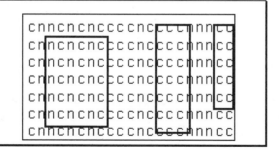

Figure 3–11
C = *Website Customer;*
N = *Not Website Customers.*

Machine Learning Your Site

Machine-learning data mining tools are specifically effective in discovering patterns within websites and identifying clusters of profitable customers, as Figure 3–11 shows.

The blocked clusters in Figure 3–11 represent common characteristics within the data and can point to key relationships and patterns hidden in your website data. They also provide to webmasters, marketing, and management easy-to-understand statements about what is occurring in a large website.

IF ZIP CODE	(93011–94123]	
AND REGISTRATION NO.	(0051–0943]	
AND USER ID NO.	(4566JK33–4558DL01]	
THEN	/WEBSELL/PRODUCT8.HTM	87%

This rule can be broken down into the following components. First, the ZIP codes point to a group of California ZIP codes 93011 through but not including 94123, for which demographic data can be matched by percentage of households for multiple consumer lifestyles. Next, a group of registration numbers was found: 0051 through but not including 0943, which represent a specific period in time, for issue dates. Finally, a cluster of cookie identification numbers was isolated that seemingly represent an unknown association. However, additional analysis may discover similarities in browsing habits. In any event, when the combined factors of these conditions occurred, the data mining process discovered a high propensity for selecting PRODUCT8.HTM, which is one of the main pages for this commercial website.

A key difference and value of machine-learning algorithms over statistical classification systems such as regression is that they are able to classify separate areas in data space. For example, these types of data mining tools can discover islands of web customers which a regression approach would find difficult to classify. There are several ways that a website visitor can be identified as profitable. One type of client may make multiple purchases of low-dollar items, while another profitable customer may make single high-dollar purchases; in both instances they represent online sales.

Machine-Learning Tools

A good strategy in selecting the right algorithm is to try multiple tools using a single data set on the same dependent variable and then seeing the results and evaluating the accuracy of the tree. Keep in mind also that you will often encounter more than one data set that may require having access to all of the main algorithms since they work on different data variables and data sets with different results.

The following data mining tools excel in their ability to handle large numbers of attributes and records, estimate statistical significance, handle both categorical and numeric attributes, learn transparent rules, and improve incrementally. This group of machine-learning-based data mining tools includes: *AC2, Alice, Business Miner, Clementine, C5.0 (RuleQuest), CART, Cognos Scenario, Data Surveyor, Decisionhouse, IDIS, IND, KATE-Tools, KnowledgeSEEKER, Preclass, PQ–>R, SAS Enterprise Miner, SuperQuery, Profiler, and WizWhy.*

Using a decision tree tool like *KnowledgeSEEKER*, a database can be segmented into statistically significant clusters very quickly. Like other high-end data mining tools, KnowledgeSEEKER contains multiple algorithms: CART, CHAID, and ID3. A unique feature of this tool is that it runs CART and CHAID concurrently. This means both continuous and discrete dependent and independent variables can be modeled without pre-processing, splitting, or scaling of your data.

Figure 3–12 *The leaves of a decision tree are classes of website customers.*

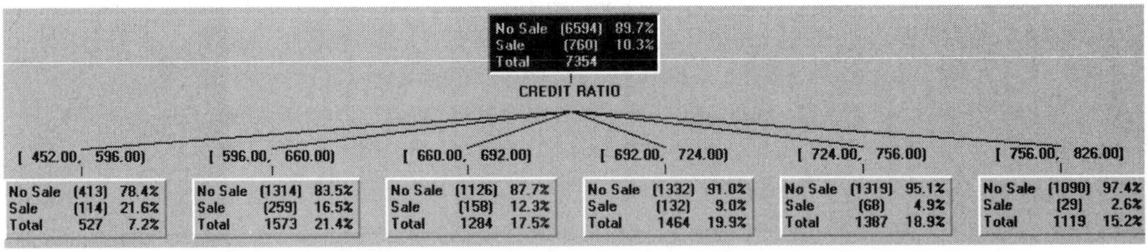

The tool generates Multivariate Decision Trees, IF-THEN rules, and SQL syntax. In the example in Figure 3–12, the data mining tool was able to generate a decision tree identifying a key *attribute* (credit ratio) and *intervals* (dollar ranges) differentiating between customers who purchased a product online and those who did not.

Genetic Algorithms

A genetic algorithm (GA) is essentially a program version of the evolutionary process. The main difference of course is that in a system a program can be modified in microseconds. GAs are really optimization program routines, guided by the principles of natural evolution. They are search procedures based on the concepts of natural selection and genetics. GAs represent a robust alternative to linear programming and mathematical optimization techniques. For an electronic retailer it represents a technology for optimizing the design and arrangement of how its website positions and communicates with its visitors.

Coupled with neural networks and machine-learning algorithms, GAs have a tremendous potential for mapping web visitor patterns and optimizing website design. Because of their inherent design they are highly malleable and well suited for the dynamic environment of the Web. John Holland developed the first GAs at the University of Michigan during the 1970s. Dr. Holland was impressed by the ease with which biological systems could perform tasks that defeated powerful computers. He observed that evolution took place in small increments at the chromosome level and that nature tended to be biased toward some chromosomes that produce a more "fit" organism. The basic concept that Holland developed involves how stochastic searches take place: rather than operating on a single solution to the problem at hand, GAs operate on a *population of solutions*.

Code of Survival

To use a GA you must encode solutions to your problem in a structure that can be stored in a computer. This encoded solution is called a *genome* or *chromosome*. These chromosomes are a population of possible solutions, in essence a set of character strings that are analogous to the base-4 chromosomes that we see in our own DNA. The trial solution—where numbers are used for the input variables—will have a result or output function, which describes the quality of the trial solution. The output is commonly called the *fitness*, since it describes how "fit" the trial solution is. The fitness function typically has a number of different inputs. For instance, the fitness function for a response to an offer in your website may have such input variables as the connect time, the number of days since last purchase, the customer's ZIP code, or the total amount of purchases.

Each population member will therefore have an identical number of genes, or input variables. The GA creates a population of genomes, then applies crossover and mutation to the individuals in the population to generate new individuals. It uses various selection criteria so that it picks the best individuals for mating and subsequent crossover. The key to GAs is the "objective function," for it determines how "good" each individual is. Also important is how genomes or chromosomes are structured as possible solutions (inputs) to a fitness function.

Genetic algorithms are based on the concept of *schemata* as developed by John Holland in the early 1970s. A schema is simply a template for representing the possible patterns of a given solution, which with GAs is represented as a genome or a chromosome. This schema is represented in a series of sequential symbols of 1s, 0s, and *'s in a fixed position. For example, the schema of **01 is the following genomes: 0001, 1001, 1101, and 0101—these chromosomes all end with 0 followed by 1. They are also encoded structural solutions to problems a computer can process. The relationship between a genome and a schema is that when they match, they survive.

The fitness of a particular schema is the average fitness of all the genomes that match the schema in a given population. For example, the fitness of the above sample is the average of the genomes 0001, 1001, 1101, and 0101. Holland found that the shorter the defining length of a schema, the more likely it was bound to survive from one generation to another. The defining length of a schema is the distance between the outermost fixed positions. For example, the defining length of 1*10111 is 6 (7 – 1). Low-order schema are the code of GAs which build from one generation to another, with the fittest surviving and mixing with others to evolve into fitter solutions. Holland's Schema Theorem explains how GAs are really searching through possible schemata to find the most fit solutions for the next generation. Holland worked primarily with strings of bits, but you can use arrays, trees, lists, or any other object. What is important is that you must define the genetic operators: reproduction, crossover, and mutation.

Reproduction

This is the process by which a program evaluates strings copied according to a desired output, with strings with high values likely to contribute an offspring or more to the next generation. GAs work by starting with relatively poor trial solutions, that is, population members with poor fitness. The first process, reproduction, involves an exchange of information between population members. Selection keeps the size of the population constant but increases the fitness of the next generation.

Selection is similar to the process of "natural selection" in nature, where only the fittest individuals in the population survive to pass their genetic material on to the next generation. The chance of the genome surviving to the next generation is proportional to its fitness value. For example, let's say you are attempting to determine the setting of x and y coordinates in order to maximize z on a surface. In this instance, your *inputs* are x and y with z being your *output*. The first step would be to create a population of random possible solutions, in this case some coordinates being better than others:

1. $x = 2.0, y = 4.0$
2. $x = 1.3, y = 3.5$
3. $x = 2.5, y = 6.0$
4. $x = 4.5, y = 5.0$
5. $x = 3.0, y = 2.5$
6. $x = 1.5, y = 4.5$

You next rank your solutions (selection) and keep the best coordinates, which yield the better results:

1.	$x = 4.5$	$y = 6.0$	keep
2.	$x = 3.0$	$y = 5.0$	keep
3.	$x = 2.5$	$y = 4.5$	eliminate
4.	$x = 2.0$	$y = 4.0$	eliminate
5.	$x = 1.5$	$y = 3.5$	eliminate
6.	$x = 1.3$	$y = 2.5$	eliminate

Crossover

When *crossover* occurs, two strings exchange information that yields new combinations of scenarios. Survival is based on choosing the genomes in a random way proportional to their fitness. This involves the selection of two individuals, the selection of a crossover site, and the exchange of values between the two strings. Crossover, which occurs in nature, creates two new genomes from two existing ones by gluing together pieces of each genome. When population members mate, they cross gene values over to their partner, resulting in a "trade" of values.

This mixes up the information in the gene values of the population members, creating new and diverse "offspring." Our example of those higher ranked coordinates would follow this process as follows:

	Prior to Crossover	After Crossover
Scenario 1.	2.5, 6.0	4.5, 2.5
Scenario 2.	4.5, 5.0	6.0, 5.0

Mutation

Mutation is a source of variation used to maintain diversity in a population of possible scenarios. In a binary-coded genetic algorithm, it is the occasional alteration of a bit position. Once the crossover has taken place, the offspring undergo mutation. The values of the individual genes of population members can be changed, or mutated. Mutation is important in evolution because unlike crossover (which merely *trades* genes), *new* gene values are introduced. This further increases the diversity of the population members.

Reproduction and crossover do a good job of searching the space for possible solutions, but they depend on initial conditions and randomness that might not happen; mutation provides the additional catalyst for new combinations to occur. Mutation, however, is held to a minimum because radical changes can be as destructive as they are productive. They should only be used to avoid premature convergence to a local optimum.

Once crossover and mutation have occurred, the new population members will replace the old ones if they are better. In this fashion, population members can have improved fitness with each new cycle (or generation) of crossover, mutation, and natural selection. Program users typically want to maximize or minimize the fitness, so the survival of the fittest action is governed by whether the new fitness is better or worse than the previous generation's fitness. The resulting process yields a steadily improving solution to the problem, often identifying the optimum solution in a surprisingly short time.

A Step-by-Step Example Using a Binary-Coded GA

1. Objective: Maximize the function.

$$F(x) = X^2 \text{ (Objective)}$$
$$\text{Where } 0 = < X = < 31 \text{ (Range)}$$

2. Code the schema. Use a binary string of length = 5.

Example: $11000 => 1 \times 2^4 + 1 \times 2^3 + 0 \times 2^2 + 0 \times 2^1 + 0 \times 2^0 = 24$

3. Reproduction of the initial population, e.g., 4 strings:

String Number	String	×	Fitness	% of Total
1	00010	2	4	1.8%
2	00011	3	9	4.0%
3	01110	14	196	87.1%
4	00100	4	16	7.1%

Average Fitness = 56.25

Initiate reproduction via a roulette wheel four times to get the following:

String Number	String	Number of Hits
1	00010	0
2	00011	1
3	01110	2
4	00100	1

4. Crossover. Members of the newly reproduced chromosomes are mated at random. Suppose string numbers 3 & 4 and 3 & 2 are mated.

For 3 and 4	Split	Before	After
String 3	01110	01110	01110
String 4	00100	00100	00100
String 2	00011	00011	01011
String 3	01110	01110	00011

5. Mutation. Supposing we selected p = .002, we would expect 20(.002) = .04 bits to undergo mutation.

6. The new population is:

String Number	String	×	Fitness	% of Total
1	01110	14	196	53.1%
2	00100	4	16	4.3%
3	00110	6	36	9.8%
4	01011	11	121	32.8%

Average Fitness = 92.25

This process continues to iterate until an acceptable solution is arrived at.

Data Mining with Genetic Algorithms

Genetic algorithms work by evolving successive generations of solutions, which get progressively better by splitting and matching. As with nature, the idea is that only the fit survive. As such, GAs are optimization engines, which are currently being used in data mining applications to improve the performance of neural networks. Most data mining tools are designed for discovery, while genetic algorithms are really tools for optimization. However, when used in tandem a GA can be used to optimize the performance of a neural network in classification and prediction. Although not as common in today's data mining tools, genetic algorithms are beginning to make their way into the standard methodology of optimizing the performance of neural networks. Several data mining tools are incorporating both neural networks and genetic algorithms, using the GA to optimize the settings, the topography, and the learning rate of the neural network in order to improve their overall performance.

Genetic algorithms can also be used in conjunction with rule generators to achieve higher performing prediction rules. The approach involves (as with most GAs) establishing a fitness function, in this case a classifier error rate. The genomes or chromosomes are the set of rules generated by a machine-learning algorithm. The idea is to focus on the generation of IF/THEN rules and then go through the recombination and mutation of these chromosomes (rules) in order to weed out the weakest ones so that the fit rules meet a minimum cluster size (accuracy rate). The process involves establishing classifier *committees*, which are sets of distinct classifiers whose predictions are averaged:

Rule 1:	0.93	IF Age 32	THEN will purchase product X
Rule 2:	0.66	IF Gender M	THEN will purchase product Y
Rule 3:	0.87	IF Prior Sale Y	THEN will purchase product Z

Committee Average: 0.82

Average propensity to purchase product groups X, Y, Z

Repeated runs of the genetic algorithm system are performed using different random number seed rules. The process involves all three steps (reproduction, crossover, and mutation) to insure poor rules (classifiers) are eliminated by the committees. The concept of using genetic algorithms with machine-learning algorithms is meant to optimize the search space and improve the overall accuracy of their predictive models.

There are few commercial genetic algorithm data mining tools in the market, making it difficult to incorporate the technology in the analysis of your web data. On the desktop level there is Evolver, an add-on to Microsoft Excel. The product has been around for some time and is quite robust and built on solid theory. From the Netherlands there is a newer package called The OMEGA Predictive Modeling System, which uses a GA to optimize the learning process. Another tool known as the NeuroGenetic Optimizer (NGO) incorporates a GA with back-propagation and Self-Organizing Map neural networks. On the high-end there is the NeoVista Solutions software, which includes a genetic algorithm module as part of its data mining suite of tools. Public code is also available from several universities on the Web for those who wish to develop their own applications.

Genetic Algorithm Applications

One of the most intriguing applications of GAs is in the area of retailing, specifically for the optimization of product shelf display size and location. Several retailers have begun to use GAs to design or improve their store and product layouts to maximize revenue opportunity given various store demographics. One of the problems retailers have, much like large e-commerce websites, is dealing with a large volume of products. Coupled with this are the changing and diverse demographics of store shoppers, each requiring a detailed and accurate reorganization of unique products for each store. E-commerce websites selling multiple products and services experience the same problem.

The current solutions require extensive planning and resources, but GAs are ideal for this type of logistics problem, which is rapidly replicating itself in a large scale on the Web with large electronic retailers. Coupled with the problem of design is the problem of inventory control, which again GAs can optimize, by reducing overstock and out-of-stocks and increase inventory forecast accuracy.

Through the use of GAs, websites can also maximize their sales by improving their web design and product (web page) organization for improved cross-selling. GAs can improve the use of inventory dollars and increase the affinity grouping of products based on website visitor demographics. Affinity grouping can also assist in the positioning of product items based on web customer profiles, much like retailers are currently doing it with the aid of GAs. The concept of evolutionary retailing is one of using GAs and neural networks to optimize the design and functionality of online storefronts and portals to maximize retail space design.

The AI Cousins: Case-Based Reasoning and Fuzzy Logic

Two other AI-based technologies have the potential of assisting you in the optimization of your electronic retailing efforts and customer service. One is *case-based reasoning* (CBR) and the other is *fuzzy logic*. Although few data mining tools include their technology, you still should know something about how they work, what they are capable of doing, and how you may be able to deploy them in the future.

Case-Based Reasoning (CBR)

A CBR system works by matching new problems to "cases" from a historical database, and then adapting successful solutions from the past to current situations. CBR has typically been used for customer support, quality assurance, and maintenance applications. In these situations, CBR maintains an institutional memory of prior problems so that when a new call comes in, old solutions are retrieved and matched to answer similar new problems. CBR is a simple yet powerful method of indexing, which is more akin to *remembering* than to *learning*, the way the other data mining technologies operate.

CBR is a collaborative system that stores case samples of solutions it then uses to recommend fixes to new problems. The most common use of this indexing system is with trouble help desks, where CBR technology is used to respond to problems by finding similar cases in its memory, and adapts the solution that worked before to the current problem. CBR technology was developed originally in the 1980s, most prominently from the work of Roger Schank at the Yale University AI lab. Obviously, a similar application can be found in the collaborative filtering software, like Firefly for recommendation of products and services based on case samples.

CBR works by maintaining a database of known records, so for example, you could store a database of prior website customers who've made large dollar purchases. Using this CBR engine you could profile new website visitors who match the prior website customers for classification and prediction. CBR uses distance and combination functions to do the matching between old customers and new visitors. CBR is also quite adaptive, so as new customers are identified new types of neighborhoods are created, permitting new web visitors to be targeted.

The whole concept is that of association: new website customers likely to respond to an offer are probably similar to previous customers that responded in the past to like offers and incentives. CBR works easily with all types of data, including nonrelational text and images. Still, there are drawbacks. CBR requires a large amount of historical data for finding neighbors. The classification of new records can require processing all the historical records to find the similar profitable neighbors. It is also highly computationally and storage intensive. The strengths of CBR are of course its simplicity, which boils down to: *"I think this website visitor will respond to this ad because he is a lot like these other website visitors who clicked on the link."*

The number of vendors offering CBR technology is limited. Inference's CBR Express is one. The most immediate application of CBR technology is to the area of customer service, where visitors can interact with a CBR engine in order to come up with solutions that have previously been resolved.

Fuzzy Logic

The name is deceptive; it should really be "continuous value logic," which provides a superior method of information modeling. Conceived in 1965 by Lotfi Zadeh, an engineer and professor at the University of California at Berkeley, fuzzy logic provides a method of reducing as well as explaining system complexity. Dr. Zadeh was concerned with the rapid decline in information afforded by traditional mathematical models as the complexity of the target system increased. He expressed his theory as follows:

As the complexity of a system increases, our ability to make precise and yet significant statements about its behavior diminishes until a threshold is reached beyond which precision and significance (or relevance) become almost mutually exclusive characteristics.

Much of this complexity, he realized, came from the way in which the variables of the system were represented and manipulated. Since these variables could only represent the state of a phenomenon as either on or off, the math necessary to evaluate operations at various "border" states became increasingly complex, which at some point became a morass of equations providing little insight about the underlying process. Zadeh called this state the *principle of incompatibility.*

Fuzzy logic is a calculus of compatibility. In fuzzy logic there is no black or white, there is instead a degree of gray in both. Everything is measured in *degrees of membership.* Fuzziness, the measure of how well an instance (value) conforms to a semantic ideal or concept, describes the degree of membership in a fuzzy set. This degree of membership can be viewed as the level of compatibility between an instance from the set's domain and the concept overlying the set. For example, in the fuzzy set WILL BUY, the value YES has a degree [.31] meaning that it is only moderately compatible with WILL BUY. This is called a "measure of fuzziness" because it is used to assess the degree of ambiguity or uncertainty attached to each fuzzy set. It is important to realize that a website visitor can be a member of different fuzzy sets simultaneously:

IF WILL BUY THEN [.31]
IF WANTS INFO THEN [.35]
IF WILL NOT BUY THEN [.34].

More and more, fuzzy logic is being used with neural networks, much like genetic algorithms. However, it is not being used at the front end of neural networks, to optimize their setting, but instead to explain their "black-box" findings. The key benefit of fuzzy logic is that it allows for imprecise states to be categorized with simple "IF/THEN" relations, which are easy to verify and optimize. Conversely, a key benefit of neural networks is that they learn from data sets; thus a combination of both technologies provides the best of both worlds. One data mining vendor who already incorporates this type of fuzzy logic and neural network mixture is DataEngine from Management Intelligenter Technologien GmbH. For the Web data miner, fuzzy logic offers a powerful technology for data compression and insight from the hundreds of thousands of online patterns. Fuzzy logic is also being used as a new method of buying and selling stocks and eventually retail products via the Web by the OptiMark system.

Conclusion

It is important to remember that today's data mining tools stem from the three branches of artificial intelligence designed to emulate human *perception, learning,* and *evolution.* It is equally important to understand how to strategically position these tools in order to enhance the value of your website and electronic retaining presence. Incorporated in today's modern data mining tools are technologies that can extract powerful knowledge and insight about your online customers in the form of business rules, C code, decision graphs for segmentation, classification, prediction, clustering, and optimization.

Don't limit yourself to just one tool or one technology; multiple tools are best for pruning your data and optimizing the process of learning. Use a tool incorporating a machine-learning algorithm to compress your data and to identify the important attributes in your data. Use a neural network to converge on a model, using the attributes identified by the machine-learning algorithm. Use a genetic algorithm to optimize your neural network to improve the accuracy of your model. Use a fuzzy logic system to extract rules from a neural network.

Finally, recognize that these core AI technologies may soon migrate to software other than data mining tools. Some of the segmentation algorithms like C5.0 or CART may soon be incorporated in web analysis software. Likewise, neural networks may soon become a part of new electronic retailing server products. What is important is that you be aware of how each of these technologies can improve your online sales by allowing you to retain and attract your current and future customers. Just as physical retailers like Wal-Mart have used genetic algorithms and neural networks to optimize their stores, so can they be utilized to optimize electronic retailing sites like Amazon.com. The core technologies of data mining are quite mature and robust, having been around for years; how they are used in the new interactive networked environment that is the Web will provide some unique new challenges for e-miners, e-marketers, and e-merchants.

4

Ten Steps to Mining Your Data

The mining of your web data starts well before you begin using a data mining tool, and it continues well after your analysis. Several steps are involved prior to the actual analysis of the data in order to ensure the data mining process is a success and a profitable endeavor. Although the data mining tools simplify and automate the analysis of databases, care must be taken in using them or they may lead to faulty findings and erroneous conclusions.

Identify Your Web Business Objective

The mining of your website involves some advanced planning about what type and level of information you intend to capture at your server and what additional data you plan to match it with. This by itself will ensure your data mining efforts will yield measurable business results. For example you need to plan with your web team what kind of log, cookie, and form information you intent to capture from your visitors and at what juncture. Next you need to involve your business, sales, and marketing teams in deciding what kind of demographic and household information you need to purchase to merge with your server data. In addition, you should consider bringing in your information system team for the possible incorporation of your datamart or data warehouse and customer database into the mix.

This advance planning can save you time and money in your data mining efforts. It can also translate into quicker results and thus ensure your success in the mining of your website. Keep in mind the principle that having more data is better than not having enough. Keep also in mind what your business and marketing goals are and what kind of data is required in order to achieve them. For example, if your goal is to prevent customer attrition, then you are likely in need of developing a "churn" model. In order to construct such a model you should secure samples of customer accounts that have recently closed or terminated so that your analysis can examine the patterns and differences between customers who are active and those who are inactive.

This preplanning step may require the use of modeling tools and techniques for building a blueprint for creating a road map to the data mining initiative. Modeling techniques can form the foundation to the mining application and ensure it meshes with the actual business requirements. This modeling initiative can also alert you to possible obstacles, such as the lack of access to certain data for the analysis. Another benefit is that it ensures you document your data mining efforts. Process-modeling tools also provide a benchmark for measuring improvement and a common language for communicating across your firm and the various teams and management. The following are a few of the modeling tools you can use to ensure a successful data mining project:

Product	Vendor	Website
Corporate Modeler	Casewise Systems	casewise.com
ProCarta	Domain Knowledge	domainknowledgeinc.com
Aris Toolset	IDS Scheer	ids-scheer.com
LiveModel	IntelliCorp	intellicorp.com
WorkFlow Modeler	Meta Software	metasoftware.com
Designer/2000	Oracle	oracle.com
Aion	Platinum Technology	platinum.com
ProVision Workbench	Proforma	proformacorp.com
Visio	Visio	visio.com

Before you begin a data mining project, be clear on what you hope to accomplish with your website analysis. The mining of your web data must be looked on as a strategic competitive move, which like all other business initiatives should have a measurable goal. Most likely you will not be performing a data mining project in a vacuum; other divisions or individuals in your firm are likely to be involved in the project. For a large retailing website this may include the following individuals:

Server Engineer	Website Analyst
Internet Engineer	Production Engineer
User Interface Designer	Production Content Manager
Web System Administrator	Design Lead
Web Technologist	Web Content Producer
User Interface Analyst	Promotions Manager
Brand Manager	Web Publisher
Internet Application Developer	Forum Manager
Online Documentation Manager	Web Content Editor
Web Partner Services	Web Marketing Editor
Web Account Manager	Web Administrator
Web Producer (Marketing)	Web Designer
Software Developer	Partner Advertising Administrator
Graphic Artist	Production Marketing Manager
Web System Designer	Web Content Publisher

Ensure they participate in the establishment of expectations, whether in terms of online sales, web traffic, or other measurable goals. Most likely you are already aware of the current state of affairs with your website, your Internet presence, and electronic retailing efforts. These are some of the questions you may want to consider at this juncture:

1. How much of an improvement do you need on your advertising or customer response rates?
2. What area of your website do you hope to improve by data mining customer transactions?
3. Is the business goal of your data mining analysis measurable, and if so, what is your baseline for success?

Recognize that you need to do some documentation regarding your data mining analysis both prior and after your analysis. The data mining of your transactional data will definitely have positive results on your website operation and overall bottom line, so the question you need to frame is "by how much?" What you need to be clear on is by how many responses, e-mail requests, online sales, clickthroughs, etc.

Baseline

One way of establishing these baselines is by looking at the current rate of sales for each of your main product lines. For example, if only 80 out of every thousand website visitors click through and purchase Product A on your website, then your baseline for that product is 8 percent, and your data mining goal will be to increase that rate for Product A. If you have multiple products, you need to establish baseline rates for each, or at a minimum do it for main product lines, so you can begin to gauge the impact your data mining analyses are having on your overall sales and marketing efforts. You need to establish some general baselines, whether it is in the form of average respond rates or average sales, in order to measure how much better data mining works over random chance. For starters here are some possible business goals for the mining of your web data.

Are you looking to identify potential new website customers? This is probably the most common data mining objective. Classification most commonly involves discovering the attributes, characteristics, or features of your website customers. This objective is best achieved by having as much information as possible about who buys and who doesn't while in your website. Classification typically involves distinguishing between revenue web visitors and nonrevenue web visitors. Classification is a clear-cut black-and-white prediction.

In order for a data mining tool, such as a neural network, to learn the unique features of your website customers, it needs to be trained with a large number of samples. You will need examples of website customers with a large number of features, which you can begin to gather in advance of the actual data mining analysis. Start by designing your registration forms to capture as much as you can about your customers. Explore how you can link your website data with existing internal databases such as your customer information file or your data warehouse. Plan to invest in the purchasing of external demographic or other third party data, which can be overlaid with your web data to enhance its value.

Are you looking to find specific website product sales trends? Are you looking to find revealing online trends or relationships between certain web pages representing individual products or services? In other words, is your data mining goal that of discovering a unique online *association*? This type of discovery can assist you in the positioning of certain web pages, offers, incentives, and links. The discovery of an association between unique products and services can in fact impact your overall website design. If they click on Product001.htm, what is the probability they will click on Product002.htm, Product003.htm, etc.? More importantly, what is the probability that if they buy Product003.htm, they have a propensity to buy Product009.htm?

Are you looking to identify specific buying patterns over time in your website? This may be a sequencing issue, which is usually an association problem with an additional dimension of time. Sequencing involves evolving trends and populations; in the case of your website, this is usually monthly or weekly sales of certain products and services. For high-traffic websites, like a search engine or a popular content provider, this may be accelerated to hourly trends or patterns. Many web marketing and electronic commerce forecasting problems involve sequencing or time-series analyses with data being sampled at fixed intervals of time.

Sequencing is generally more involved, since instead of looking at a single recorded web transaction with one measured value for each feature, are you instead looking at that same feature measured at different times. One of the most common web management problems is attempting to anticipate traffic in the future: How many visits or sales are you likely to have based on observed patterns over time? This is clearly a sequencing problem. Another sequencing problem involves online patterns once a web visitor or customer logs into your site. Here the sequencing problem, which may be tracked by your cookies, is trying to map the movement of your website visitors. This involves mapping the path of your website visitors, which is very much like association, but involving the additional element of time.

Keep in mind that prediction, association, classification, clustering, and sequencing are not exclusive goals and in fact may overlap as a result of your data mining analysis. What is important, however, is to be clear about the business objective, since it will influence both how you select your data and tool and, more importantly, the format of your solution. Have a clear focus on the business goal you are trying to obtain.

- Are you trying to increase response rate to a web campaign?
- Are you trying to identify what products tend to sell together?
- Are you trying to identify the features of large shopping carts?
- Are you trying to identify the features of your most profitable clients?

Select Your Data

Once you've defined your business objective, your next step is to choose the web server and company data for meeting this goal. Here is a quick checklist:

- Is the data adequate to describe the phenomena the data mining analysis is attempting to model?
- Is a common field in your web data being used for linking to other databases?

- Can the data from your web be consolidated with your data warehouse?
- Will the data being mined be the same and available after the analysis?
- What internal and external information is available for the analysis?
- How current and relevant is the data to the business objective?
- Are the data sets being merged consistent with each other?
- Who is knowledgeable about the data being gathered?
- Is there redundancy in the data sets being merged?
- What joints are needed for the various databases?
- Is there lifestyle or demographic data available?

Creating Customer Data

One of the advantages of mining your website is that the customer data can be created on the fly. For example, several advertising models provide methods by which to sell your products and services on the web. However, they also provide methods by which to generate customer data for mining. Among the several marketing models, the most common are brand sites, banners, buttons, pop ups, chat, push, e-mail, and agents.

Brand Sites

These were some of the first websites set up—where a company wanted a site simply because everybody else was doing it. Originally, few were doing any electronic commerce. They were simply on the Internet to build brand awareness. Brand sites usually contain useful content with some type of contest, game, newsletter, or promotion, and are usually on the Web for purposes of building customer loyalty and recognition.

These sites span the realm of products and services, as the examples in Figures 4–1 and 4–2 demonstrate. Figure 4–1 typifies the new genera-

tion of sites, which are already doing some merchandising. Even these websites have the ability to gather data for mining through the use of log and cookie files as well as forms. They can also use other web-specific commercial software and services such as BroadVision's Relational, GuestTrack, DoubleClick, LikeMinds, and FireFly to further profile their visitors and their propensity or affinity toward their products and services. These branding sites, simply by their presence, can begin to interact and capture some general demographics about their visitors.

Figure 4–1
This site provides games, information, and a shop for making purchases.

Figure 4–2
An elegant brand building site.

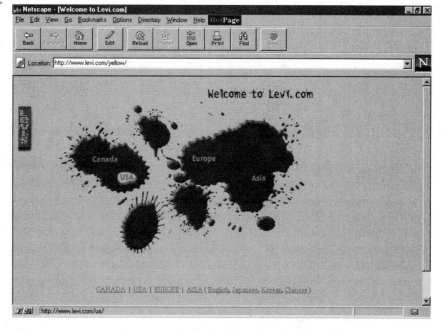

Banners

Banners are rectangular, static, and dynamic billboards commonly found on the top of search engines, online directories, and other popular websites (Figure 4–3). They commonly entice the users to click through the ad, which will take them to another website. These types of advertisements can attract visitors by interacting with them, which again leads to the generation of visitor information for data mining.

Typically, clickthrough for most banners is around 2 percent through general rotation, but in some instances banners can improve this rate to 6 percent by linking the type of banner to presets on the basis of "keywords" input by the user of search engines or online directories. A rate of around 9 percent can be achieved on the basis of topic directions. Special ad servers like SelectCast from Aptex, using neural network and proprietary indexing technology, claim rates of up to 14 percent. Other techniques for improving clickthroughs are the use of traditional marketing words like "new," "free," or "click here" or by the use of motion or certain bright colors. Studies indicate that animation improves clickthrough rates by as much as 15 percent over static billboards. Other web design techniques include pull down menus and interactive games and ticker messages.

Figure 4–3
This banner sits atop a popular search engine and rotates with each visit.

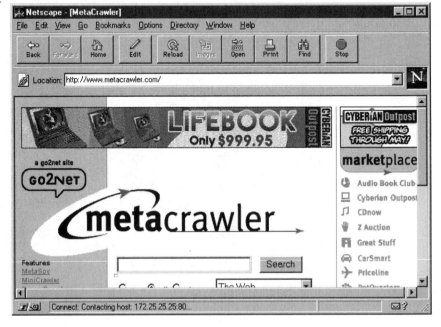

Buttons

Buttons windows, usually about a quarter of the size of the normal-sized banners, typically are very limited in the information they provide and are narrowly targeted to a very small audience. For example, you may find them on a website designed to sell software or hardware with a button designed to take the visitor to a computer brand site or a browser site like Netscape or Microsoft (Figure 4–4).

Other ways of getting additional clickthroughs include positioning buttons in popular online magazines or industry-specific websites. They are product- or service-specific and can be closed by the user so that they are not as intrusive as a banner. They are, however, another method of attracting visitors and aggregating customer data for mining.

Figure 4–4
Note the two browser buttons at the bottom of this page.

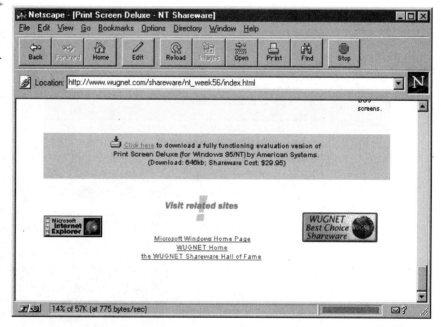

Pop Ups

Like buttons, pop ups are a novel concept of advertising and promotion. They are often launched within a website for purposes of pitching a special product or service. The difference between buttons and pop up windows is that they are self-contained and generally cover a square of the browser window. They are designed to grab the attention of the visitors while at the same time not taking them away from the main home page (Figure 4–5). Visitors can interact with the pop up either with a self-contained form or banner while at the same time remain at the main website where they can also interact or shop. The pop ups, like the buttons and banners, have the ability to gather personal customer information about potential prospects which can be mined.

Figure 4–5
This pop up window can be accessed without the need to leave the website.

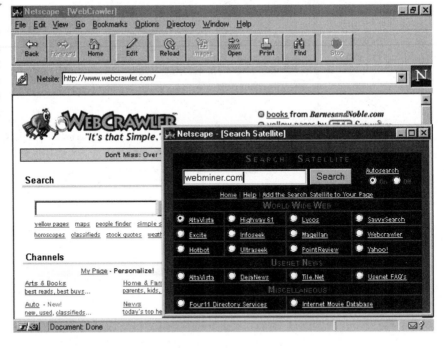

Push

Also known as "webcasting" or channels, users are allowed to select the type of content they want "pushed" to them. As with chat, most push sites like PointCast require some initial registration and selection of specific topics, which again is important in gathering information for data mining. Because visitors select and reveal what information they are interested in getting pushed to them in a registration form often requiring gender, age, and ZIP code, important data is compiled for data analysis. When visitors sign up with a channel provider they fill out a menu of topics and interests, which becomes their preference profile. Some of the key players in push technology are BackWeb, Intermind, NETdelivery, and Marimba.

- *BackWeb* is able to push personalized content from multiple sources, including legacy files, in real-time.

- *Intermind* is able to integrate legacy and intranet systems via Notes/Domino. Extranet channels are also available for customer-support applications.

- *NETdelivery* is a special delivery service that can provide mailbox icons on the user's screen.

- *Marimba* and its Castanet technology is designed to reduce bandwidth demand by only updating content that has changed. Castanet is designed to distribute and manage itself automatically.

E-mail

E-mail provides the ability to communicate easily with visitors, prospects, and customers. While e-mail enables a relationship to form and increases purchases or visits, it can also capture data about customer interests or concerns. E-mail enhances a site's ability to form loyal relationships with customers through personalized dialog. The more a site knows about its visitors and customers, the easier it is to provide them with the products and services they desire. E-mail is a very effective and inexpensive way to acquire and maintain a customer. It is non-intrusive and ubiquitous.

Care must be taken, however, when using e-mail to capture client data. You must make sure you allow the customers to sign up voluntarily and to only send them the information they request at the intervals they request, and most important, give them the ability to get off your mailing list. Several mail servers exist allowing you the ability to create a database of recipients based on customer profile information. Servers and software products such as Aptex, Egain, Majordomo, Pegasus, Revnet, ListProc, AltaVista, Arial, InfoPress, and UnityMail allow you to build forms for capturing customer data directly into a database for mining. The Kana Customer Messaging System e-mail software contains a module that uses AI to analyze inbound messages and sort them correctly.

Chat

Yet another model for attracting visitors and data gathering for mining are the chat sites found in high traffic locations like search engines and online directories. Since most chat sites require registration information about visitors, data can be gathered and used for targeting ads based on demographics, psychographics, gender, age, income, and of course the chat discussion topic. Chats also tend to be topic-specific, which can provide a method for data gathering about visitor interests.

Agents

Agents or "collaborative filtering" software programs make recommendations based on prior web activity by individuals with similar demographic or psychographic profiles. Affinity or collaborative programs are designed to make recommendations on the basis of what other people have liked with similar likes and dislikes to those of you. They make their recommendations based on your preference input and the activity of a community of users similar to you. The most prevalent of these collaborative filtering sites and software is FireFly, a pioneer in using AI technology for commercial purposes. These types of collaborative filtering applications are usually deployed in websites selling music, videos, books, and other types of recreational products and services.

Some agents act as filters, browsing through large amounts of data and providing their owners only the information that matches their criteria. Most intelligent agents are typically not website-specific. They instead involve the retrieval of the specific type of intelligence you furnish during the registration phase. There are several types of "agents." Some are server-specific while others are designed to cruise the Web in your behalf. For example, some agents are designed to roam the Web for specific information you are interested in. This can be keyword-specific or industry- or company name-driven, or take the form of information on a specific technology, news topic, product announcement, stock price or activity, company name, etc.

The intelligence of these agents varies. Some are simply able to search on specific topics the owner specifies, and others, which are smarter, are able to look over your shoulder and cue on the specific keywords you typically search on, gradually "learning" what your interests are and through these observations suggest or search for information, products, or services in your behalf. Because agents require user registration and specific personal information and topics or keywords they represent yet another method of gathering important personal information for data mining.

Dealing with Transactional Data

When you first encounter transactional data gathered from your website, find out exactly how it was done, what guidelines are in place, and how often the logs and forms databases are updated. As in the case of constructing a data warehouse, bringing together data from diverse systems often involves dealing with flat-files, relational tables, and hierarchical and relational systems from multiple operational systems that at times deal with the same attributes (such as dates) in different ways. The coordination and selection of these data sets will involve considerable effort and time. In fact, this may be the most time-consuming part of the entire data mining effort.

Key issues likely to drive your decisions in the selection of your web data are the portability and cost of both internal and external databases. A related issue may include security and privacy, especially in the use of any information provided by your website customers. Keep in mind that some of the information required for profiling your customer might not be available—be prepared to do some data gathering. Be prepared also to deal with inconsistent data definitions, different encodings of data, and inconsistent values when selecting and merging your data from multiple sources.

The data requirements for your mining analysis are directly linked to the output or desired insight that you wish to obtain from your web database. For most analyses, the general rule is the more the better. A second rule in the selection of your web data is that you should strive to have a good sampling of both types of customers or accounts, both positive and negative samples: sales and no-sales. Keep in mind that in your analyses the more descriptive information you have on a website visitor and customer, the better the predictive models you are likely to obtain. First and foremost you must recognize why you are accumulating the data which you will be mining—similarly be prepared to acknowledge that you may need additional data you don't currently have.

The bottom line is simply *know the data!* If you are not conversant with the data, you may want to enlist the service of someone who has knowledge of the problem domain. It is important to select the important variables in the data, such as the dependent (outputs) and independent (inputs) variables. When dealing with files or databases from some other departments, find out why the information was gathered in the first place. It is important to have the participation and involvement of the retailing, marketing, shipping, sales, and of course, the web team members during this process.

Prepare Your Data

Once the data has been assembled and visually inspected, some decisions must be made regarding which attributes to exclude and which attributes need to be converted into usable formats.

- What condition is the data in, and what steps are needed to prepare it for analysis?
- What conversions and mapping of the data is required prior to the analysis?
- Are these processes acceptable to the users and the deliverable solution?
- What strategies must be taken for handling missing data and noise or outliers?
- How skewed is the data? Are logarithm or square transformation needed?
- Do you need to do 1-of-N conversion for categorical fields?
- Do you need to normalize dollar fields by dividing them by 1000?
- Do you need to convert purchase dates to continuous values?
- Do you need to convert addresses to sectors?
- Do you need to convert Yes/No fields to 1/0?

A graphical tool or a good file editor can assist you in inspecting the physical state of the data. A visual inspection should provide you an overview of the number and percentage of blank fields in the data set. Also, a statistical tool can assist you in identifying important relations between variables in the data. This, however, may not help in large data sets. Operational data is organized to be compact for speed and efficiency; it is not organized for analysis. Carefully review its format and be prepared to convert it into a format that will yield insight from its analysis. For example, it may be efficient to have an account establish date in the format of MM/DD/YY, but it may be necessary to transform this field to one that equates to "Total Number of Establish Account Days: NNNN."

If you are dealing with a very large database, don't do wholesale conversions on the entire data set. It is safer to first do a random extract, perform the transactions, mine the data, and evaluate the results. If you are considering using a neural network tool, additional conversion of the data will be required so that categorical values are converted to 1-of-N values and all continuous values are converted to ranges between 0 and 1 or into log or square functions. One common method of smoothing data is to reduce the number of distinct values for a feature. A similar technique can be used to "discretize" continuous features into a set of true-or-false features, each covering a fixed range of values.

Missing data presents a unique problem, especially if you are using a neural network tool, since they cannot deal with missing values. Most modern data mining tools provide options on how to deal with missing values. Care should be taken, however, on whether a missing value represents a negative response that needs to be re-coded and used. Consider replacing all missing values with a zero or an average mean. The drawback to this is that the replaced value is not correct. Lastly, randomly extract a sample of the data, especially if you are dealing with a large database, and start with a small prototype model. Start small and expand with your data mining analysis. For example, rather than constructing multiple response models for all the products in your retailing site, you may want to test only a few for your major product lines.

Enhancing Your Data

One of the strategies you may want to take in preparing your data for mining is linking it to other databases your company may already have from production files. For example, here are a few file types with their content:

Company File Types	Content
Transactional Data	Type of Products or Services Sold
ZIP Code or Customer Demographics	Gender, Age, Income Level, Children
Outbound Mail	Response, Location, Household Data
Telemarketing	Response Rate, Number or Mailings
Customer Information	Total Number of Sales, Client Since Date
Data Warehouse	Customer Profile by Product and Service
Datamart	Customer Profile by Division or Branch
Consumer Credit Report	Credit/Debit Cards, Occupation, Mortgage

Evaluate Your Data

A structural evaluation of your data should be performed in order to determine what type of data mining tools to use for your analysis.

- What is the ratio of categorical/binary attributes in the database?
- What is the nature and structure of the database?
- What is the overall condition of the data set?
- What is the distribution of the data set?
- How skewed is the data set?

Utility Tools for Preparing and Viewing Your Data

Quite often during this phase of a data mining project you will be required to visually inspect large text data sets, such as a server log file. Sometimes you may experience import errors, which can only be detected by physically opening an ASCII file and scanning down to a line item. The following software tools are quite useful for doing these types of tasks:

UltraEdit-32
This is a powerful and useful text editor with the following database handling features:

- Disk-based text editing—up to 2GB file size with minimum RAM used even for multi-megabyte files
- Insert string feature at every increment (ideal for formatting DB records and inserting hard returns)
- Insert/fill columns, insert line numbers and sum columns/ selection feature

- Column/block editing—allows insertion/removal of columns of data

When dealing with databases from different sources, you are bound to have to deal with different file formats. As such you will need to import data sets and convert them into a uniform format which you can then import into your data mining tool. The following tool is very good in doing these types of conversions.

Data Junction
This data conversion utility tool permits users to translate data to or from almost any structured file format, including databases, flat files, spreadsheets, ASCII, binary, EBCDIC, reports and text files, SQL, ODBC, COBOL, ISAMs, vertical applications, mailmerge, Stats/Math, and many others. Data Junction has filter, edit, and mapping capabilities for modifying characters, fields, and records into the exact format you required. Specifications can be selected interactively through a powerful GUI, or via batch automation.

As a general rule, neural networks work best on data sets with a large number of numeric attributes. Machine-learning algorithms incorporated in most decision tree and rule-generating data mining tools work best with data sets with a large number of records and a large number of attributes. Empirical studies have shown that the structure of the data critically impacts the accuracy of a data mining tool. For example, data sets with extreme distributions (skew > 1 and kurtosis > 7) and with many binary/categorical attributes (> 38%) tend to favor machine-learning-based data mining tools.

Often, derived ratios of input fields may be required in order to capture the impact or the true value of the inputs—to capture the velocity of a client value, such as profit or propensity to buy. For example, a commonly derived ratio is one of debt-to-income: rather than using simply the debt and income attributes as inputs, more can be gained by the ratio rather than the individual values. In your web analysis, the number of site visits or the number of purchases made over time may provide a better insight into the true value of website customers:

Number of purchases/Number of visits:	$7/9 = .77$ Propensity to Purchase Ratio
Total amount of sales/Total number of visits:	$\$39/5 = 7.8$ Profit Ratio

Format the Solution

In conjunction with the evaluation of your web data and your business objective is the issue of the format your business solution is going to take.

- What is the desired format of your solution, decision tree, rules, C code, graph, map?
- What is the goal of the solution, classification, regression, clustering, segmentation?
- How will you distribute the knowledge gained by the data mining process?
- What are the available format options from the data mining process?
- What does management really need, insight or sales?
- What do you need from the data mining process?

Multiple tools may be required to come up with the ideal data mining form for your website. For example, you may need to extract rules from a clustering analysis. To do so you will need to first perform the clustering analysis using a Self-Organization Map or Kohonen Network. Next you will run the identified clusters through a machine-learning algorithm in order to generate the descriptive IF/THEN rules that "profile" the extracted clusters. Conversely, you may have to first do an analysis using a machine-learning algorithm on a data set with a large number of attributes in order to compress it and/or to identify a few significant attributes, and then run those significant attributes through a neural network for the final classification model.

Tradeoffs may be in order, but you must weigh your options with respect to what your business and website needs are and what tools you will need in your analysis. What are you after, insight or results? Often the format of your data mining solution will determine what data mining tool you will use. If you need to explain how and why you uncovered a pattern in your web data, you may need to use a machine-learning algorithm such as a decision tree or rule generator data mining tool. If all that matters is accuracy and efficiency, a neural network tool will do. For an e-commerce site, most likely both paradigms will be advantageous, since knowing the demographics of customers and increased sales are both desired goals.

Select the Tools

The selection of the right tool is clearly dependent on the task you are trying to accomplish. For example, the following matrix describes what each data mining technology is best suited for:

Tool Type	Classification	Clustering	Description
Genetic Algorithms	Yes	No	No
Machine Learning	Yes	Yes	Yes
Neural Networks	Yes	Yes	No
Self-Organizing Maps	No	Yes	No

Along with selecting the right technology, the characteristics and structure of your data must also be considered when selecting the right tool for the job. Here is a checklist of data-related issues you need to consider when selecting a data mining tool:

- number of continuous value fields
- number of dependent variables
- number of categorical fields
- length and type of records
- skewness of the data set

As a rule, machine-learning algorithms perform better on skewed data sets with a high number of categorical attributes and with a high number of fields per records. Neural networks, on the other hand, do better with numeric data. The following are a dozen criteria you need to consider in the selection of the right data mining tool. They involve software issues and hardware requirements:

Scalability

As a website and its log files and forms database get larger, a tool's performance should improve accordingly. Scalability means that by taking advantage of parallel database management systems and additional CPUs, the user is able to work with more data, build more models, and improve overall accuracy by adding additional processors. As the data increases so does the complexity, not only in the number of records but also in the number of attributes, variables, and possible website patterns. If a platform lacks the ability to scale, the computationally intensive nature of data mining will slow and eventually kill the decision support system.

The number of interactions among variables and amount of nonlinearity of parameters also contribute to the scalability of complexity. As the patterns become more subtle among the noise, the need for accuracy rises. At this juncture it is important to evaluate what kind of parallelism the tool supports. Find out if the tool supports a symmetric multiprocessing system (SMP) or massively parallel processing system (MPP). Technical factors affecting scalability include database size, model complexity, performance monitoring and tuning, as well as effective model validation. The issue of scalability in a data mining tool is how well it takes advantage of hardware design, including parallel algorithms and their direct access to parallel DBMSs. A high-end data mining tool needs to be able to run on a scalable hardware platform.

Accuracy

Accuracy is measured in the error rate of the algorithm or network for predictive modeling. There are several ways to evaluation accuracy. It can be measured as the *degree* of error, that is, determining *how* wrong the incorrect answers were. For some applications, it is of interest to know if the system responded with "no answers" or "wrong answers," and for what values of the condition attributes this happened. The structure of the data set being used to test it must be appropriately noted. See R. D. King, C. Feng, and A. Sutherland, "STATLOG: Comparison of Classification Algorithms on Large Real-World Problems," *Applied Artificial Intelligence* 9(3):289–333, May-June 1995.

- How does the algorithm of the tool determine if the characteristics of the problem match?
- What provisions are made for handling missing values, noise, and cost computations?
- How fast does it train and how does it work on the new data?
- How does it treat the dependent and independent variables?
- How much noise can it handle before accuracy drops?
- How sensitive is the algorithm to noise?
- How sensitive is it to missing data?

Formats

A data mining tool incorporating a machine-learning algorithm should provide a feature for viewing the most important rules or factors it discovers. The tool should not only be effective in detecting patterns, it should also provide you an insight into what is happening in your website and allow for easy and quick interaction with the data. The simplest explanation to the activity in your website is the preferable solution in discovering the nature of the customer transactions under analysis. A data mining tool should generate its results—trees, formulas, weights, graphs, or rules—as simply as possible in order to uncover as many unseen objects as possible. For a data set of some size, such as one from a large web retailing site, reading through all the rules will be an impossible mission for a user, even if each rule is simple to understand. For this reason a tool should generalize a simple solution while at the same time incorporate features to avoid overfitting. That is to say, general rules should describe what activity is taking place at a high level at your website.

You must ask if your tool incorporates a feature for prioritizing its results and, if it does, how it accomplishes this: what factors does it use, what significance level does it use, what is the percentage of its probability and accuracy, how many numbers of cases does it incorporate in its rule, and so forth. Does the tool offer some form of visualization aid, such as histogram of errors by business graphs, or can its market segments be mapped to geographic maps? Is the tool designed to work on a desktop or in a client/server environment? Size is not a true measurement of the complexity it can handle—quite simply the only thing a tool's architecture may indicate is the amount of data it can process and not the complexity it can mine.

Solutions

A data mining tool should help you understand the results of its analysis by providing simple yet exact measurements, such as predicted error rates, level of significance, and/or rate of accuracy. What kind of output (solutions) does the tool generate: decision tree, C code, IF/THEN rules, narrative reports, graphs, visualization, SQL syntax? Some tools produce results that are relatively easy to interpret, such as decision trees that can be expressed as rules. Other tools, such as a back-propagation neural network, may make good predictions but may be difficult to understand. Ideally, both understanding and accuracy should be balanced in the format of the tool's solution.

The tool should also incorporate adequate instruments to allow the user to perform a sensitivity analysis on its output results. Does the tool include some interface for exporting the results of its models to other visualization or OLAP tools? What kind of GUI is provided for model building? Does the tool provide an API, which can be used embedded in a production system, in C, Visual Basic, or PowerBuilder?

Preprocessing

Preparing the data for analysis is one of the most time-consuming aspects of data mining. Your web server log files generally are comma-delimited, so the tool you select should be able to read this format without difficulty. Your forms database is most likely housed in some relational database, which again your tool should be able to connect to. Any special features a tool can perform to ease this process will greatly expedite the development of knowledge extraction and the construction of your predictive models. Some preprocessing functions to consider in evaluating a tool should include its ability to do some of the following:

- data cleaning
- data selection
- data description
- data transformation

A key feature of a data mining tool is its ability to cope or handle the data "as-is" in order to do some autonomous data cleaning, such as dealing with missing values, by giving you the options to "discard," "average," "alert," "exclude," etc. The tool you select should be able to provide some descriptive report on the quality of the data to the user.

- How well does it describe the data, row and value counts and distribution of values?
- Can it "sense" the difference between continuous value and categorical fields?
- Can the tool recognize and deal accordingly with integers, real numbers, etc.?
- How does the tool handle missing data or identify integrity violations?
- Can the tool explode categorical variables into dichotomous variables?
- Can the tool "map" fields or change them on the fly?
- Can the tool group continuous variables into ranges?
- Can the tool do calculations of existing columns?
- Does the tool require extensive data preparation?

Connectivity

Some data mining tools require that the data being mined be extracted from the target databases into their internal file format, whereas others can work directly against the database. A scalable data mining tool that can directly access your web server using its native SQL can maximize performance and take advantage of special performance features, such as parallel database access. Consideration should be given to those tools that can optimize performance by allowing the data mining processing at the server level. Although you likely will want to mine your data on a dedicated server set aside exclusively for data analysis.

- Can the tool consolidate data from multiple sources for individual analysis?
- If the tool is currently ODBC compliant, what drivers does it support?
- Does the tool incorporate an HTML or a JAVA interface?

Import/Export

Data mining tools that provide an easy integration path with other products offer additional ways to get the most out of the total data mining and knowledge discovery process. Related to connectivity is the feature of importing data: does the tool support multiple formats such as ASCII, Access, Excel, comma or tab delimited, SAS, SPSS, and other specific DBMS, etc.? What conversion does the tool make with the original data it imports and at what ratio? Does the tool allow for the exporting of code, syntax, rules, etc.? Many database products (including traditional query, reporting, graphics, and visualization tools) can assist in the understanding of the data before and after the data mining process. The tool should provide the capability to easily link its results to an exportable format that can be visually enhanced for a presentation to management or others.

Memory Management

Normally a data mining tool's memory requirement will only be linear, depending on the size of the data set. The time complexity of the learning phase is a very limiting factor for many of today's data mining tools. If the algorithm used, for instance, uses exponential time growth, the maximum size of the training set will be quite limited. When considering the memory usage of a data mining tool, only the complexity matters, as for time usage. Still, the memory usage could give an indication as to what kind of system is necessary in order to handle "normal" amounts of data, in terms of number of records and rows.

On the other hand, whether a complex system uses one or two hours is usually of less importance. For a tool using iteration to achieve better and better accuracy, the time taken into evaluation must be the time to reach a certain level of accuracy. In the evaluation of a tool, consideration should be given to this time/complexity factor. Know in advance that certain tools, such as those based on an SOM network or a genetic algorithm, operate on a data set in such a way that they are very computationally intensive—meaning results may not be available for several hours.

Performance

Speed and accuracy both contribute to the evaluation of a data mining tool's overall performance. Speed is measured by how fast a model is built, as well as how fast a deployed predictive model can evaluate new data. Given the tool's design network or algorithm, how does it process the data, via single or multiple passes? Another factor impacting performance is cost—that is, the cost of providing a learning data set in the development of a model. This cost includes the number of examples necessary and the cost of assuring a needed accuracy in the learning set of a model. In most instances the sheer volume of transactions for a large website dictates that this will not be a factor or concern. The cost factor should be considered in the evaluation of a tool's overall performance. Somewhat related to this criteria is the issue of data limitations, that is, whether the tool restricts the type of variables it is capable of processing.

- What are the limits to the number of ranges or intervals it can group?
- Can the tool assist in the understanding of the results of the analysis?
- Does the tool require numeric or discrete data fields?
- Can the tool present results in a graphical format?
- How many categories can the tool process?

Noise

Tool accuracy is often affected by noise, which is the result of irrelevant columns, missing or incorrect values, or cases that don't conform to an underlying pattern. In evaluating the robustness of a data mining product, you must answer the question of how much of this noise the tool can stand before its accuracy drops. Instead of evaluating a data mining tool based on a bell-shaped training set, one should also measure a system's noise-handling capabilities. Different levels of noise should be added to the training set, and the number of correct classifications with the new rules should be noted. If the noise added to the training set created inconsistencies, the resulting classification errors should be studied carefully, as some systems, for instance, will create conflicting rules with no hints to which one to choose in a particular situation.

Paradigms

A key criterion for a data mining tool is the data mining technologies it supports. For example, can the results of analyses be linked or passed from one classification system to another, in order to develop a hybrid solution? An example of this is being able to do clustering using an SOM (Kohonen Network) and then generating rules from a sub-cluster using a machine-learning algorithm (C5.0)—all within one data mining suite is an ideal feature. In the analysis of the data mining tool, specific references on the type of technologies should be noted in order to optimize its results.

- What are the underlying technologies and techniques of the tool? Are they proprietary or generic? And most importantly, are they linked?

- Can the tool split the data into training and testing sets? Can the user select the ratio of this split?
- Is the analysis entirely automated and closed, or does it allow for some degree of customization?
- Does the data mining incorporate more than one classification algorithm or network?
- Does the interface allow for the close evaluation of results of the analysis?
- How intuitive is the tool? Does it require extensive training?
- Is there an application program interface (API)?
- What is the current version of the tool?

Efficiency

Finally, consider the criteria of the data mining tool's efficiency. Will it take much time to take a decision based on the data mining process? For example, in developing a set of weights or rules, what matters is how we find the formula or rule to use. If the rules are sorted somehow, it may be possible to use indexing or search methods to find the most general and robust rule quickly. Otherwise, the complexity of taking the decision could be higher than if, for instance, all rules must be compared pair-by-pair. Some tools offer solutions in the form of hundreds of rules, which defeats the purpose of data mining—uncovering a simple pattern from a massive amount of customer online transaction data. For example in a decision tree, the complexity of decision-making is usually some function of its width and height. In the evaluation of a data mining tool, how it handles this issue of complexity and efficiency needs to be addressed and considered.

Tool Selection

Other nontechnical issues are of course platform and price, as well as the availability of training, consulting, and support. The range in prices for data mining tools vary greatly, starting from a $5,000 desktop single technology system to a multiple paradigm suite with each module costing in excess of $135,000. Keep in mind, however, that both of these systems may be based on the same core technology, such as a variation of the CART algorithm or a back-propagation neural network. The difference in price is really dependent on the platform each of the systems is designed for deployment on, as well as the scope and size of the web data set each system is required to mine. Some data mining companies are new and small and may not be around for long. What is important to note, however, is the technology that their tools are based on, such as neural networks and machine-learning and genetic algorithms, is a mature and robust technology that will survive over time.

Lastly, you need to step back and consider outsourcing rather than purchasing a data mining tool and the related training it may require of your staff. As with other information system projects, outsourcing or consulting is always an option. This may be more cost effective over time; after all, you are not buying software as much as buying

Figure 4–6
How machine-learning algorithm tools identify customer clusters.

Machine-Learning Algorithms

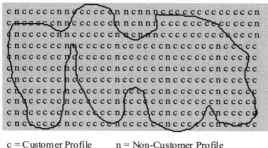

c = Customer Profile   n = Non-Customer Profile

Figure 4–7
How neural network tools identify customer clusters.

Neural Networks

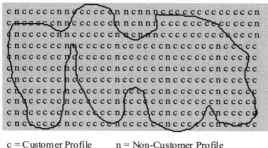

c = Customer Profile   n = Non-Customer Profile

Figure 4–8
How neural network tools, optimized with a genetic algorithm tool, identifies customer clusters.

Genetic Algorithm + Neural Network

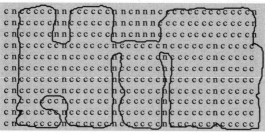

c = Customer Profile   n = Non-Customer Profile

the knowledge and insight it provides from your transactional data. However, as previously stated, data mining is an iterative process, which means that you may be churning data on a fairly regular basis from your website, mandating that you incorporate data mining as part of your everyday operation.

If your data is highly skewed, you may want to use a machine-learning algorithm tool, which can locate profitable customer clusters distinctly independent of one another (Figure 4–6). If your data is nonlinear, you may want to use a back-propagation neural network tool, which can map a data space more efficiently than linear regression (Figure 4–7). You may want to optimize your neural network tool with a genetic algorithm tool (Figure 4–8).

A Tool Shopping Tip: Kick the Tires before Buying

You may want to start by browsing the Web for samples of evaluation copies of data mining tools. A key site is www.kdnuggets.com, a data mining directory of companies, tools, and reference materials. Keep in mind the platform requirements in the selection of tools and the various features each provides. Keep in mind also that you may require more than one tool—consider the benefits of a data mining suite which incorporates multiple paradigms. Finally, ask for a Proof-of-Concept evaluation copy of the software. For example, some vendors will provide special pricing for a 90-day "try-out" deal of their tool.

Construct the Models

It is not until this stage that the actual data mining of your website files begin. This is the process of searching for patterns in a data set and the generation of classification rules, decision trees, clustering, scores, weights, and evaluation and comparison of error rates.

- Is additional data available which could help the performance of the models?
- What are the model error rates? Are they acceptable? Can they be improved?
- Is a different methodology necessary to improve model performance?
- How many models do you require for your entire website?
- Train and test models using a random number seed?
- Output SQL syntax for distribution to end-users?
- Supervised learning or unsupervised learning?

- Incorporate C code into a production system?
- Integrate rules in a decision support system?
- Purge noisy and redundant data attributes?
- Classification, prediction, or clustering?
- Monitor and evaluate results?

Will you be developing a model via supervised learning? This is a situation where you have samples of both negative and positive cases: website buyers vs. website non-buyers, web visitor respondents vs. web visitor nonrespondents, etc. In most instances, especially for a large electronic retailing site, you will have thousands of samples from which you can develop your models, in which case you will be performing supervised learning for classification or prediction. However, if you have multiple products and services, most likely you will need to construct separate models for each. For example, the propensity to buy one category of products, say BeatlesCD.htm, will be different from StonesCD.htm or PoliceCD.htm. Furthermore the propensity for each product line will also require a specific model, so that a model for AbbeyRoadCD.htm will be different from WhiteAlbumCD.htm. To what extent you want to refine your modeling efforts depends on your resources and time.

If you don't have a sample of both positive and negative cases, you will most likely be performing clustering, or unsupervised learning. This process is much more difficult to do than classification, but it may be necessary. Clustering is often done to discover consumer patterns. Retailers often do a type of data mining clustering commonly known as "market basket" analysis to better position certain products that tend to sell in unison or to offer special incentives. For example, a clustering analysis might discover that consumers who buy premium wine tend to also buy deli cheese, while those who buy microbrewery beer tend to instead purchase deli meats.

Similar purchasing patterns can be uncovered in a commercial website, for example, where certain products tend to be bought at the same time. Sequencing may be involved between a point in time when one product is purchased, such as an ink-jet printer this month and ink-jet cartridges 30 or 60 days later. An exhaustive amount of purchasing associations and patterns exist in large websites such as one selling relatively inexpensive consumer items like books, CDs, toys, and software. Visual associations can be explored, which can lead to cross-selling opportunities.

Both supervised and unsupervised learning require that you split your data into training and testing sets. This can be in a 90/10, 70/30, or 60/40 ratio. The splitting of the original data must be done using a random seed number; almost all modern data mining tools incorporate a feature for splitting your data and evaluating the results of the models you create. Once the training set has been used to construct a model, the test set is run through the data mining model in order to evaluate its accuracy. Dividing the number of incorrect classifications by the total number of instances produces the model's error rate. Dividing the number of correct classifications by the total number of instances gives the model's accuracy rate.

Almost all of the current data mining tools provide a method by which you can measure the accuracy of the models you can construct with them. They facilitate the process by which you can split your data into training and testing data sets. They each also provide methods by which you can randomly test and compare the results of your training and testing data results. Decision tree tools, for example, provide detailed output designed to show the differences between the current tree and the alternate data set. Some tools allow for the "resubstitution" of data so you can test on the same data that you trained your model on. However, it is always best to test with an alternate "unseen" data set to perform the test. This alternate data set can come from a hold back sample created by partitioning your data or from an imported, external file.

Validate the Findings

As previously mentioned, a data mining analysis of your website will most likely involve individuals from several departments, such as Information Systems, Marketing, Sales, Inventory, etc. It most definitely will involve the administrators, designers, analysts, managers, and engineers responsible for designing and maintaining the day-to-day operations of your website. It is important after you have completed your data mining analysis that you share and discuss your findings with all of them. Domain experts (people who are the specialists in their area) need to be briefed on the results of the analysis to ensure the findings are correct and appropriate to your site's business objectives. This is the sanity check: You need to be objective and focused on your initial goal for mining your website. If your data mining results are faulty—whether it is due to the data, tool, or methodology—you may need to do another analysis and reconstruct a new set of models with their participation and input.

What important relationships were discovered between the independent and dependent variables? For example, do the demographics you discovered about your website visitors and customers match those of prior marketing analyses? A website selling game software will likely have totally different customers from those of an investment brokerage site. Keep in mind too some of the inherent demographics about who uses the Web in general, for this may skew your perception of who your website customers are. People on the Web tend to be better educated and a bit more affluent than average, but this is also slowly changing every month as more and more people get "wired."

Another side issue at this time may be presenting the results to management and the various departments in your company, including your web administrators and designers. It is important that they understand the implications of the data mining analysis. In other words, now that you have identified unique consumer patterns or identified a specific web consumer profile—how are you going to validate it? The validation of the findings often involves testing a model with "real bullets" in field situations. For example, a field test may involve making a special offer on your site, or doing a special e-mailing campaign. You will need to do a test to measure how well your data mining findings or models improve your business bottom line, like response rates and/or sales figures. To minimize risk you may want to do a control test to measure how well your data mining models perform and how well they improve existing baselines prior to full implementation involving all product lines.

Deliver the Findings

A data mining report should be prepared documenting the entire data mining process, including the steps you took in selecting and preparing your data, the tools you used and why, the tool settings, your findings, and an explanation of what the code that was generated is supposed to do. As with any business process, you need to establish both baselines and procedures. In your analysis report you need to comment on the results of the data mining analysis, stating whether it meets the business objective of your website. If for some reasons it doesn't, you should state why not. You may want to include in your report how the data mining analysis results can be improved. Is different or new data warranted? Perhaps external demographic and household information should be brought in, or you could capture better information via newly designed registration forms or cookies in your website.

You should include some recommendation for action stemming from the data mining analysis. For example, if you found that most of your website customers are young professionals, you may want to suggest some subtle changes to the content and design of your site. Data mining is an iterative process, and its documentation will ensure that improvement in the effectiveness of your website, especially if you are involved in electronic commerce, will continue over time. These incremental improvements will occur not only in how data mining takes place in your website and your company but also in the accuracy of the models and in the improvement of your online sales and marketing.

Integrate the Solutions

This final step in the data mining of your website data project is really a commitment to continue the process of learning from your firm's online transactions. This process involves incorporating the findings into your firm's business practices, marketing efforts, and strategic planning. Data mining is a pattern-recognition process involving hundreds, thousands, or maybe millions of daily transactions in your website.

Integrating Your Website and Data Warehouse

The integration of your website data with your company information file or data warehouse can assist your company in knowing how your current customers match in characteristics with those of your website visitors. As with the mining of your data warehouse, the integration of your website data will further enrich your insight about the attributes of your current and potential customers.

Through the integration of your website with your internal production company databases, you can provide website visitors timely information about your inventory, services, and customer support. While doing this you can also begin to learn who they are and what they like and dislike about your products and services. By mining the data collected about your website visitors you can begin to serve them with the type of information their demographics indicate they want to possess.

Your company can communicate to its customers in a highly personalized tone and manner. By integrating web purchasing information with your data warehouse, you can acknowledge purchases, remind customers about similar products, and cross-sell related or complementary services. Several measurements can be mined, including the date of the most recent purchases, the dates of those purchases, and the total amount of money each customer has spent at your site. The mining of these measurements can be used to calibrate customer value, profitability, and loyalty.

Through the merger of your data warehouse and website, several deliverables are possible, including the identification of your most profitable customers and potential future clients. With this profile you can move to target and develop new potential clients while they visit your website. Comparisons of several attributes can be made between your existing customers and those of your site visitors in order to fine tune or alter your ads, offers, incentives, pricing, messages, banners, and other communications. Through this matching you can also make some informed decisions about marketing campaigns and the overall design of your website. For example, you can investigate how your current customers compare to your web visitors in terms of the following attributes:

- Age
- Gender
- Income
- Hobbies
- Occupation
- Marital Status
- Home Location
- Education Level
- Recreational Interest
- Disposable Income Ratio
- Psychographics and Demographics

Psychographics are measurements of individual's attitudes and lifestyle characteristics. Such measurements are excellent indicators on how website visitors and customers are thinking and where they are going with their lives. SRI International, an independent nonprofit research institute, has developed eight Values and Lifestyles (VALS) categories for consumer types:

- Actualizers
- Fullfilleds
- Achievers
- Experiencers
- Believers
- Strivers
- Makers
- Strugglers

VALS categorizes U.S. adult consumers into mutually exclusive groups based on their psychology and several key demographics.

VALS is unique because it highlights factors that motivate consumer-buying behavior. VALS looks at the underlying psychological make-up of people. It looks at the human side of the equation, for example, preferences for such values as control or freedom, tradition or novelty, information or stimulation, hands-on activity, or intellectual abstractions. One of the SRI's recent developments is iVALS, which is a profiling system designed to enhance the usefulness and quality of online environments for end users, content providers, and intermediaries. iVALS profiles web users and clusters them along the following categories:

- Wizards
- Pioneers
- Upstreamers
- Socialites
- Workers
- Surfers
- Mainstreamers
- Sociables
- Seekers
- Immigrants

This is an example of an iVALS profile:

The iVALS Wizards Profile

Wizards are the most active and skilled Internet users. Computers are a key aspect of their lifestyles, and mastery of technology figures prominently in their identities.

More than 80% of Wizards have been on the Internet for three or more years. Although Wizards report meeting many new people during their years online, it is likely that such friendships often stay virtual. That is, Wizards are not necessarily seeking to meet people in the traditional sense. Rather, their sociability appears as a byproduct to their heavy involvement in so many aspects of Net culture.

Nearly everyone in the Wizard group has performed relatively esoteric functions such as videoconferencing on the Internet or creating Web pages. Half have participated in a MUD or MOO. Most would call themselves computer power users. Many have used WWW retail sites, and all own a lot of games or multimedia, especially for adults.

Wizards are nearly all males, and relatively young, with a median age under 30. Despite their age, many work as computer technicians, professors, middle managers, consultants, or industry analysts, and therefore earn a medium to high household income.

Wizards are a prime target for sophisticated technical information, beta test software, authoring tools, computer and software industry conferences and trade shows, and other computer-related professional or product communications. They like software with lots of options and enjoy climbing a learning curve if it leads to interesting new abilities.

Through the data mining of your website a new understanding of your visitors and customers will emerge, especially when merged with psychographic profiles like iVALS. Through the mining of this data, a profile or several composites can emerge which will assist you in tailoring their experience during their time in your site to more closely meet their needs.

This final step of your data mining analysis requires that you monitor the performance of the models that you have generated. All models will age and their performance will disintegrate, so you need to ensure you monitor the accuracy of your data mining models.

The data mining process can involve some if not all of the above steps, and in many cases they may not be sequential. There will be instances where certain steps can be entirely skipped. However, the basic idea in the process is to ensure that the data mining is heavily dependent on recognizing the business objectives of your website and the limitations of the data and the tools.

The integration of the data mining solutions usually means taking action. A data mining analysis can lead to making some organizational changes on how your website resources are deployed, or what recommendations are made to management and what alliances and partnerships you may want to consider. The integration of a data mining analysis may impact how your online inventory is arranged, or how your website promotions are planned, or which website visitors and customers get what offers. It may involve a closely integrated e-mail system incorporating personalized notification of products and services based on your data mining analyses. This integration may involve how accounts are scored, graded, or grouped. The integration of a data mining solution may be done on a case-by-case basis or on a batch process, so that, for example, you profile your entire website customer account file on a weekly, monthly, or quarterly basis.

The data mining effort that you conduct will likely include a lingering question: *"now what?"* Are you prepared to use the knowledge of your data mining analysis to change your business and your e-commerce site? Are you prepared to make major marketing and business process changes? Are you prepared and do you have the support of management to re-design your website should your analysis support this action? All or some of these questions are likely to result from the mining of your website and you should plan to deal with them accordingly.

Data mining is a process, not a project. As such you need to consider who will be doing it, when is it required, and what data will you be mining. Data is not static. As such you need to plan on conducting periodic analysis of it, at what intervals depends on how often and dramatically it changes. For example, a bank may need to mine its data warehouse every quarter for its customer acquisition models. A cellular telephone company may want to mine its warehouse every month in order to keep its churn model fresh and accurate. An electronic retailer may want to mine its website every week—why? Because the business environment each of these entities is attempting to anticipate and model changes at very different rates: customers do not change checking accounts as often as they do cellular carriers or online booksellers.

One way of determining how often you need to mine your data is to periodically check the accuracy of your models against current customer data. If the accuracy has deteriorated significantly since the creation of the model, it is time to build a new one. Knowing all of these lingering questions before you start will hopefully lead to a smoother incorporation of data mining into your business and the optimization of your website. Just remember that data mining will definitely benefit any firm with an e-commerce site. A standard process model is being developed by several interest groups known as the CRISP-DM (Cross-Industry Standard Process for Data Mining), which is aimed at moving away from the focus on the technology and instead concentrates on the business problems: http://www.ncr.dk/CRISP/.

5

The Tools

In this chapter we will discuss several data mining tools. Data mining tools are commercial programs incorporating an AI technology for visualization, association, segmentation, classification, prediction, clustering, optimization, and modeling. Some tools incorporate multiple technologies, such as neural networks and machine-learning algorithms within a suite, with the capabilities of linking their results.

Criteria

The tools selected represent a cross section of commercial products based on different technologies, each formatting business solutions in a unique manner. This side-by-side discussion will demonstrate how two tools using a variation of the same technology, such as a neural network, can format a solution in a dramatically different manner. In a relatively young industry such as data mining, there are currently no standards. As such the results of their processes can at times be quite different.

All of the software products are designed to run on desktop environments or high-end servers. They vary in price from a couple of thousand to well over a hundred thousand dollars. There are other tools on the market that were not included in this review but are equally good at data mining and modeling.

This sampling will demonstrate the wide range of features, performance, and approaches in today's data mining software vendor market. Our purpose is also to demonstrate that the main criterion in your tool selection should be based on how well it answers your website business needs. Keep in mind the dozen criteria from the prior chapter on tool selection:

1. Scalability
2. Accuracy
3. Formats
4. Solutions
5. Preprocessing
6. Connectivity
7. Import/Export
8. Memory Management
9. Performance
10. Noise
11. Paradigms
12. Efficiency

Simply having the "right" technology in a data mining tool is not enough. Having a tool with multiple paradigms has its obvious advantages. For example, you can "link" the results from one to another, enabling you to benefit from two technologies rather than a stand-alone solution. For example, Clementine from SPSS enables you to do cluster analysis using a Kohonen network, then link the segments to a C5.0 machine-learning algorithm for the generation of rules describing the attributes of those clusters. Another tool, Decisionhouse, enables you to use a machine-learning algorithm to segment your data set in a decision tree, and then view the market segment it discovered via a geographic map, for the entire United States down to the ZIP code level. The point is that multiple paradigm tools provide more *useable* business results, which are greater than their single technology parts.

Some large end data mining tool vendors are able to ask and get $150,000 for their base package, because they are able to deliver technologies in a manner a company can incorporate into their business processes and systems. NeoVista, a high-end data mining vendor, will virtually customize their software to meet their customers' needs, most of which are Fortune 100 firms. Simply incorporating an algorithm in a package does not mean it is a very effective business tool. In order for a tool to truly be effective it must be scalable and robust software able to handle large data sets in a client server environment and deliver business solutions in a format that can be deployed over the enterprise. This includes the tools you use for analyzing your website data.

You should select a tool that is going to provide you the business solution you require in leveraging your website to its full marketing and sales potential, and provide you the insight you need about your online customers and the transactions they generate. The tools we look at in this section range from desktop systems to large multitasking, multi-parallel server powerhouses, which can benefit websites of all sizes, from single product/single person websites to major portals of electronic commerce.

To demonstrate the different approaches of some of these tools, we performed multiple analyses on a single data set containing a small random sample of 1,472 records, the output from a small electronic commerce web server for a single day. From this sample data set we attempted to identify specific website patterns leading to online sales and to identify some of the demographics of these visitors and customers. There were three possible outcomes to the sessions, which were identified by specific pages on the site:

JustBrowsing.htm	*This results in a no sale visit.*
E-mailMe.htm	*This is a potential lead to a sale.*
OrderForm.htm	*This is a sale, and the desired outcome*

The primary objective of the analysis then is to identify the characteristics of those website visitors who selected the OrderForm.htm. To do this we linked the forms database, which contained the visitor's ZIP code, and the server log file to a demographic data set from CACI known as the ACORN database.

The ACORN Consumer Classification System provides a percentage of distribution by consumer type for all the ZIP codes in the United States. ACORN analyzes demographic profiles and classifies consumers according to the type of residential area in which they live. ACORN is a database designed to identify consumer profiles on 226,000 neighborhoods sorted by 60 lifestyle characteristics, such as income, home value, occupation, education, age, and other key determinants of consumer behavior. The ACORN is a neighborhood segmentation system containing 43 clusters, or consumer segments, which can be used to determine the lifestyle of customers on the basis of their ZIP code. For example, the ZIP code 94502 is categorized by the ACORN system as consisting of the following consumer segments:

37.4% Wealthy Seaboard Suburbs—This type is located along the eastern seaboard and in California. Residents are married, middle-aged professionals at the peak of their lifetime earnings. They rank among the highest for auto club memberships and travel extensively. Media preferences include Metropolitan, Boating and Yachting, and the *New York Times*. This market's share of disposable income is relatively high.

62.6% Successful Suburbanites—Members of this type have achieved their success with families, home ownership, and prosperity by dint of hard work. Upward mobility characterizes this market. Essentially suburban, they drive new cars and spend money on sports, exercise equipment, and personal computers. They are likely to have loans. They do not watch a lot of TV, but read daily newspapers.

Keep in mind that other types of visitor attributes are available for this type of inductive analysis both from within your website's log files and forms databases and from external data providers such as Equifax, MetroMail, LikeMinds, NetPerceptions, and NetCount, which can further describe the psychographics and household features of website visitors, such as their income ranges or the presence of children. (See Figure 5–1.)

Single Record Sample by Field Name

Top One Percent ZIP %, Wealthy Seaboard Suburbs ZIP %, Upper Income Empty Nesters ZIP %, Successful Suburbanites ZIP %, Prosperous Baby Boomers ZIP %, Semirural Lifestyle ZIP %, Urban Professional Couple ZIP %, Baby Boomers with Children ZIP %, Thriving Immigrants ZIP %, Pacific Heights ZIP %, Older Married Couples ZIP %, High Rise Renters ZIP %, Enterprising Young Singles ZIP %, Retirement Communities ZIP %, Active Senior Singles ZIP %, Prosperous Older Couples ZIP %, Wealthiest Seniors ZIP %, Rural Resort Dwellers ZIP %, Senior Sun Seekers ZIP %, Twentysomethings

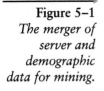

Figure 5–1
The merger of server and demographic data for mining.

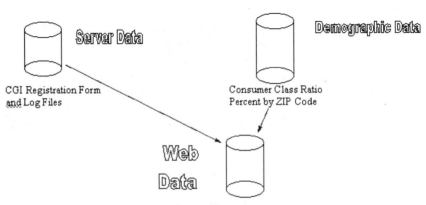

Combined Databases for Data Mining

ZIP %, College Campuses ZIP %, Military Proximity ZIP %, East Coast Immigrants ZIP %, Middle Class Families ZIP %, Newly Formed Households ZIP %, Settle Southwestern Families ZIP %, West Coast Immigrants ZIP %, Low Income: Young & Old ZIP %, Middle America ZIP %, Young Frequent Movers ZIP %, Rural Industrial Workers ZIP %, Prairie Farmers ZIP %, Small Town Working Families ZIP %, Rustbelt Neighborhoods ZIP %, Heartland Communities ZIP %, Young Immigrants ZIP %, SSN Dependents ZIP %, Distressed Neighborhoods ZIP %, Hard Times ZIP %, Urban Working Families ZIP %,**Subdomain,Income,ZIP,Gender,Product,HTM**

Single Record Sample Content

0,3,0,0,56,0,0,20,0,10,0,5,0,5,0,0,0,0,0,0,0,0,0,0,0,0,0,0,0,0,0,0, 0,0,0,0,0,0,0, "com", "10265", "10452", "Male", "Notebooks", "JustBrowsing.htm"

Single Paradigm Tools

We begin by looking at single paradigm tools; these are data mining products incorporating a single technology, such as a neural network or a machine-learning algorithm like ID3.

Tool	Vendor	Platform	Technology
DM Marksman	HNC Software	NT with card	Neural Network
4Thought	Right Info	WIN95/NT	Neural Network
KnowledgeSEEKER	ANGOSS	WIN95/NT/Unix	CART, CHAID, ID3
NGO	BioComp	WIN95/NT	Neural Network, Genetic Algorithm
WizWhy	WizWhy	WIN95/NT	Proprietary Algorithm

Database Mining Marksman

Along with NeuralWare and Nestor, HNC is one of the pioneering neural network software companies to emerge in the mid-1980s. However, unlike the other two, HNC has been very successful and is now a public company. Its success, however, has not come from selling data mining software. In the 1990s the company changed its business strategy from selling tools to selling business solutions based on neural network technology, specifically in the area of credit card fraud detection. HNC's flagship product, Falcon, currently monitors millions of credit card accounts, representing about 80 percent of cards issued in the United States, for fraud. Following in this vertical approach to providing solutions rather than software, HNC today sells ProfitMax, a credit card profitability management system. It has also recently spun off a company called Aptex, which is marketing products like SelectCast for Internet advertising and marketing using proprietary text recognition and neural network technologies.

Database Mining Marksman

Best at: Classification, direct marketing applications.

Cost Factor: No

Current Version: 1.1

Data Access: Can import ASCII and most file formats, also ODBC-compliant interface.

Data Preprocessing: Missing value substitution, conversion of symbol strings, symbol mapping.

Distinguishing Feature: Hardware processor allows for optimal performance of network.

File Limitations: Output must be binary categorical. Inputs: 250,000 rows X 100 columns. Limit of 15 to 20 symbols per categorical variables.

Format of Solution: The software generates reports on *lift*. It also shows which variables impact the most on output results. A sensitivity analysis feature allows for the prioritization of input drivers.

Installed Base: 25

Memory Required: 64 MB

Parallel Processing Support: No

Pricing: $48,750 software and PC with 16 node SNAP parallel processor with 3 days training.

Space Required: 3 MB

Training/Consulting: Yes, $7,500 per session plus travel and expenses.

Technology Paradigm: Back-propagation and Kohonen neural networks.

HNC also produces Database Mining Marksman, a product designed for direct mail marketers combining neural network software with a hardware accelerator card. Marksman contains three components: the Marksman GUI, a link to Microsoft's Excel spreadsheet, and DBMS/COPY. Excel is used for report generation and DBMS/COPY is used for data preparation, extraction, and importing. Marksman supports classification using the back-propagation neural network and clustering using the Kohonen network. Most of the reports generated by Marksman are geared toward direct marketing; hence they are designed to help set cutoff points for direct mail campaigns, based on desired response rate, and maximized return or budget limits. The reports include Gains by Score, Gains by Percentile, Acquisition Cost, Lift Chart, and the Rollup Report.

A wizard feature in the software guides the user through each "project" which is the start to finish concept of a complete analysis. From the Analyze button in the main screen the user is provided the following options:

File Definition ... define the data to be mined

Data Preparation ... how is the data to be cleaned and mapped

Relationship Discovery ... what fields are to be used

Modeling ... set the parameter for the model

Analyze Data ... execute the modeling process

Importing data into Marksman involves the use of DBMS/COPY, a stand-alone software product, to export graphs and reports. Models can be binary where the dependent variable must be two-valued, or they can be categorical "Yes" or "No" and lastly continuous with value predictions. There is no way to export code from Marksman; for this you need a companion product HNC sells called DeployNet. This is a distinct disadvantage for a tool that is so expensive.

This data mining tool demonstrates some of the limitations of the breed. It is singular in its approach to a specific data mining task—direct marketing. It is also limited in the technology it incorporates: a neural network from which you cannot export the results of the analysis, that is, the weights in the form of C code. The other limitation of this tool is that it relies on another software product for the importing of data and the exporting of graphical solutions. Clearly it would be difficult to use this type of tool for the analysis of web-based data since its reports are narrowly aimed at the direct mail industry. When selecting your tools, beware of industry-specific applications with designed features that may limit their usefulness when mining website databases.

4Thought

4Thought is like another data mining tool from the United Kingdom (Profiler from Attar Software Ltd.), in that it requires a hardware security key that connects to the parallel port. Although this may be a standard in England where both of these products come from, these software keys can be a deterrent to using the programs. Although vendors' desires for protection against unauthorized duplication are justified, which the companies claim is much more common in Europe, these keys can be a significant problem. When you are working in a net-

4Thought

Best at: Time series modeling

Cost Factor: No

Current Version: 3.21

Data Access: Can import ASCII, ODBC support, Excel, Lotus, SPSS

Data Preprocessing: Outlier detection, interpolation, eliminates highly correlated columns, supports functions

Distinguishing Feature: Spreadsheet interface

File Limitations: Dependent variable must be numeric, limited to 256 categorical variables

Format of Solution: Statistical and reports

Installed Base: 500

Memory Required: 20 MB

Parallel Processing Support: No

Pricing: $9,900 plus 20% support service annually

Space Required: 3 MB

Training/Consulting: Consulting services $2,000 daily

Technology Paradigm: Back-propagation neural network

worked environment with both desktops and notebooks, you must disconnect and reconnect the software key to each machine as you do your analysis; crawling under desks to get to the port to get to the software key should not be a task of the data mining process.

4Thought has a somewhat simplistic interface. It presents the data in a spreadsheet format, which after a model is created adds a column with the predicted results. Changes to the data can be made in the spreadsheet environment, so that a graph can easily be created. 4Thought can import fixed and delimited ASCII, Excel, Lotus, and SPSS formats. It is also ODBC compliant and can link to Excel, Btrieve, dBase, and XDB. An ample number of functions are provided for data transformation, which is especially good since it is a neural network tool. It has a wizard-like feature called Autolog, which applies a logarithm to those columns that have a distribution that looks more like a log-normal distribution than a normal distribution. During the construction of a model, dynamic feedback is provided allowing for the user to see how the training and testing are progressing. Once the model is built, a predicted value column is created in the spreadsheet. If new input values are typed in a blank row at the end of the spreadsheet, a new predicted value is automatically computed. In addition, the neural network weights can be exported as a macro function to Excel, Lotus, and SPSS. Several graphs are available for pre- and post-modeling and the comparison between the inputs and the generated outputs.

4Thought is clearly aimed at the business analyst and the power spreadsheet user. It provides the functionality of a neural network in a spreadsheet format. In fact 4Thought is similar to other low-end data mining tools that work as add-ons to Excel. These tools, such as NeuralWare's Predict, Braincel, and Evolver use the Excel environment as an attempt to isolate the user from most of the complexities of data preparation and modeling. The strategy is a good one, for it takes advantage of the large installed base and the graphical capabilities of Excel. However, in choosing such a strategy they also limit themselves to the number of rows and cells Excel can import. The mining of a web database with 4Thought would necessitate the importing of it into Excel prior to analysis, which would be highly unlikely for a large e-commerce website with thousands of daily transactions.

KnowledgeSEEKER

KnowledgeSEEKER, which was originally introduced by FirstMark Software prior to its sale to AGNOSS, is one of the most mature data mining tools in today's market, and the current version is one of the industry's most flexible and powerful desktop decision-tree tool builders. Among KnowledgeSEEKER's strengths are its ease of use and its robust method of importing data from multiple data sources in different formats. KnowledgeSEEKER can import from multiple ASCII and DB formats and it is also ODBC compliant. Once the data has been imported into KnowledgeSEEKER, the user can view all

---

KnowledgeSEEKER

Best at: Ease of use

Cost Factor: Yes

Current Version: 5.0

Data Access: ASCII text fixed-length and delimited, dBase, Excel, Gauss, Lotus, Paradox, QuattroPro, SAS, Sawtooth, SmartWare, Splus, SPSS, Stata, Systat, and ODBC

Data Preprocessing: Emphasis on interaction with data

Distinguishing Feature: Very mature and robust tool

File Limitations: Scalable to hardware

Installed Base: 800

Memory Required: 640 K

Parallel Processing Support: No

Pricing: $5,000

Solution Format: Decision trees, IF/THEN rules, SQL syntax

Space Required: 4 MB

Training/Consulting: Yes

Technology Paradigm: CART, CHAID, and ID3

attributes, with the user being given the flexibility to do force splits on any variable in the data to create a decision tree.

The tool attempts to guess at the type of data imported, but the user can change this both during import or once loaded in KnowledgeSEEKER. Attributes can also be changed on the fly through what KnowledgeSEEKER calls "Mapping"—in this process several fields can be merged, renamed, or created. Once a decision tree is generated, the nodes created can be viewed textually and graphically. KnowledgeSEEKER allows for decision trees to be created via three possible ways:

Auto—A complete decision tree is generated until no interesting splits can be found.

Find Split—The user controls the depth and direction of the decision tree.

Force Split—The user forces the splits on a variable they select.

Multiple branch trees can be created with total flexibility, allowing the user to select specific nodes of interest and developing sub-branches on the fly. In the decision tree in Figure 5–2, the data splits on the variable "Product" from which the user can further drill down. In this case we selected "Drives." We asked the software to search and create a decision tree, which in this example splits for "Rural Industrial Workers," an ACORN consumer class.

Figure 5–2
Knowledge-SEEKER provides excellent control over the splits in the trees it generates.

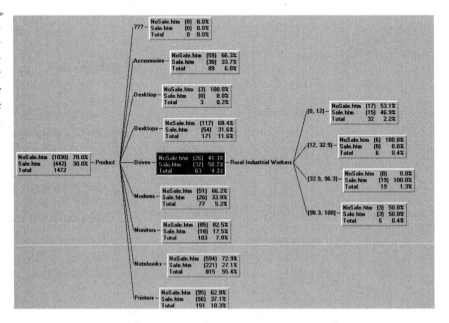

Once a decision tree is created there are two ways it can be vali-dated. The simplest and fastest way is by going to the *Test* menu and selecting the *Resubstitution* option, which provides you both a Misclassification Rate and an Accuracy figure. The other method of evaluating a decision tree is by splitting your data set by whatever ratio you want, and then testing it:

```
KnowledgeSEEKER test results of partitioned data set.
Error Rate Profile :: Test Partition
           Learning      Testing       Dropped
 Category    Freq  %    Freq   %    Diff. Freq %
 ─────   ──. ──.   ──. ──.   ──  │ ──
 NoSale.htm   776 70.3   254 69.0    -1.3 │0 0.0
  Sale.htm    328 29.7   114 31.0     1.3 │0 0.0
 ─────   ──. ──.   ──. ──.   ──  │ ──
            1104         368           0
Misclassification Rate: 0.290761
Accuracy: 70.9239
```

Decision tree settings can be adjusted via the Tree Configuration menu. For example, the *Filter Threshold* (percent error) can be set to the following settings:

Decision	1%
Prediction	5%
Exploration	20%

The *Decision* support setting of 1 percent means that erroneous effects will be produced only 1 time in 100. It is a setting requiring an exceptionally high level of confidence in tree results. The *Prediction* is the default setting confirming that the displayed rela-tionships are valid with a 95 percent certainty rating. This is the rec-ommended setting for most data mining tasks by ANGOSS. The *Exploration* setting is the most relaxed and is designed to let you explore relationships in your data. It allows you to be wrong in about 20 times out of 100 when using this filter level. Lastly, KnowledgeSEEKER gives you the option to specify your own filter threshold for any value between 0 and 1. Other tree configuration options include *Split Search Algorithm*:

Cluster	finds groups that maximize similarity within groups
Exhaustive	finds groups that maximize statistical significance

Another setting is for the Split Search Criterion, which lets you change the criterion used to guide the split search for any field as well as change how to display significance values. The default method is the adjusted level of significance. This method is the most statistically sound approach since it reduces the possibility of producing chance results and puts all the fields on a common statistical footing. These are the options:

Adjusted	this setting is designed to ensure the integrity of the classification tree
Unadjusted	this setting is prone to a bias towards fields with a lot of categories
Entropy/Variance	this setting simulates the ID3 machine-learning algorithm

KnowledgeSEEKER incorporates both CART and CHAID algorithms concurrently, which allow the user to segment a data set on either a categorical or continuous value variable. Another useful feature of KnowledgeSEEKER is the ability to *Reshape* any decision tree, which enables the user to page through various splits of their data set. For example, Figure 5–3 is a view on an ACORN consumer class "Successful Suburbanites" from our sample data set. Figure 5–4 is another decision tree of the same data set, split by another consumer class, "High Rise Renters."

KnowledgeSEEKER not only generates decision tree, but can also produce Crosstabs, IF/THEN rules, and SQL syntax for export use. For example, the following rules and syntax were generated from the decision tree in Figure 5–4.

Figure 5–3
Knowledge-SEEKER's split of the web data of a specific consumer class: Successful Suburbanites.

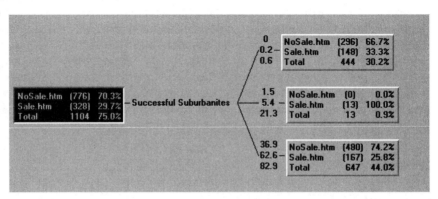

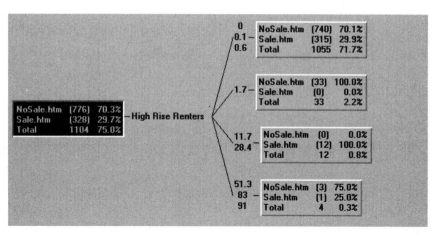

Figure 5–4
*Knowledge-
SEEKER's split
of the web data
of a specific con-
sumer class:
High Rise
Renters.*

RULE_1 IF	High Rise Renters =	0, 0.1 or 0.6
THEN	HTM = NoSale.htm	70.1%
	HTM = Sale.htm	29.9%
RULE_2 IF	High Rise Renters =	1.7
THEN	HTM = NoSale.htm	100.0%
	HTM = Sale.htm	0.0%
RULE_3 IF	High Rise Renters =	11.7 or 28.4
THEN	HTM = NoSale.htm	0.0%
	HTM = Sale.htm	100.0%
RULE_4 IF	High Rise Renters =	51.3, 83 or 91
THEN	HTM = NoSale.htm	75.0%
	HTM = Sale.htm	25.0%

Overall, KnowledgeSEEKER is one of the best decision tree tools in the market. The tool has a very clean and easy-to-use interface, it is very fast and accurate, and it provides the users plenty of options in modifying their data and in generating different trees and subsequent IF/THEN rules. KnowledgeSEEKER is very robust and makes a very good tool for segmenting web databases, offering multiple solutions in various formats for rapid deployment by web administrators and business and marketing analysts. A new product, knowledgeSTUDIO by AGNOSS, incorporates a neural network.

NGO NeuroGenetic Optimizer

Best at: Classification and Prediction	**Memory Required:** 16 MB
Cost Factor: No	**Parallel Processing Support:** Yes
Current Version: 2.1	**Pricing:** $295 and up
Data Access: ASCII delimited	**Solution Format:** API
Data Preprocessing: Yes, with EMS	**Space Required:** 5 MB
Distinguishing Feature: Accuracy	**Training/Consulting:** Yes
File Limitations: None	**Technology Paradigm:** Genetic Algorithm and Multiple Neural Networks
Installed Base: 350	

NGO NeuroGenetic Optimizer

The NeuroGenetic Optimizer (NGO) is a self-optimizing neural network model-generating tool. It uses a genetic algorithm component to select key data variables and optimize the structure of a back-propagation, a Self-Organizing Map, and other neural network architectures to maximize the predictive accuracy of its models.

The concept behind this tool is that rather than building one model at a time, you build multiple ones simultaneously. This particular approach to data mining and model construction lends itself quite well to dynamic business applications requiring multiple forecasting models. For example, BioComp's Enterprise Modeling Server can generate multiple models for each product an e-commerce site may carry. Another feature this tool has going for it is that of combating model deterioration. As with any other types of models, neural network models tend to decay with time. Having the ability to quickly refresh them with new data is clearly an asset, which this tool delivers.

The NGO uses genetic algorithms to evolve neural network structures while simultaneously searching for significant input variables to maximize the predictive accuracy of its neural network models. The effectiveness of the genetic algorithms' search capabilities in optimizing the settings of a neural network is an excellent idea. For example, a problem consisting of finding the best combination (subset) of 20 inputs and up to 15 hidden nodes in a back-propagation neural network is a combinatorial problem with over 16 million permutations. According to BioComp Systems, an excellent solution often appears in less than 1500 evaluations, which is 0.009 percent of the total possible configurations of a neural network. Commonly highly fit networks are often found in the first 30 to 50 neural networks evaluated. This is clearly an efficient means for discovering effective network structure/input combinations. The one drawback to this approach is one of time. A complex analysis, say of 10 or 20 web pages on your site, will likely take hours or even days to complete. The other drawback of the NGO is that it can only construct models on less than 32,000 observations.

This adaptive multimodeling capability is a good pragmatic approach to data mining highly dynamic data such as a web-generated database. The result of this process is higher accuracy neural networks that are optimized for the entire website with less effort on your part. The NGO automates much of the modeling development and data mining process. Some of the tedious tasks like the splitting of the testing/training data sets, determining which input variables to use and the overall neural network architectural design, are all automatically done for the user by the software. The NGO uses its genetic algorithms to evolve the neural network structures and select which input variables are the most important to what you are trying to predict, such as total sales for each product on your website. Once NGO has produced a model that fits the data, that is, learned the relationships between multiple inputs and a desired output, you need a separate product called the Predictor to view and use the resulting network. Predictor is shipped with the NGO and allows you to view graphs resulting from the network. It also allows you to enter data for predictions or load files to create scores that can be saved to disk.

Using the NGO can be as simple as opening a data file and running the software. The tool prompts you for your data format type and loads it into memory. Next it prompts you for the identification of inputs and desired output. Since you are likely going to be dealing with an ASCII comma-delimited flat file, generated from your server, you must tell NGO which fields to use as inputs and what field will be your output. From that point NGO goes on to build and validates the training and testing data sets, providing a variety of methods for viewing the modeling processes. NGO provides multiple graphs for monitoring its modeling activity, such as *Predicted vs. Desired* or *Accuracy vs. Error Trend* results, *Status* and *Report* screens—all of them can be viewed from multiple screens. This is a good feature since once you start the mining process you need to know that the training and testing of the data are taking place in the background.

The NGO also creates a population of candidate-input variables and neural structures, training them and evaluating them. It next selects the top networks and pairs up the genetic material representing the inputs and neural structure of the networks and does the exchanges of the genetic material between them. As with all proper genetic algorithms it also throws in a few mutations for a flavor of random searches before it goes back into the training/testing cycle again. These processes continue for a defined number of cycles (generations), for a defined period of time, or until a neural accuracy goal is reached.

If you leave the training at the default settings, NGO will continue running, splitting, pairing, and recycling for several hours. In our sample data set of 1472 observations with seven fields as inputs/outputs, the NGO ran for over six hours before it converged on an answer. This process is clearly computationally intensive, but the effectiveness of genetic algorithms combinatorial search capabilities with neural networks is truly great. During a run, the NGO provides you the ability to view the status of what is happening, view the evolving population, see the configurations and the statistics of the top ten networks. You can also observe learning curves and watch the neural outputs match your desired data for the network being trained and view and/or print reports on the specifics of the system setup and the resulting top networks. After several hours NGO found that being from a ZIP code with a high percentage of "Successful Suburbanite" consumer class was the most important attribute for predicting online sales.

WizWhy

WizWhy is a data mining tool originally developed and marketed in Israel. It uses a proprietary algorithm to generate IF/THEN rules and predictions. This algorithm is very extensive, meaning that the more data samples you have the longer it takes to generate rules. Another minor concern about WizWhy is that it generates a very large number of rules, which luckily, the user is able to reduce at the end of the data mining analysis. The interface is fairly straightforward, prompting you

WizWhy

Best at: Classification	**Installed Base:** 100
Cost Factor: Yes	**Memory Required:** 640 K
Current Version: 1.1	**Parallel Processing Support:** No
Data Access: ASCII/dBASE	**Pricing:** $5,000
Data Preprocessing: None	**Solution Format:** IF/THEN rules
Distinguishing Feature: Provides rule probability, count, and significance level	**Space Required:** 1.5 MB
	Training/Consulting: Yes
File Limitations: None	**Technology Paradigm:** Proprietary Algorithm

for the location and type of file format to import. Once imported, the tool lists all the fields, prompting you for the field to predict and an option to "Analyze if Empty" and "Ignore Field" for all the other fields in your imported database. Once you are done with your selections, you click on the *Rule Type,* where you can select the parameters for the rules you want WizWhy to generate. If you like, you can simply leave WizWhy at the default settings and select the *Issue Rules* button.

The following is a sample of the type of Rule Report generated by WizWhy, using the default settings. The settings can be modified to increase the accuracy of the rules and to reduce the number of rules. For example, this analysis generated 33 rules, which we reduced to 20 for brevity; the settings for reducing them are also adjustable. After some time a report and a group of rules will be generated directly from your web data. Here are the top five rules extracted from our sample data set:

WizWhy REPORT

Total Number of Records: **1472** Minimum probability of the:

1) if-then rules: **0.410**
2) if-then-not rules: **0.820**

Minimum Number of Cases in a Rule: **20**

Field to Predict: **Webminer.HTM**
Field to Predict is analyzed as Boolean in reference to the following value:

OrderForm.htm
Prediction error costs:
Error of the first kind: 1
Error of the second kind: 1
Mean probability of the predicted value is 0.300

PREDICTION ON THE PRESENT FILE Decision point:
Predict OrderForm.htm when conclusive probability is more than **0.449**

Number of errors of the first kind (misses): 339

Number of errors of the second kind (false alarms): 64

Total number of errors: 403

Success rate when predicting **OrderForm.htm: 0.600**

Success rate when predicting **NOT OrderForm.htm: 0.736**

Total cost of errors: 403

Number of records with no relevant rules: 26

Average cost (per record): 0.279

1) *If* **Subdomain** *is* <u>net</u>
   and **Product** *is* <u>Printers</u>
   Then
   Webminer.HTM *is* <u>OrderForm.htm</u>
   Rule's probability: **0.793**
   The rule exists in **23** *records.*
   Significance level: Error probability < 0.01

2) *If* **Income** *is* <u>**789.00 ± 617.00**</u>
   and **Product** *is* <u>Drives</u>
   Then
   Webminer.HTM *is* <u>OrderForm.htm</u>
   Rule's probability: **0.639**
   The rule exists in **23** *records.*
   Significance level: Error probability < 0.1

3) *If* **High Rise Renters** *is* <u>1.00</u>
   Then
   Webminer.HTM *is* not <u>OrderForm.htm</u>
   Rule's probability: **1.000**

WizWhy REPORT *(continued)*

The rule exists in **45** records.
Significance level: Error probability < 0.1

4) *If* **Enterprising Young Singles** *is*
98.00
Then
Webminer.HTM *is not*
OrderForm.htm
Rule's probability: **1.000**
The rule exists in **45** records.

Significance level: Error probability < 0.1

5) *If* **ZIP** *is* **94105**
Then
Webminer.HTM *is not*
OrderForm.htm
Rule's probability: **1.000**
The rule exists in **45** records.
Significance level: Error proba-
bility < 0.1

Because of WizWhy's relative slowness, it would not be appropriate for a large website. However, a small to medium site that does not require daily analysis will find WizWhy to be an excellent tool for generating rules with probability rates, record counts, and significance measurements. Note also that it has the ability to generate IF/THEN as well as IF/THEN NOT rules, and is able to tell you the probability of the rules and the number of instances as they appear on your training data set.

An important point to consider in the evaluation and selection of data mining tools is that these products and their results can be linked in order to obtain a hybrid solution. For example, you may want to use a decision-tree tool like KnowledgeSEEKER or WizWhy to segment and identify the key variables in your data set, especially if you are dealing with a large number of data fields. Then using the more compressed data set, with a reduced number of variables, you can use a neural network tool like NGO for classification—which with its embedded genetic algorithm can further optimize the accuracy of the final models for your website. (See Figure 5–5.)

Figure 5–5
Single technology data mining tools can be linked to maximize their solutions.

Machine Learning Tool   Neural Network Tool   Genetic Algorithm Tool

Data →

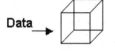

Compression   Classification   Optimization

The Data Mining Suites

The sum is often greater than its parts, and in data mining this becomes quite obvious when multiple technology tools are combined in a suite of paradigms. The following section showcases this new breed of multiple paradigm products.

These tools can combine features and technologies and are capable of linking analyses and their results in formats that can segment your website visitors by their demographic or lifestyle features, then present them in the form of SQL syntax, C code, or a 3D ZIP code map. Incorporated in these new tools are multiple technologies including statistics, neural networks, genetic algorithms, decision trees, and visualization modules enabling users to view relationships, extract patterns, and construct predictive models from their data.

Using one or two of these high-end tools you can do visualization, segmentation, association, classification, prediction, clustering, and optimization. Some are capable of running on scalable servers and take full advantage of their multiprocessor architectures. These data mining vendors recognize that no single technology can answer all the business questions a data warehouse or a large electronic commerce site may have about their data and as such, their products are designed to provide multiple solutions. Specifically built to deliver business results, most of these tools are able to generate C code, SQL syntax, three-dimensional graphs and maps for presentations and exporting into production systems. Some have the ability to base their analysis on millions of observations.

Tool	Vendor	Platform	Technologies
Clementine	SPSS	NT/UNIX	Back-propagation, SOM, C5.0
DataEngine	MIT	WIN95/UNIX	SOM, Fuzzy Logic
Decisionhouse	Quadstone	WIN95/NT/UNIX	CART/ID3, Regression, GIS

One of the advantages of these types of tools is that you are able to search through data space in a different way. (See Figure 5–6.)

Figure 5–6   *Slicing and dicing data spaces with multiple processes.*

Machine-Learning Algorithms 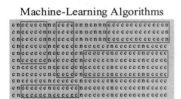 Neural Networks 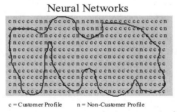 Genetic Algorithm + Neural Network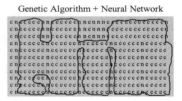

c = Customer Profile   n = Non-Customer Profile

Clementine

Best at: Clustering and Classification

Cost Factor: Yes

Current Version: 5.0

Data Access: ASCII and ODBC

Data Preprocessing: Yes

Distinguishing Feature: GUI Interface

File Limitations: None

Installed Base: 500

Memory Required: 40 MB

Parallel Processing Support: Yes

Pricing: $43,000 single license, one-year maintenance

Solution Format: C code

Space Required: 65 MB

Training/Consulting: Yes

Technology Paradigm: Regression, back-propagation/Kohonen neural networks and ID3/C5.0 machine-learning algorithm

Clementine

Clementine from SPSS combines several data mining technologies in one product, including visualization, statistics, neural networks and machine-learning algorithms. Data can be imported as a flat file or connected via ODBC, from which several manipulations and processes can be performed simply by connecting icons from the main panel. The most impressive feature of this tool is the ability to perform all aspects of data preparation, graphing, analysis, and modeling by dragging, connecting, and dropping icons on its main panel—through what SPSS calls "visual programming." The Clementine icon-based programming environment is accessed from the main window (see Figure 5–7).

Data preparation is accomplished using nodes from three palettes: Source, Record Operations, and Field Operations. These nodes give the user the capability to link and import data, to view the data in a table, and to transform the data. The Record Operators allow the user to select, merge, sample, and balance the records used for the analysis. They can be used to select a subset of the records based on a specific condition, to join records from multiple files, or do random

Figure 5–7
*The Clementine
"canvas" for
mining data.*

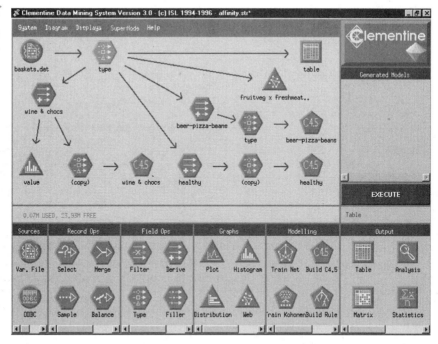

selections and other types of data manipulation. The Field Operators allow the user to filter records, create record types, and derive fields as well as other preprocessing transformations. A graphical group of nodes allow the user to generate plots, histograms, distribution charts, and generate a link association graph it calls "the web."

The modeling nodes allow the user to perform several operations including classification, segmentation, and clustering. Classification models can be constructed either via standard regression or a back-propagation neural network. Segmentation can be done via the C5.0 or ID3 machine-learning algorithms. The clustering is done with the Kohonen (SOM) neural network and the standard statistical nearest neighbor method. Several Output nodes are included to explore the results of the modeling processes as well as to generate C code for use by production systems.

To build a model the user simply selects and links the various Records, Field, Modeling, Graph, and Output nodes. Through this linking process procedures are created labeled "streams" by Clementine. These streams control data preparation, selection, partitioning, model building, testing, evaluation, and deployment. The stream pane is the primary work area, and the palettes across the bottom of the main panel contain the nodes and the "nuggets" that

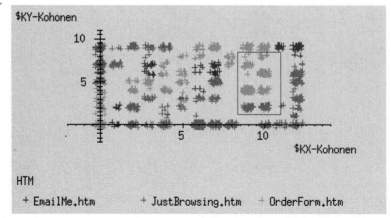

Figure 5–8
By marking the green cluster we were able to create a derived variable.

are the result of the modeling process. Multiple streams can be created on a pane, and stream diagrams can flow in any direction and be rerun from any point along the stream. Streams plus the contents of the generated models can be saved (as a state) and recalled. The user is isolated from the code creating process; in the Clementine environment, data mining is accomplished via click, link, and run.

One powerful feature of Clementine is its ability to link a clustering network to a rule-generating algorithm. For example, let's say you want to do an exploratory analysis of your website visitors from your log files—but you have no clear idea of where to start. Using one of the modeling nodes in Clementine known as Kohonen or Self-Organizing Map, you can build a cluster from your data, then "grab" it in the graphical environment and create a "derive" node. From there the derived node can then be routed through the C5.0 machine-learning algorithm, which can generate rules describing the features of the cluster discovered by the SOM. Using the SOM component, the sample data set was used to train the Kohonen Network, and several clusters were created (Figure 5–8).

Using the derived variable created from the clustering process we next generated a set of rules describing that grouping:

Rules for T:

Rule #1 for T:

    if HTM == OrderForm.htm

    and Subdomain == com

    then –> T (172.0 Instances, 1.0 Confidence)

This rule is indicating a high number of orders occur with .com domain types

Rule #2 for T:

> if HTM == OrderForm.htm
>
> and Subdomain == gov
>
> then -> T (0.0 Instances, 1.0 Confidence)

This rule is indicating no orders are being made to government: .gov domain types.

Rule #3 for T:

> if HTM == OrderForm.htm
> and Subdomain == edu
> and Product == Desktops
> then -> T (54.0 Instances, 1.0 Confidence)

This rule is indicating that academic .edu domain types are making desktop orders

Rule #4 for T:

> if HTM == OrderForm.htm
> and Subdomain == edu
> and Product == Monitors
> and % of Wealthy Seaboard Suburb Consumer ZIP is > 16.7
> then -> T (9.0 Instances, 1.0 Confidence)

This rule is indicating some monitor orders are being placed by schools in specific geographic neighborhood areas in Connecticut and New Jersey, where the consumer types "Wealthy Seaboard Suburb" reside.

Through this process the user can literally discover rules from a blank data space in a totally autonomous and unbiased manner. This process is especially effective in situations where the objective of data mining is exploratory in nature. It is also effective in situations for which there are no positive and negative samples from which to train a neural network or construct a decision tree. This feature clearly illustrates the power of integrated data mining tools—where the user can pass the results from one technology to another for refinement or for conversion into the desired format. In this example, we did not want the weights (formulas) from the neural network; we instead wanted the insight in the form of easy to understand rules, which described the attributes of clusters in the website database.

Clementine's visual programming interface is unique and powerful. It is intuitive enough so that nonstatisticians can construct and compare multiple models very quickly on website data. Very complex data mining processes, which if done manually would take time and experience, can be accomplished with the click-and-drag functions of the Clementine environment. The preprocessing abilities and the ability to construct parallel models and compare results side-by-side are very powerful features, which most single paradigm tools are not able to do.

One of Clementine's drawbacks is its inability to generate graphical decision trees. This makes for a very poor interface when viewing the results of the machine-learning algorithms. The most powerful feature of this tool is the ability to link the clustering Self-Organizing Map (Kohonen) neural network with the machine-learning algorithm C5.0—enabling the user to generate rules describing clusters. This is a unique feature that few tools can do: *the linking of unsupervised learning to supervised learning.* Clementine runs on Sun and other major Unix platforms, and it uses Hummingbird for emulation on Windows workstations where is runs on NT.

The ability to link data mining processes makes tools such as Clementine worthwhile. Clementine's easy-to-use visual interface enables web administrators, marketing, and business users to build models for prediction, forecasting, clustering, visualizing, estimation, and classification directly from their website data.

DataEngine

DataEngine is a tool from Germany incorporating several clustering types of technologies, including the following modeling techniques:

- Fuzzy Rule Base SystemMultilayer Perception
- Fuzzy C-Means
- Kohonen Network Fuzzy Kohonen Network

DataEngine

Best at: Clustering and Association	**Memory Required:** 32 MB
Cost Factor: Yes	**Parallel Processing Support:** Yes
Current Version: 2.1	**Pricing:** $10,000
Data Access: ASCII, Excel, and ODBC	**Solution Format:** API
Data Preprocessing: Yes	**Space Required:** 47 MB
Distinguishing Feature: Clustering	**Training/Consulting:** Yes
File Limitations: None	**Technology Paradigm:** Kohonen neural networks and Fuzzy Logic
Installed Base: 100	

Figure 5-9
DataEngine
readily provides
data parameters
to the user.

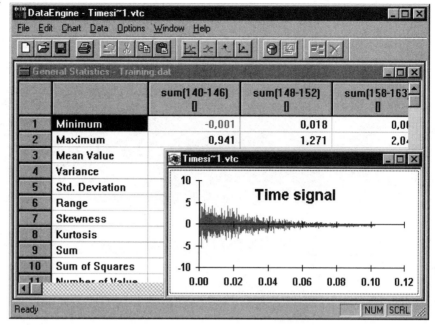

Each of these modeling methods can be configured to perform an analysis of your web databases, but although the importing of the data is fairly straightforward, deciding which clustering method to use is not. DataEngine has several useful components for data acquisition, preprocessing, and visualization. It also contains an extensive list of mathematical functions for scaling your data and a statistical component for correlation and regression analysis as well as general descriptive statistics. (See Figures 5-9 and 5-10.)

Several statistics functions are included in DataEngine for the treatment of your data, such as: moving average, moving minimum, moving maximum, moving variance, and moving standard deviation. This type of tool is optimized for control problems rather than the exploratory mining of web data. For example, because of the need to deal exclusively with numeric data, when it comes to using a Kohonen network there is a need to convert the original data. This can be done within most data mining tools or outside of them such as in a spreadsheet or database program. One common method of converting "string" fields like domain types, is as follows:

Figure 5–10
*DataEngine pro-
vides multiple
data analysis
processes to
the user.*

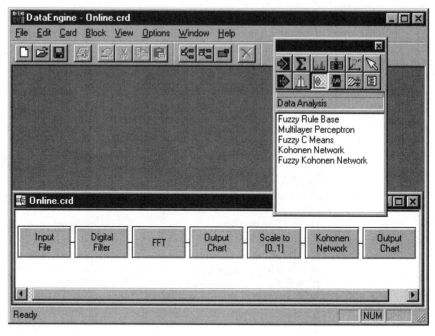

Figure 5–11
*DataEngine
enables users to
evaluate and
map the data
mining process.*

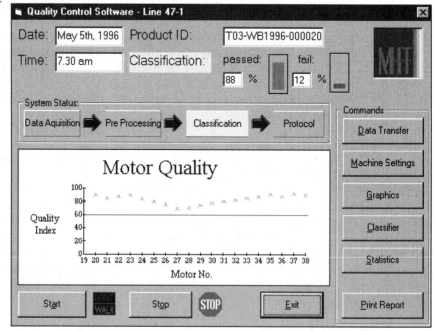

Original Subdomain	Converted Value
COM	0000001
GOV	0000010
JP	0000100
NET	0001000
ORG	0010000
UK	0100000
EDU	1000000

The same holds true for our desired output:

Possible Outputs	Converted Value
E-mailMe.htm	001
JustBrowsing.htm	010
OrderForm.htm	100

Although DataEngine contains a suite of very powerful clustering and association techniques and features (see Figure 5–11), the user should be well versed in their use prior to attempting to mine web data with this tool.

Decisionhouse

Decisionhouse is a powerful multiple-paradigm data mining tool from Quadstone Ltd. in Scotland. Decisionhouse incorporates several components

Decisionhouse

Best at: Visualization	**Memory Required:** 40 MB
Cost Factor: Yes	**Parallel Processing Support:** Yes
Current Version: 1.2	**Pricing:** $150,000
Data Access: ASCII and ODBC	**Solution Format:** Scores and graphs
Data Preprocessing: Yes	**Space Required:** 65 MB
Distinguishing Feature: Tool Following	**Training/Consulting:** Yes
File Limitations: None	**Technology Paradigm:** Machine-learning algorithm and regression
Installed Base: 50	

for data preprocessing, segmenting, visualizing, reporting, and classifying in a seamless integrated system. The tool is highly scalable, capable of running on advanced parallel computing platforms, and operates in a three-dimensional environment. All the components in Decisionhouse are fully interoperable, making it easy to pick out data of interest from any view, and to "drill it" further using other parts of the software:

- Binning Editor
- Decision Tree Builder
- Crossdistribution Viewer
- Crosstab Viewer
- Map Viewer

Scorecard Builder

A powerful feature of this tool is the ability to let the user interact with the data from a single record view to a view incorporating millions of records. The interface allows for a quick method by which the user can view, rotate, and drill down on very large databases. In the Decisionhouse environment, the user can quickly look at the distribution of any field in the database and analyze it with a high degree

Figure 5–12
A three-dimensional Decisionhouse decision tree, in which volume and color reflect content and rates.

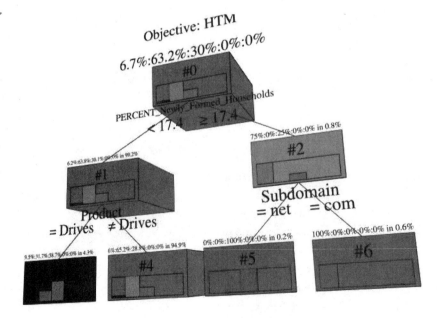

Figure 5–13
*Decisionhouse
users can map
market segments
from their web-
site data with
ZIP codes.*

of flexibility. The tool provides the ability to segment the data, to create scenarios, and to pose quick questions against a database.

In the Decisionhouse environment the graphics and segments are represented by color and mass to reflect a high frequency rate. This enhances a "feeling for the data" as the user interacts with it during the mining analysis. From several of the Decisionhouse components the user has the options of selecting a group of attributes in the data and generating ad hoc views on millions of records almost instantly. This can be done either from the Binning Editor, the Crossdistribution Viewer, or the Map Viewer. The Decision Tree Builder performs the segmentation of the data, with the ability to link its results to the other components. For example, in the three-dimensional decision tree in Figure 5–12, two market segments (in red) were identified by the consumer class "Newly Formed Households" and domain types NET and COM.

The market segment identified in the decision tree can be mapped on a U.S. map or on one of a state, such as Texas or California, and viewed down to the ZIP code level. This market segment can also be viewed by other components, such as the Crossdistribution Viewer to explore more closely these newly discovered clusters. Because of its integrated designs and functionality a user can "fly over" the data from a web database and at any time drill down for further exploration using a variety of tools, including the generation of a map and/or SQL syntax.

For classification, Decisionhouse uses another component called the Scorecard Builder, which uses several types of regression. A retailing site that wants to predict propensity to purchase scores for site visitors could use the Scorecard Builder module. As with other integrated software suites, the power to link all of the components enables the user to segment, classify, visualize, and map the data in one seamless process. Another innovation of this product is its "tool following" feature. That is, the result of one tool can be passed or followed by another, so that for example by selecting from the above decision tree the node #6, that market segment can be viewed in a geographic map. See Figure 5–13.

Other Tools

Darwin (Thinking Machines). Darwin is a set of tools oriented toward classification and regression. Like other suites it incorporates multiple paradigms. StarTree is used for building decision trees using a CART-based algorithm. StarNet is included for creating models using several neural networks. It supports five possible training architectures: back-propagation, steepest descent, conjugate gradient, and modified Newton. Darwin also contains a genetic algorithm for optimization problems called StarGene. Another component called StarMatch produces clustering models using the k-nearest neighbor algorithm. A final component, StarData, is used for data preparation and analysis. A scripting facility lets users record and play back data mining analyses.

Darwin has a GUI for building models using each of these components. The algorithms are parallelized for handling large amounts of data. Darwin's use of multiple algorithms for model building broadens the range of problems on which the product can effectively work. Although developed by Thinking Machines to take advantage of scalable platforms, the weakness of this tool is its output, specifically the format of its solutions—it lacks visualization. For reporting its modeling results Darwin relies on the spreadsheet Excel, through integration with MS Office.

Decision Series (NeoVista). Decision Series is basically a custom built set of applications bundled with their Professional Services consultancy. Their Decision Series is a suite of customized data mining tools that provide different models and technologies. DecisionNet is a back-propagation neural network tool, employing a proprietary technique closely related to radial basis functions, and can be used for classification and regression. DecisionAR can be used for association and sequencing discovery. DecisionCL is used for clustering, employing a proprietary technique closely related to k-means. DecisionAccess provides data-preparation functions, and Decision Series accesses data in ASCII files.

NeoVista offers Decision Series only in a bundle package with its knowledge engineering services. Consequently, NeoVista does not have a GUI for model development, although the company develops a custom GUI for most applications. Each of their four applications—Neural Nets, Clustering, Genetic Algorithms, and Association Rules—costs $135,000. NeoVista is currently providing decision support software and services to large retailers, banks, and telcos. A typical NeoVista install involves several weeks of on-site interviews by its knowledge engineers for purposes of identifying the business problems, which their data mining solutions have been purchased to solve.

Enterprise Miner (SAS). Enterprise Miner is an SAS System entry into the data mining market. As with everything SAS sells, Enterprise Miner is an add-on module to the SAS base system. It provides a GUI to three mining modules: the SAS Neural Network Application and the SAS Decision Tree Application, for building CHAID-based decision trees, and an SAS Regression Application. Bundled with the product is the SAS/Insight visualization tool for data exploration. A useful feature of EM is its integrated methodology that allows users to run regression, a back-propagation neural network, and a decision tree side by side and then integrate their results in a visualization module. The technology is very basic with no special algorithms or features in the neural network or decision tree modules. The most powerful feature of EM is the installed base of SAS users, which is sizeable, especially with financial related firms.

GainSmarts (Urban Sciences). GainSmarts provides data analysis, statistical modeling, and financial measurement for vertical market segments, including the automotive and financial services industries. For the automotive sector it lets dealers and sales managers "see" their best opportunities in an array of useful charts, maps, and reports. Their tool provides "what-if" scenarios for new and used vehicle sales departments. Gain guides users to the hidden potential in automotive dealerships through advanced data visualization, mapping, and intelligent performance benchmarking. For the financial sector it provides a turnkey system specifically designed for prospect targeting, response prediction, customer retention, loyalty measurement, cross-selling, and offer management. Gain uses decision tress, genetic algorithms, and gain tables to chart expected profitability for mail campaigns. It uses genetic algorithms to optimize the CHAID decision trees, a technique, although computationally intensive, that does improve results.

Intelligent Miner (IBM). IBM's Intelligent Miner is a set of tools for classification, association, and sequence discovery, time series, clustering, and regression. For classification it uses a decision tree and neural networks and for clustering it uses a Kohonen neural net. Most of the algorithms have been parallelized for scalability. Models can be built using either a GUI or an API. Intelligent Miner is tightly coupled with DB2, which also must be installed, but Miner supports input from sources such as ASCII files.

MineSet (SGI). MineSet from Silicon Graphics Inc. is a set of data mining tools that combine classification and association algorithms with a high degree of visualization. Their strongest and most notable features are in the integration of data mining analytic tools with high-end visualization tools for user exploration and navigation of data sets and mining results. The product's data mining tools include the Association Rule Generator, Decision Tree Inducer for classification, Evidence Inducer, and Column Importance determination utility. All the algorithms, except association, are based on the Machine-Learning Library in C++ (MLC++) code developed at Stanford University.

Visualizers, such as the Map Visualizer and the Scatter Visualizer, work directly with data to explore relationships and trends. Models are presented to the user for analysis using 3D visualization. Model results are displayed with visualizers such as the Tree Visualizer, which lets the user explore a decision tree model in a 3D format. The tools present several dimensions of data simultaneously by using color, size, and animation. The visualizers support filtering, querying, rotation, zooming, and panning, and can be customized by the user. SGI has added k-means and iterative k-means algorithms for clustering and has developed graphical outputs for clustering in its visualizer. MineSet 2.5 also supports regression trees for the generation of decision trees. The software can now create decision tree models on continuous variables.

Orchestrate (Torrent Systems). Orchestrate is an excellent object-oriented application environment designed for building and deploying scalable data processing software systems. Based on the data-flow model of application programming and execution, Orchestrate consists of two parts: the Orchestrate Application Framework and Runtime System and Orchestrate Components. Developers build Orchestrate Applications using standard UNIX shell-scripting techniques to combine existing sequential programs with Orchestrate components to construct a sequential data-flow Orchestrate program. Developers build Orchestrate Components using Orchestrate's robust C++ Component Development Interface. The Orchestrate Application Framework and Runtime System is a parallel software infrastructure which maps the sequential Orchestrate data-flow application to the underlying hardware architecture and manages run-time execution of the system as a single UNIX program.

Pattern Recognition Workbench/Model 1. PRW from Unica Technologies is a set of tools for building classification, clustering, time-series, and regression models. In addition to building models with back-propagation neural networks, it provides algorithms for logistic regression and linear regression. PRW builds clustering models using k-means. The tool set is the basis of Model 1, a package for database marketing modeling and analysis sold by Group 1 Software and Unica.

PRW provides a GUI based on a spreadsheet-style interface. The data must be brought into one or more spreadsheets, after which the data is prepared for mining via the product's extensive set of functions. PRW will automatically generate alternative models and search for a best solution. It also provides a variety of visualization tools for monitoring model building and the interpretation of its results. A model can be deployed as a spreadsheet function, as a dynamic link library, or as C code.

DecisionCentre and the Future. The future of data mining tools may well resemble those of DecisionCentre, an experimental tool developed at the Imperial College in the U.K. It uses a three-tiered architecture to perform parallel data mining anywhere on the Web. The tool uses Java and CORBA to provide a web-centered approach to data mining. The DecisionCentre server and the command and visualization client will run on any platform that supports Java, and can access data sources anywhere on the Web or on a corporate intranet. DecisionCentre supports several parallel data mining algorithms, implemented with the standard MPI. The Data Mining services currently available include:

- Decision Tree-Based Classification (four different parallel options)
- Bayesian Classification with Parallel Autoclass
- Parallel Self-Organizing Maps for Clustering
- Back-Propagation Neural Networks Association Rule Discovery

The Java-based visualization tools are integrated in the client interface. They can be used to view the data source as well as the output models from the data mining process. The visualization tool set contains a Self-Organizing Map Visualization Classification Tree Browser and a 3D Visual Data Mining.

The DecisionCentre three-tier architecture offers scalability, accessibility and extensibility. It is written in pure Java, providing portabil-

Figure 5–14
*The
DecisionCenter
Java client pro-
vides a view of
the data being
mined over
the Web.*

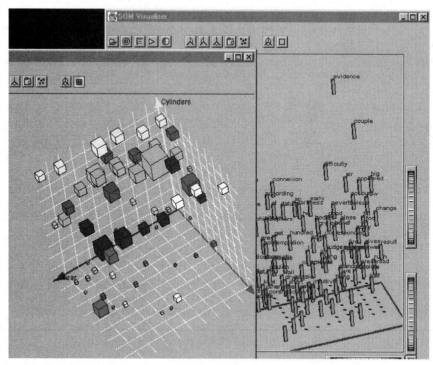

ity and ease-of-use. Parallel data analysis applications are embedded via CORBA distributed object technology. (See Figure 5–14.)

Final Tool Tip

As you can see, there is a diverse and extensive assortment of features to the current data mining tool products. You will need to do some personal experimentation prior to deciding on which tool(s) are right for mining your web data. It is quite likely that you will need more than one tool and that you will need additional software for the extraction and preparation of your data *prior* to mining it. Likewise, you will likely need some additional tools in the integration of your data mining solutions. This may be in web design and database integration tools or bulk e-mail software. However, the data mining tools that you do use will be very important and integrated components in the operation of your website—especially if you are involved in e-commerce. New tools continue to appear in the market. See Tables 5–1 and 5–2.

Table 5-1 *Leading data mining tools.*

Product (Vendor)	O/S	Paradigm
4Thought (Right Information Systems)	WIN95, NT	Neural Network
Answer Tree (SPSS)	WIN95, NT	CART, CHAID, QUEST
BusinessMiner (Business Objects)	WIN95	Machine-Learning
Clementine (ISL)	NT, Unix	Machine-Learning and Neural Network
Darwin (Thinking Machines)	Unix	Machine-Learning and Neural Network
Data Mining Tool (Syllogic)	SGI, NT	Machine-Learning and Nearest Neighbor
Database Mining Marksman (HNC)	NT	Neural Network
DataCruncher (DataMind)	WIN95, NT, Unix	Machine-Learning
DataEngine (MIT)	WIN95, NT, Unix	Neural Network and Fuzzy Logic
Datasage (Datasage)	NT, Unix	Open API
Data Surveyor (Data Distilleries)	Unix	Machine-Learning and Bayesian Network
DbProphet (Trajecta)	NT, Unix	Neural Network
Decision Series (NeoVista)	Unix	Machine-Learning and Neural Network
Decisionhouse (Quadstone)	NT, Unix	Machine-Learning and Regression
Delta Miner (Bizzantz)	WIN95, NT	Neural Network and OLAP
//Discovery (HyperParallel)	Unix	Machine-Learning and Neural Network
Discovery Server (Pilot)	NT, Unix	Machine-Learning
Enterprise Miner (SAS)	NT, Unix	Machine-Learning and Neural Network
Enterprise Modeling Server (BioComp)	NT, Unix	Neural Network and Genetic Algorithm
GainSmarts (Urban Sciences)	NT, Unix	Genetic Algorithm, CHAID, Regression

Product (Vendor)	O/S	Paradigm
IDIS Data Mining Suite (IDIS)	NT, Unix	Proprietary Algorithm
KDD Explorer (SRA)	Unix	Proprietary Algorithm
Kepler (Dialogis)	WIN95, Unix	Open API
Knowledge Discovery Workbench (NCR)	NT, Unix	Neural Network and Machine-Learning
KnowedgeSEEKER (AGNOSS)	NT, Unix	CART, CHAID, ID3
Intelligent Miner (IBM)	RS6000, AS/400, MVS	Machine-Learning and Neural Network
MindSet (Silicon Graphics)	SGI, NT	Machine-Learning and Naïve Bayes
Model 1 (Group 1)	WIN95, NT	Networks, CHAID, Regression, GAs
ModelQuest Enterprise (AbTech)	WIN95, NT, Unix	Polynomial Networks
Nuggets (Data Mining Technologies)	WIN95, NT	Proprietary Algorithm
Orchestrate (Torrent)	Unix	Machine-Learning and Neural Network
Partek (Partek)	Unix	Neural Network and Genetic Algorithm
PATTERN (Magnify)	Unix	Proprietary Algorithm, ART
Polyanalyst (Megaputer)	Unix	Proprietary Algorithm
Predict (NeuralWare)	WIN95, NT, Unix	Neural Network
PRW PRO+ (Unica Technologies)	WIN95, NT	Neural Network, k-nearest, regression
Scenario (Cognos)	WIN95	Machine-Learning
Xpertrule Profiler (Attar)	WIN95, NT, Unix	Neural Network, ID3
WizWhy (WizSoft)	WIN95, NT	Proprietary Algorithm

Table 5–2 *Leading data mining suites.*

TOOL (COMPANY)	OS	Parallelized	Segmentation	Optimization	Classification
Clementine (ISL)	NT, Unix	No	C5.0	None	Neural Network
Darwin (Thinking Machines)	Unix	Yes	CART	GA	Neural Network
Data Mining Tool (Syllogic)	SGI, NT	No	Proprietary	None	Proprietary
DataEngine (MIT)	NT, Unix	No	None	Fuzzy Logic	Neural Network
DataSage (DataSage)	NT, Unix	Yes	No	No	No
Data Surveyor (Data Distilleries)	Unix	No	Proprietary	None	Bayesian
Decision Series (NeoVista)	Unix	Yes	Proprietary	GA	Neural Network
Delta Miner (Bizzantz)	WIN95, NT	No	OLAP	None	Neural Network
//Discovery (HyperParallel)	Unix	Yes	Proprietary	GA	Neural Network
Enterprise Miner (SAS)	NT, Unix	No	CHAID	None	Neural Network
Enterprise Modeling Server (BioComp)	NT, Unix	Yes	None	GA	Neural Network
GainSmarts (Urban Sciences)	NT, Unix	No	CHAID	GA	Regression
Knowledge Discovery Workbench (NCR)	NT, Unix	No	C5.0	None	Neural Network
Intelligent Miner (IBM)	RS6000, AS/400	Yes	Proprietary	None	Neural Network
MindSet (Silicon Graphics)	SGI, NT	No	C4.5	k-nearest	Naïve Bayes
Model 1 (Group 1)	WIN95, NT	No	CHAID	GA	Regression
Orchestrate (Torrent)	Unix	Yes	Proprietary	None	Neural Network

TOOL (COMPANY)	OS	Parallelized	Segmentation	Optimization	Classification
Partek (Partek)	Unix	No	None	GA	Neural Network
PRW PRO+ (Unica Technologies)	WIN95, NT	No	None	k-nearest	Neural Network
Knowledge Discovery Solutions (SRA)	Unix	Yes	Proprietary	None	Proprietary
Xpertrule Profiler (Attar)	NT, Unix	No	ID3	None	Neural Network

6

The Data Components

Every visit to your website creates a record of absolutely *everything* that happens during that session. Depending on how your website is configured, a significant amount of visitor and customer information can be captured and stored on your server log files or some other type of database for data mining. As your website increasingly becomes the first point of contact between your company and your current and future customers, a careful analysis of this web-based information can be quite important. For example, most likely your company wants to know who's visiting your site, what draws them there, and how they got there. You certainly would like to know what your website visitors are looking at, as well as what it is they are buying and most importantly *who they are*. Your website data is the most direct source of information about your current and potential future customers. In fact it is your company dynamic customer information file creating itself with every visit and online transaction. In this chapter we will discuss the important data components captured at your website that can provide valuable insight through data mining.

The single most time-consuming part of mining your website will involve the capturing, extraction, aggregation, and preparation of your server data for analysis. This will likely involve some preliminary planning by your web administrator or team in coordination with your sales, marketing, and other business groups in your company. At issue will be the methods and the type of customer and transactional information you want to capture at your website. There are various methods by which you can effectively capture very valuable customer information at the server level. This includes data from several types of web log files, cookies, databases linked to your website forms, dynamic tracking, and even third party vendors. Several technologies can also be used to capture website visitor and customer information, including the popular Common Gateway Interface (CGI), Java, and JavaScript. New web standards and features are also evolving, affecting how new browsers will interact and provide customer information as electronic commerce transactions occur with new servers from such vendors as Netscape and Microsoft.

Data mining is an elaborate process involving not just the use of powerful pattern-recognition algorithms, but also planning how you will capture important transactional data, how you can append additional information to it, and finally how you can prepare it for actual analysis. In order to gain the most intelligence from your web data, it is important to know what files are available and what programs you can use to collect this information. The brick and mortar of your data mining analysis starts with your website data, more specifically several components that are used to create your server log files and other web-based databases, including transfer (access) logs, cookies, and forms.

Server Log Files

When a visitor first accesses your website, that single request can generate multiple transactions, which get recorded in your log files. First there is a recorded transaction for the requested page, such as info.htm, and then there are multiple "hits" for each graphical (gif) image on that page. Almost all web servers generate these log files as ASCII comma-, space-, or tab-delimited text files. Almost every web server incorporates, at a minimum, these two files: a *transfer log,* which tells you what your visitors saw, and an *error log,* which tells you about disconnects. Most servers also support two additional log files, which can tell you from where your website visitors originated: a *referrer log,* which tells you how your visitors found you, and an *agent log,* which tells you what browsers they used.

Depending on how your website is configured and what program you are using, your log files can be the starting point for finding out who your visitors and customers are. These files can assist you in finding where they came from and what "keywords" they used to find you, what path they followed through your website, and how long they stayed.

Transfer Log File

One of the most important sources of information about your website visitors starts with your server transfer log file, also known as the access log. This is where every transaction between the server and browsers is recorded with a date and time, the domain name or IP address of the server making the request for each page on your site, the status of that request, and the number of bytes transferred to that requester. At the minimum, almost every server records some of this information. The standard method by which servers record access by browsers and other automated spider programs is the "Common Log Format" as created by the National Center for Supercomputing Applications (NCSA). The data fields in the transfer access_log file used by most web servers takes the following format:

1. Internet provider IP address (*webminer.com* or *204.58.155.58*)

2. Identification field (always a hyphen, or "-")

3. AuthUser (usually the ID or password required for accessing a protected area)

4. Date, time, and GMT (Greenwich Mean Time) of transaction (*Thu July 17 12:38:09 1999*)

5. Method of transaction (*"GET"* or *"POST"* with filename such as */index.html/products.htm*)

6. Status or error code (usually *200* (success) of transaction)

7. Size in bytes of transaction (file size)

The following is a detailed breakdown of the standard log file format and its seven standard data fields.

Host Field

This is the first field of the common log format, which is usually the remote server making the request from your website, it is usually in the format of a domain name sun51.cs.standford.edu or an IP address like 207.171.194.2.

Depending on how your server is configured, you will get either the domain name or an IP address in this first field. In order to obtain a name rather than an IP address, your server has to make a request to resolve (translate) the IP address into a hostname using the Internet Domain Name System (DNS). However, even when your server is configured to do these lookups with DNS of IP addresses, not every search will succeed. The reason is that most Internet Service Providers (ISPs) assign IP addresses dynamically to their clients from a reserved pool. This is especially true of large ISPs such as Earthlink, MindSpring, FlashNet, etc.

Identification Field

The second field in the Common Log Format is almost always a hyphen, due to the fact it is never used. The original Request for Comment (RFC 931) was for an authentication service back in 1984 laying out a proposal for a query/response protocol that would identify the owner of a

TCP connection between two computers on the Internet, specifically, to identify UNIX systems directly connected to the Internet. This RFC preceded the age of web browsers, when connections were mainly between FTP, ARCHIE, telnet, and mail servers. Several versions of the original RFC have occurred since 1984 with the current version being 1431 The Identification Protocol. The name of the actual program that implements the "ident server" is identd.

Authuser Field

This field was designed to contain the authenticated username that a visitor needs to gain access to a protected directory accessible only by password. For example, an administrator may create a special billing database where only authorized customers can gain access via the use of their usernames and passwords.

Time Stamp

This field contains the date, time, and the Greenwich Mean Time (GMT). The format for the date is DD/Mon/YYYY (i.e., "06/Jul/1999"), and the format for the time is HH:MM:SS. The GMT uses a plus or minus sign to indicate the number of hours the local time for the server differs from the Greenwich Mean Time.

HTTP Request

The transactional and fifth field contains the usual GET command, which is blocked by quotation marks. The GET method tells the server which document the visiting browser is requesting. The other two commands are used less often. They are the POST command, which is used with forms when the *Submit* button is pressed. POST tells the server to expect some data and what program or script can be used for handling it. A less used command is the HEAD, which works the same way as the GET method except that the server only returns the <HEAD> section of any document. HEAD commands are generated usually by special indexing programs, such as *WebCrawler*, one of the earliest search engines. The last part of the HTTP request field is the name and version number of the protocol, such as version 1.1.

Status Code Field

The sixth field in the Common Log Format describes what happened with the transaction, which is usually "GET" and its status code of 200, which stands for "Success." This simply means the server successfully delivered the web page selected by the browser. There are various classes of status codes, the main ones are:

Class	Purpose	Descriptions
200	Success	201 Created
		202 Accepted
		204 No Content
300	Redirect	301 Permanently
		302 Temporarily
		304 Not Modified
400	Failure	401 Unauthorized
		403 Forbidden
		404 Not Found
500	Server errors	501 Not Implemented
		502 Bad Gateway
		503 Service Unavailable

Transfer Volume

The seventh and final field of the Common Log Format provides the total number of bytes transferred by the server to the client during the transaction. Only the GET requests with status 200 will have a value in this field, all others will only show a hyphen or a zero.

These seven fields are the standard fields generated by most servers. However, additional fields can be appended. Two of the most common ones are the Referrer Log and Agent Log files. A cookie field can also be appended, which can be used to track the activity of visitors while at a website, or upon their return.

Error Log

When a transaction in your website results in an error or failure to download, it gets recorded in the error log file. This can be useful in alerting you to a design problem, that is, situations in which visitors are canceling downloads in mid-process. Here is a sample of a line from an error log:

```
[Tue June 16 06:57:09 1999] send lost connection to client 165.133.159.28
```

Referrer Log

This log file contains the URL from which the requests for your web pages originated. In other words, this log captures the location your website visitors came from and how they found you. This can be a link from another page or a search engine "hit." For example, if they found you through a search engine like Yahoo! or Excite, this log can tell you what keywords they used to locate your website. This is very important information, which in a data mining analysis can reveal useful insight into possible strategic marketing initiatives and campaigns. This is a sample output:

```
http://search.yahoo.com/bin/search?p=data+mining+websites → /index.html
```

The complete URL for the search engine (Yahoo!) and the keywords used in the search (data mining websites) are to the left of the → symbol, with the link to your website (usually the opening page) on the right, in this case the common default of index.html.

Agent Log

This file records the name and version number of the browser making the request. It can also contain the name of robots, spiders, and other search engine indexing tracks.

```
Mozilla/2.0 (Win95; I)
Mozilla/2.0 (Macintosh; I; PRC)
MetaCrawler/1.2b libwww/4.0D
```

Extended Log Format

Rather than generating individual and separate referrer and agent logs, your server can be configured to append this information to the original seven fields found in the Common Log Format. For example, a rather common extension is the Referrer log which can tell you where your website visitors are coming from and what keywords they are using to find your site. Additional customer information can be generated about their movements within your site with server-set cookies, which can be appended to your log file.

IF	They were referred from Yahoo! and Keyword was "new film videos"
THEN	The propensity to buy Product Y is 65%
or	
IF	They buy Product A
THEN	The propensity to buy Product X is 74%

Configuring Your Server

There are a variety of settings for UNIX and NT servers that need to be set in order to optimize the amount of customer information you are capturing. These settings involved various server software, including the NCSA, the Apache, the CERN, the Netscape, and the NT WebSite. Because there are many settings, some of which are likely to change with each new version of the software, I will not go into detail on the configuration of each. I will note, however, some of the more important settings, which you are likely to want to ensure are correctly set either by you or your technical team. UNIX servers are configured via files containing directives that control basic settings, such as authorization and paths. Netscape is configured through HTML forms, while the WebSite uses a series of dialog boxes and wizards.

Server Configuration Tips

All servers can be configured to produce user agent and referrer log output. For example, to configure this on the popular Apache web server, the following settings are needed:

1. Make sure the mod_log_config Apache "module" is compiled into your server.

2. Add the following line to your httpd.conf file in the Apache conf directory:

```
FOR APACHE 1.2 OR BETTER, WITH THE MOD_USERTRACK MODULE:
LogFormat "%h %l %u %t \"%r\" %s %b \"%{Referrer}i\" \"%{User-
    agent}i\" \"%{Cookie}n\""
FOR APACHE WITHOUT THE MOD_USERTRACK MODULE:
LogFormat "%h %l %u %t \"%r\" %s %b \"%{Referrer}i\" \"%{User-
    agent}i\""
```

3. When you have done both of these things, restart the Apache server on the fly using the kill -1 Unix command.

The Apache server will now log in the usual "common log format," with the addition of two new fields, referrer and user agent, and a third "cookie field" uniquely identifying the user if you have compiled Apache with the mod_usertrack module installed. This is an example of the common log format, extended to include referrer and user agent information.

```
foo.bar.com - - [02/Jul/1998:16:48:44 -0744] "GET /webminer/index.html
    HTTP/1.0" 200 5898 "http://www.altavista.digital.com/query"
    "Mozilla/3.01 (Macintosh; I; PPC)"
```

Apache and NCSA Server Configurations

These directives should be checked in the *httpd.con* file:

Settings	Function
AgentLog *filename*	Specifies the location of the log file that identifies the client program used for each request, such as: `AgentLog logs/agent_log`
ErrorLog *filename*	Specifies the location of the error file, such as: `ErrorLog logs/error_log`
DNSMode *options*	Controls under what conditions the server will attempt to do reverse DNS lookups of the client browsers, the options are:
None	No DNS lookup.
Minimum	DNS lookup only for resolving access permissions.
Standard	DNS lookup for every request (this is the default).
LogOptions *options*	Specifies how log information should be written to the various log files. The options are as follows:
Separate	Agent and refer log files will be split into two separate files as specified by the AgentLog and ReferLog directives.
Date	Puts a date stamp on both the separate agent and referrer logs.
Combined	Combines and appends both the agent and referrer fields in the transfer log (recommended).
ReferrerLog *filename*	Specifies the location of the referring URL log file. It can be set either as an absolute path or as a relative path from the ServerLog directory, the default is: `ReferrerLog logs/referrer_log`
Script *method cgi_script*	Specifies the type of scripts which may be executed. The methods are: GET, POST, PUT, or DELETE.
TransferLog *filename*	Specifies the location of the transfer log file, either as an absolute path or a relative path to the ServerRoot directory. The default is: `TransferLog logs/access_log`

CERN Server Configurations

The following group of directives govern the logging in CERN used to specify the location of log files and their configurations:

Settings	Function
AccessLog *filename*	Specifies the location of the access log file, as an absolute or relative path from the ServerRoot directory. The common default setting being: `AccessLog logs/http:log`
ErrorLog *filename*	Same path and location as the AccessLog, most common setting is: `ErrorLog logs/http:error`
LogFileDateExt *suffix*	This directive specifies the extension to be used for log file names, such as time date format. `LogFileDateExt %H:%T`
LogFormat *format*	Specifies the format of the transfer log: Old, Common, or New.
LogTime timezone	Specifies the timestamp for the log files: `LocalTime or GMT`
NoLog *expression*	Specifies no logs for selected directories: `NoLog /for_your_eyes_only`

Netscape Server Configurations

Netscape uses the AddLog directive to set the transaction log and record the user-agent for server transactions. The options are as follows:

common-log	This records transaction data in the common NCSA log format, with the following parameters: Name=*logname* This specifies the name of the log to use and it must be the logfile name that you initialized with Init fn=init-clf name=... at the top of the *obj.conf* file. Iponly=*n* This parameter sets the server not to perform host-name lookup. Any value will do, since the Server Manager by default creates iponly="1".
flex-log	This records transactions in the extended or flexible logging format. This format is also set in the Int directives with the flex-init function. It uses the same parameters as the common-log function.

WebSite Server Configurations

The Server Admin tool is used for administering the WebSite server. WebSite uses the Windows 95 or Windows NT Registry to maintain information about the server. From the *Properties* section of the server's Control menu the configuration for several components can be set, including *Logging*, which specify the location of logging files, the type of access file format, and tracing options for the server log. WebSite has three main logs:

Error Log	This log records access errors, such a failed authentication.
Server Log	This log records each time the server is restarted or a new configuration is updated.
Access Log	This log records each request made to the server and its response in one of three formats: *Common Format:* This is the older NCSA/CERN standard web log format used by most servers. It is the default setting. *Combined:* This format uses a more practical web log format with fields delimited by quotation marks. This format incorporates two additional fields, the referrer and user_agent information. *Window (WebSite Extended):* This format is designed to collect data in a format that can be easily imported into Microsoft's *Access* and *Excite* packages. The data is tab delimited, which tends to create larger files.

The Multiplicity of a Visit

A single visit to your website might look like the following in your server log file:

```
204.58.155.58 - [06/Jul/1999:11:27:45 -0900] "GET /products/ad.html
    HTTP/1.0" 200 2887
```

However, any single visit is actually registered as multiple "hits" all dependent on the number of graphic and Java programs residing on that single ad.html page. Thus the above visit may actually look like this in your log file:

```
204.58.155.58 - [06/Jul/1999:11:27:45 -0900] "GET /products/ad.html
    HTTP/1.0" 200 2887204.58.155.58 - [06/Jul/1999:11:27:45 -0900] "GET
    /images/hotstuff.gif HTTP/1.0" 200 327
204.58.155.58 - [06/Jul/1999:11:27:57 -0900] "GET /images/sale.gif
    HTTP/1.0" 200 129204.58.155.58 - [06/Jul/1999:11:27:59 -0900] "GET
    /images/today_only.gif HTTP/1.0" 200 281
204.58.155.58 - [06/Jul/1999:11:27:59 -0900] "GET /images/ad2.gif
    HTTP/1.0" 200 350204.58.155.58 - [06/Jul/1999:11:27:59 -0900] "GET
    /images/and_more.gif HTTP/1.0" 200 275
```

As we found out, the host field in the Transfer Log File can be in the format of the IP address or domain name of the server accessing your website. The reason domain names may not be included in the log files is the extra processing and bandwidth required for looking up the name, which can be obtained via the nslookup command.

Aside from counting visitors to your website, the most important information you want to obtain from the host field is the number of unique *sessions*, determined by the different and unique IP addresses in your access log file. The IP address of visitors is the single best method of determining the number of individuals accessing your site. However, this can be misleading due to the fact that dial-up users are usually assigned "dynamic" IP addresses by their Internet service providers (ISP) from a reserved lot. Also, users of large online services like America Online access the Web from a limited number of "gateways" with their own IP addresses. Lastly, corporate users typically connect through proxy servers, which means groups of individuals use the same computer.

This means that it is very difficult to identify an individual with a unique IP address. This fact leads to two conclusions: (1) sessions are more important than individual addresses, and (2) tracking by other means is necessary whether by cookies or forms.

One of the patterns you may be interested in discovering is the path taken by your website visitors and customers both from outside and inside your website. As we learned, these types of patterns can be revealed from two different sources. To find out how web visitors got your site and what "keywords" were used at a search engine, the referrer log can be used. The referrer log tells how your website visitors found your website and what search criteria they used at Yahoo!, InfoSeek, Excite, etc.

Cookie Files

To find out what paths visitors took while *in* your website, a form of tracking will need to be implemented. This can be done by setting up cookies or some other type of CGI program. *Cookies* are small text files created by servers on visiting browsers' hard disks that contain an identification code. They are passed by servers to browsers so that each time a website visitor returns to a server that passed the cookie it can recognize it and read what it wrote before, such as what pages were visited during the prior session. Netscape developed cookies as a means for servers to identify a specific browser, with the specification that only the server that provided the cookie can be the one that can access it and retrieve it. This means that identification cookie codes sent to your cookie.txt file by another server could not be accessed by a different website. Cookies unfortunately are limited to identifying browsers, not individuals.

Every visit by your customers to your website is a separate event, totally unconnected or related to any previous connection or event. Cookies are a technique by which you can make these unrelated events link into a semblance of a real-world transaction, such as the shopping experience. In fact, cookies were developed by Netscape software developers in an effort to create a shopping cart application. The shopping cart analogy works this way: it allows shoppers to buy more than one item at a session as they wander through the store (website) and pay at the cash register (form) as they leave the store. What is also important is that the store now has a record of which person went where in the store and what items were purchased. Similar to the way you order from a cataloger, a website using cookies is able to record what items you like and purchase over time and how you pay for them.

Cookies are a hack solution to a problem of "statelessness" caused by the nature of the Web and its protocol, the Hyper Text Transfer Protocol (HTTP). HTTP allows for communications to take place instantaneously without the need to maintain open connections, which may not be needed again. An effective client/server design, but poor retailing environment—hence the need to maintain "state"—cookies. (See Figure 6–1.)

The usual way cookies work is when a CGI script identifies a new user, it adds an extra header to its response with an identifier for that web visitor and other information that the server may capture from the client's input. This new header data informs the browser to add this information to the client's cookie file. In Netscape it is added to the cookie.txt file; in Internet Explorer, cookies are kept in a cookie directory under the Windows directory, associated with the username taken from the login name for the operating system (e.g., "mena@excite.txt").

Any subsequent request to that URL from the browser will include the cookie information as an extra header in the request. The CGI script uses this information to return a document targeted to that specific web visitor or returning customer. Since the cookie information

Figure 6–1   *A Sample Cookie.txt File*

A Sample Cookie.txt File

```
# Netscape HTTP Cookie File# http://www.netscape.com/newsref/std/cookie_spec.html# This is a
generated file!  Do not edit.
.excite.com     TRUE      /      FALSE  946641600             UID
    867CE396354734CB.preferences.com              TRUE      /      FALSE  1182140421
    PreferencesID      XHphq2JpN264wr8hBTHkSG.focalink.com      TRUE   /    FALSE
    946641600          SB_ID  0893859081000014623110905400052.go2net.com      TRUE  /
    FALSE   917824360      preferences   32qQ00hCOAw89U.infoseek.com       TRUE  /
    FALSE   925398460      InfoseekUserId 7BBEDA1C15F0696DCFB611F729A5C544.yahoo.com
    TRUE    /      FALSE  915145200      Y         v=1&n=dnnef14bek7pl.doubleclick.net
    TRUE    /      FALSE  1920499140     id        285bff29www.cdnow.com   FALSE /
    FALSE   942189160      cookTrack      283498007-893877542.netscape.com  TRUE  /
    FALSE   946684799 NETSCAPE_ID   10010408,11fc8400
```

is stored on the client's hard disk, the information remains even after the browser is closed and the computer is turned off. One of the most common methods of using cookies is to "recognize" prior visitors through preassigned headers, enabling the server to present "fresh" content to that visitor or customer, which they have not seen before. Cookies cannot be over four kilobytes in size, and only the issuing domain name server can have access to them. There can be no more than 100 cookies on your hard disk.

Here is the information stored by a typical cookie:

```
.snap.com  TRUE  /  FALSE  946684799  u_vid_0_0  00ed7085
```

.snap.com	This is the domain for the cookie. This by default is usually the server that created and issued the cookie to the client. Only pages from the original server are allowed to read that cookie. This means snap.com cannot read the cookies issued by yahoo.com or infoseek.com.
TRUE	Indicates whether the cookie was set by an HTTP header (TRUE) or a JavaScript (FALSE).
/	This path is variable, allowing for any page in the website snap.com to access this cookie. Same as the domain, it restricts access to cookies to those that created it. Cookies without a set / path will be deleted when the user exits the browser.
FALSE	Indicates whether it is a secured cookie or not. There is an option for encryption using HTTPS, SSL. This attribute has no value; unless it appears when created, the cookie will travel without any security.

946684799	The expiration date, expressed in seconds since midnight GMT, January 1, 1970. Another, different format has the expiration date set to Greenwich Mean Time (GMT) in the format "Wdy, DD—Mon - YYYY HH:MM:SS GMT", where Wdy is Weekday (optional), DD is Day, Mon is Month, YYYY is Year, HH is Hour in 24-hour format, MM is Minutes, and SS is Seconds.
u_vid_0_0	This is the critical name which identifies the cookie. The name of the cookie cannot contain commas, semicolons, or white space. The latest cookie replaces the older cookie with the same domain, path and name.
00ed7085	This is the value of the cookie, where the issuer of the cookie stores its information. It cannot contain commas, semicolons, or white spaces.

A Cookie Future

As the Web increasingly becomes a retailing channel of choice for millions of users, a new proposal has been advanced for improving cookies and through it online shopping, relational marketing, and electronic commerce. A Request for Comment 2109 proposes "a way to create a stateful session with HTTP requests and responses. It describes two new headers, Cookie and Set-Cookie, which carry state information between participating origin servers and user agents." Basically RFC 2109 proposes a Version 1 of cookies which will extend their abilities and provide extra information that will make it easier for users to manage them. This new version of cookies will expand their structure to include the following components:

Name. Same as Version 0, a cookie name is required. Except that for this version it cannot begin with the dollar sign ($), all other restrictions apply: no commas, semicolons, or white space.

Comment. This is a new attribute which allows the issuer of a cookie to tell the browser recipient the purpose of the cookie: *"This cookie* 'group_discount_cookie A1' *is being set to identify you as a frequent and valued customer entitling you to special discounts."* This optional feature allows the website server to tell the recipient browser the purpose of the cookie. If the user has set the browser to ask the dispensing server for the purpose of the cookie before accepting it, a message will appear in a browser dialog box. The user can inspect the information to decide whether to initiate or discontinue a session with the server.

CommentURL. Similar to the comment field but with more detailed information on the purpose of the cookie and the processing of them at the server level.

Domain. Although optional, it would work the same as Version 0 with a twist. The domain attribute still specifies the domain for which the cookie is valid, which is usually the dispensing site. However in Version 1 a subsection domain name can be set. For example, the domain *www.isuzu.amigo.com* could specify a cookie for the subdomain *.amigo.com*. An explicitly specified domain must always start with a dot, the same as in Version 0.

Discard. This attribute mandates that cookies be discarded no matter what the maximum age of the cookie may be when present.

Max-Age. The Max-Age attribute defines the lifetime of the cookie, in seconds. The delta-seconds value is a decimal nonnegative integer. After delta-seconds elapse, the client should discard the cookie. A value of zero means the cookie should be discarded immediately, which means that cookies could be discarded during a transaction.

Path. Same as Version 0, the Path attribute specifies the subset of URLs to which this cookie applies. If a path is specified, only URLs that contain that complete path / are allowed to read or modify the cookie.

Port. The Port is an additional feature of the new cookie standard which can be specified for specific system applications, such as FTP for 21, Telnet 23, and web server on port 80.

Secure. The Secure attribute (with no value) directs the user agent to use only (unspecified) secure means to contact the origin server whenever it sends back this cookie.

Version. This attribute is required and should be set to Version=1. The Version attribute, a decimal integer, identifies to which version of the state management specification the cookie conforms.

Cookie Applications

One of the most common uses of cookies is for the tracking of visitors as they navigate through a website. By collecting a visitor's cookie every time a page is requested, say for a different product or service in your site, specific patterns or paths can be mined to determine what parts of your website are the most popular. Also, you may begin the process of profiling your online customers by linking cookies to referrer log and demographic data or registration information on your visitors and customers. This profile can then be used for subsequent analysis and marketing applications. Cookies can also be used to record what type of products and services a visitor has seen and purchased so that subsequent visits can be personalized to match their specific tastes and interests. Cookies can be used to make the visitor feel welcomed and important.

To give you an idea of how cookies work and how they can be used to enhance the value of mining log files, follow this shopping site scenario. When a visitor enters your website, your server issues an identifying user number (USERID=1234) in the following response header:

HTTP/1.1 200 OK
Server: CERN/3.0 libww/2.17
Set-cookie: USERID=1234; path=/
Content-type: text/html
Content-length: 2742
<Entity body>

This tells the browser to save the contents of the cookie, the visitor identification number (USERID=1234) and associated it with the issuing server that sent it. In this example, the server that sent the cookie is www.store.com, meaning the browser associates this cookie exclusively with store.com. Netscape Navigator will store this header identification number in the cookies.txt file, while Microsoft Explorer will put it in a cookie directory. The next request that the browser makes to the store.com server will include a request header that contains the content of the cookie. Here is how it might look:

```
GET / HTTP/1.1
Cookie: USERID=1234; path=/
If-modified-since: Fri 12 Jun 1998 10:57:22 GMT
Referrer: http://store.com/index.html
User-Agent: Mozilla/4.0 (Windows 95)
```

Once the cookie is set, the browser returns a "Cookies" header. Thereafter, the server doesn't need to send any more, except to set additional cookies for special purposes, such as identifying this as a new visitor or for observing what areas of the website this customer wanders into, what this visitor views and asks information about, and of course what she puts in her shopping cart and purchases. Through these streams of ongoing transactions the exchanges of cookies are able to maintain a semblance of continuity that is absent in the HTTP protocol.

A Cookies Scenario: The Transactional Exchange of HTTP Requests and Responses

1. BROWSER: Request Headers

   GET /index.html HTTP/1.1

   If-modified-since: Fri 12 Dec 1998 12:34:22 GMT

   Referrer: http://www.kdnuggets.com/companies.html#W

   User-Agent: Mozila/4.0 (Windows 95)

2. SERVER: Response Headers

   HTTP/1.1 200 OK

   Server: CERN/3.0 libwww/2.17

   * Set-cookie: USERID=1234; path=/

   Content-type: text/html

   Content-length: 3284

   <Entity body>

3. BROWSER: Request Headers

   GET /HTTP/1.1

   * Cookie: USERID=1234; path=/

   If-modified-since: Fri, 12 Jun 1999 12:35:23 GMT

   Referrer: http:/www.webminer.com/index.html

   User-Agent: Mozilla/4.0 (Windows 95)

4. SERVER: Request Headers

   HTTP/1.1 200 OK

   Server: CERN/3.0 libwww/2.17

   Content-type: text/html

   Content-length: 2149

   <Entity body>

5. BROWSER: Request Headers

   GET /products/info.html HTTP/1.1

   * Cookie: USERID=1234; path=/

   Referrer: http:/www.webminer.com/index.html

   User-Agent: Mozilla/4.0 (Windows 95)

6. SERVER: Request Headers

   HTTP/1.1 200 OK

   Server: CERN/3.0 libwww/2.17

   Content-type: text/htmlContent-length: 4951

   <Entity body>

The dispensing and tracking of cookies continue until the visitors select the check-out form signaling they are ready for a secured transaction and payment of goods and services. Cookies can store user interests via a unique identification tag, which websites can correlate with a database on the web server or advertising network. This also means that each time a customer visits a website, the server looks for the associated information on clickthroughs, transactions, and registration entries. Cookies can be used to target and rotate ads, for example, so that when you visit a site like your favorite search engine, you don't get hit with the same banner ad. The limitations of cookies, however, are obvious: they track browsers, not people—the cookies in a customer's office PC may be quite different from the iMac at home.

Aggregate cookies can be used for mining visitor patterns while they maneuver through your website, enabling you to make it convenient for them to return again and again. The experience should be as similar to going into a small corner shop where the clerk remembers what you like and how you like it. As part of your privacy policy you should disclose how you are using cookies—to improve your visitors' navigating experience and content value—while ensuring your integrity. As part of this policy you should also use cookies only when needed and for as short a period of time as is needed to accomplish your task. If, for example, you only need to issue cookies for single session tracking, then you should destroy your cookies at the end of your visitors' browsing session. The objective of mining cookies should be to discover online tendencies and to reinforce and personalize your customers' experience every time they visit your website.

Configuring Cookies

In the mining of web data it is important that website activity be captured for analysis, which means configuring your server to write to the Transfer Log file the cookie as well as the referrer and agent information you will need for your data mining analysis. For the Netscape servers this is a simple matter of selecting a configuration option to log cookie information in the transfer log. For Unix servers such as the popular Apache, you use a source code module for implementing cookies. You need to modify the log-reporting module to include the cookie information on each line of the transfer log. This is how you configure your server LogFormat string in the source code to write the referrer, agent, and cookie information:

```
LogFormat "%h %l %u %t \"%r\" %s %b \"%{Referrer}i \" \"%{User-
    agent}i"\"%{Cookie}i\""
```

For Unix servers these cookie-dispensing modules are in C code, which must be compiled prior to integrating. For NT servers the modules are in the format of DLL files, which must be updated on your registry. However, since cookies are set simply by adding an additional response header, they can be done through CGI scripts or other Java or Javascript programs. These "virtual cookies" work well in shopping cart applications, where a purchase selection for a specific product sets up a cookie until a purchase transaction is com-

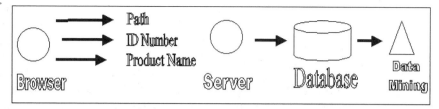

Figure 6–2
*Important cus-
tomer informa-
tion can be
stored and
mined for
analysis.*

pleted. The final CGI or Java program to process the purchase will reset the cookie to clear out all information. This application, however, does not write a cookie to the log file, which is really what is of interest in a data mining analysis.

CGI and Java can also be used to track visitors dynamically. For example, a CGI program can be used to create and send HTTP headers to set cookies. Similarly, CGI can be used to dynamically serve specific content based on the type of product a user selects. Numerous websites offer the code for doing this. Aside from serving content dynamically, what is of more relevance to the analysis of your website traffic is the ability to use the same type of CGI programming to issue your visitors a unique identification number, with the objective being to code that number into every link on that html page as an extra argument. This way every time a visitor clicks on a link in that page, their browser sends the path and product name of the file they are requesting with their unique tracking user identification number (Figure 6–2).

Cookies and CGI

Although cookies can be created via several types of technologies, such as VBScript, JavaScript, and Java, both on the server and client-side, most of today's cookies are created using CGI.

The CGI provides a set of web standards that allow the servers and programs to communicate with clients. It takes the information from the browser in an HTTP request format and passes it to the program as a set of variables. When the server receives and processes the request, it parses the headers and transforms them into a list of variables that is sent to the CGI program as standard input when the program first begins. One of the most important uses of forms is the interaction with website visitors and customers. The residue of these transactions is important customer information that is ideal for data mining.

A CGI script consists mainly as a translation program between a browser and server, matching outputs to inputs. When a request is submitted, the CGI script parses the information it receives, extracting the data such as a query string from a registration form sent by a POST request or cookie, which based on a pre-set routine, can generate a response for the website visitor, usually a set of headers followed by some HTML. This response is passed back to the server when the program concludes, with the server passing the response back to the visitor. Every time a visitor makes a call to a CGI program, the server builds the CGI request and runs that program—usually as a separate application. CGI program can be written in any language, although a large percentage of them are written in Perl, a language good at managing arrays and text.

The following are some quick examples of cookie settings, so that if you want to reach the HTTP_COOKIE variable for your own direct manipulation you can use either cgi.pm's raw_cookie() method or $ENV{'HTTP_COOKIE'}.

Retrieving a cookie value can be done within a CGI script with the following statement:

```
$myvalue=cookie('mycookie');
```

or

```
$myvalue=cookie(-name=>'mycookie');
```

Setting a cookie involves creating a cookie name and value:

```
$myCookie=cookie(-name=>'mycookie',-value=>'myvalue');
```

or

```
$myCookie=cookie('mycookie'.'myvalue');
```

This will create a cookie, which will expire at the end of the session, while the following call will last for a year before expiring:

```
$myCookie=cookie(        -name=>'mycookie',
                         -value=>'myvalue',
                         -path=>'/'
                         -domain=>'mydomain.com'.
                         -expires=>'+1y'
                         -secure=>1);
```

This is an example of how a cookie may be set up for first-time visitors. Looking for a firstVisit cookie, the CGI script, using Perl, will first check to see if a cookie is set before dispensing one to the visitor:

```perl
#!/usr/bin/perl
use CGI qw(:standard) :
# check for the firstVisit cookie
if (cookie('firstVisit')) {
    #if one exists, this is a returning visitor
    #collect the cookie value
    $firstVisit=cookie('firstVisit');
    $first="not ";
    #print header with no cookies.
    print header();
} else {
    #set firstVisit cookie
    $firstVisit=localtime;
    $cookie = cookie(-name=>'firstVisit',
            -value=>$firstVisit,
            -expire=>'+2y',
            -path=>'/');
#print header with firstVisit cookie
print header(-cookie=>$cookie);
$first="";
}
$currentDate=localtime;
#use cgi-pm's method for creating HTML.
print start_html("First Visit Check"), hl("Visitor Status");
print p("Welcome $first to The Online Shop.");#use Perl's .
    concatenation operator to split
#print p("Check out our daily sales");
print hr();
print p("It is now $currentDate.");
print end_html();
```

Open Profiling System (OPS)

The proposed Version 1.0 of cookies RFC 2109 would allow users more control over what cookies get passed to their browser and would expand their ability to reject cookies. It would also require website administrators and developers to explain why they are issuing cookies to their visitors and customers. Furthermore, the Open Profiling System as proposed by Netscape, Firefly (now owned by Microsoft), and VeriSign would set new standards designed to encourage users of new browsers to provide personal information as part of their setup options. At the same time it would provide them expanded control over who would be allowed access to their personal, home, and business information. OPS provides for the preloading of personal information at the browser level, one time only, then it allows the user to share that information only at those websites where they want to establish a one-to-one relationship—for personalized products, news, and services. The following is from the opening section of the OPS standards submission:

Introduction

As more and more users, and more and more services come to the Internet, users are finding themselves increasingly overwhelmed with the richness of new possibilities, and new service providers are discovering that rapidly building systems to fit these users' information needs becomes ever more challenging.

In general, a solution to these problems often involves delivery of highly customized and personalized information to end users, which raises the profound and valid concern about making and keeping explicit commitments to users about how their most sensitive personal information, choices, preferences, and interest will be protected in these exchanges.

Companies and service organizations worldwide want to take advantage of the 1-to-1 nature of communications on the Internet or within intranets to provide their customers, employees and visitors with individualized information, entertainment and services. However, there are two barriers to the feasibility and widespread adoption of such products and services:

1. *The potential threat to individual privacy makes end users wary of sharing any information. Today, there are few measures or safeguards that offer an end user any awareness of or any control over the usage of his or her personal information. This concern often outweighs the incentive of a personalized service and makes a person justifiably cautious about revealing any personal information.*

2. *Gathering the information that makes this personalization possible is inefficient. Service providers need to ask their visitors for information—who they are, where they live, what they do, what they like—in order to personalize the user experience. This data collection can be very time consuming for both the service provider and the end user, and can't be leveraged for their mutual benefit. Furthermore, a single individual might provide much the same information to dozens or even hundreds of parties over time—an inefficient and frustrating experience.*

The Open Profiling Standard (or OPS) is a proposed standard for exchanging profile information between individuals and service-providing parties, with built-in safeguards for individual privacy.

The OPS basically proposes the use of a Set-Profile header similar to the current Set-Cookie header, but with extensively much more information. Instead of a header with a few thousand bytes of name-value pairs for a single site, the Set-Profile header would contain a number of standardized groups of fields (with user permission) to multiple commercial sites with various security levels. The following is from the Netscape press release at the time OPS was announced:

> *Personal Profiles contains a wide range of descriptive information about an individual, such as name, address, ZIP code, phone number, and e-mail address. Personal Profiles can also contain information on an individual's age, marital status, interests, hobbies, and user identification/password. Internet sites and software products that support OPS and Personal Profiles will enable users to be aware of and in control of what profile information they divulge to Internet sites. In addition, OPS enables users to grant permission to specific Internet sites to share their PersonalProfiles with other Internet sites.*

Clearly OPS is aimed at personalizing the Web and making online transactions transparent to the website visitors and websites. The personal information or identity of visitors and customers would reside with the browser settings, much like the setting of your font preferences and other options. OPS would eliminate the need to complete registration forms and the constant retyping of personal information and preferences. For the website administrator it would make available a far greater amount of detailed demographic data for mining, and the enabling of responsive one-to-one service and customer customization.

Browsers such as Microsoft's Internet Explorer already include new options that allow for the setting and storing of user information at the personal, home, and business levels (Figures 6–3 through 6–5).

New server software is also enabling web administrators a variety of methods for personalizing their sites, while at the same time capturing important information about their visitors' and customers' usage patterns. For example, new server software like the Microsoft Personalization System (MPS) allows administrators to capture and store web visitor information between sessions linked by cookies. MPS also allows developers to create globally unique identification cookies (GUIDs) that are identical in multiple websites, allowing for the sharing of cookies between multiple domains. This feature allows for the "networking" of cookie information. The way this feature works is when a visitor appears at a server using this feature instead of sending a cookie, the MPS redirects the user to a different server. This second server then checks for a cookie, assigns a cookie if required, and bounces the visitor back to the original server with a message for that server about the cookie it set up. The original server then assigns a cookie that matches the cookie set by the master server. The result is a set of persistent cookies for two different domains with the same value.

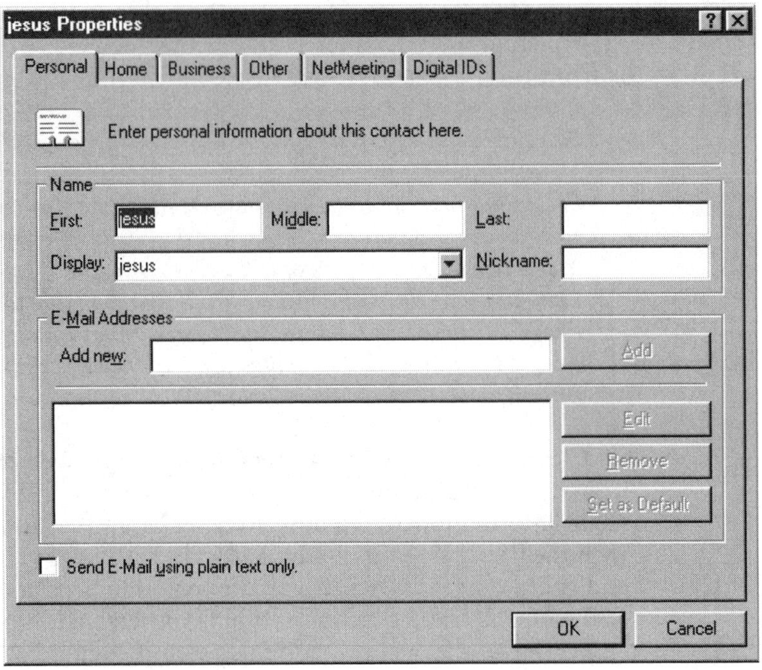

Figure 6–3
Personal information can be set in Microsoft Internet Explorer.

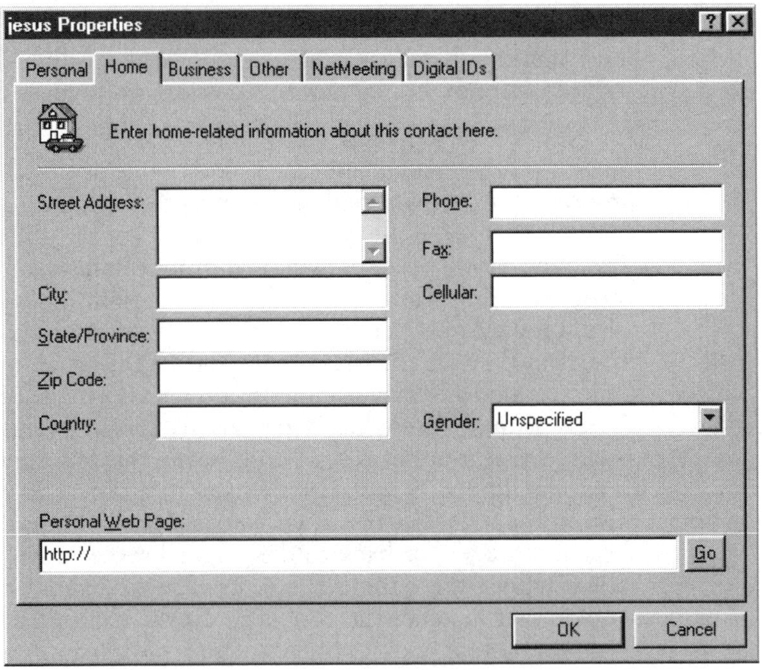

Figure 6–4
Home information can be preset on Microsoft Internet Explorer.

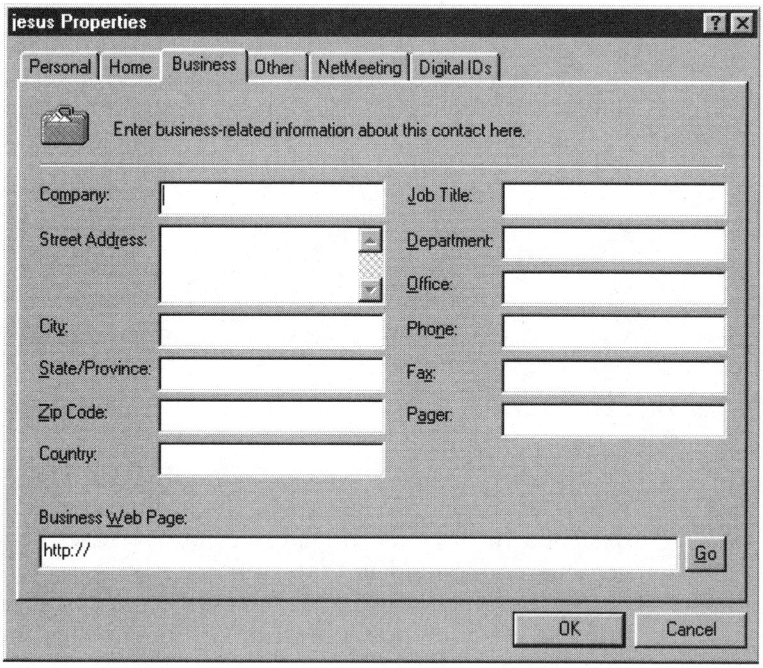

Figure 6–5
Business information can also be set for Explorer.

In essence this defeats the concept originally established by Netscape, which limited the setting, viewing, and modifying of cookies to only the original domain issuer. This Microsoft feature in effect allows for the networking of cookies via multiple servers.

The Commerce Server tools from the Site Server Enterprise edition also use cookies to keep track of shopper accounts, affording returning customers convenient access to account information and personalized messages captured from previous transactions. MPS provides for cookies to be set for tracking website visitors quite easily; allowing for the storing of personalized information by specific customers in the PropertyDatabase server component. The Microsoft User Properties Database Object has a number of properties and methods that an administrator can use to add information. Loading the UPD information into a database facilitates the linking, massaging, and mining of the data.

Although cookies are an excellent way to track individual sessions by browsers at the server level, they provide little value in data mining, unless they are used in aggregates. This is because cookies generally represent an individual identification number, which like your social security number is useless in a data mining analysis of a customer database. A social security number, like an individual cookie user identification number, is a single observation that is too unique to be generalized into a useable pattern. However, by grouping certain types of cookies, important clusters or patterns can be mined, which can lead to important insight about visitor and customer activity in your website. For example, retailer websites tend to issue cookies in several sequential steps, for purposes of identifying first-time shoppers:

Website Activity	Cookie Settings Issued
Visitors arrive at the site's home page	=on
Visitor selects a product category	=1stVisit=Welcome
Visitor selects a specific product	=Session_ID=1BABV317MEN

Sequential segments can be identified through the use of various types of data mining tools, including decision tree programs designed to discover key clusters in databases. The important concept to understand is that your website has the unique ability to both generate relational marketing messages and information when you use log and cookie files, or CGI forms designed to capture visitor profiles.

Forms

By far the most effective method of gathering website visitor and customer information is via registration forms. However, care must be taken in asking only for the most essential information; nobody likes to complete lengthy and intrusive questionnaires, especially those pertaining to income and other personal information. Keep in mind that there are various optional methods and sources of gathering demographic information rather than asking for it directly from your customers. In any event, asking too many nosy questions will only ensure that you will get no information or intentionally incorrect information from respondents.

Server processing of form submissions can take several directions, the most common of which are the launching of a CGI program that executes and returns a response to the website visitor. This is usually some form of response to the website visitor, such as some text or HTML. However, from this simple request and response mechanism a complex array of website and customer interaction and relationships can evolve. The most important is the circular feedback from consumer to retailer and the gathering of real-time vital client information. The transmission of information back and forth between client and server in hidden form fields establishes a relationship with your website visitors and customers and can track their browsing actions.

The two most important HTML tags are <FORM> and <INPUT>. The <FORM> tag is used to map the section of the HTML file to be used for user input. It is how most HTML pages call a CGI script—the tag tells the program the type of encoding being used and the method being used to transfer the data:

```
<FORM ACTION="url" METHOD=[POST|GET] ENCTYPE="...">
```

The ACTION attribute references the URL of the CGI program so that after the web visitor completes the form, all of the information is encoded and passed to the CGI script for decoding and processing. The METHOD attribute tells the CGI script how to receive the input: GET or POST (in most forms it will be POST). The POST method is the recommended way of getting information from forms since it sets no size limitations. Forms use text-input bars, radio buttons, check-boxes, and other means of accepting input by using the <INPUT> HTML tag. This is a sample of a text-input field in a form:

```
<INPUT TYPE=text NAME="..." VALUE="..." SIZE=...MAXLENGTH=...>
```

NAME assigns the value entered by the user. VALUE places the default text in the input field. The SIZE specifies the length of the input field, MAXLENGTH sets the maximum number of characters allowed to be input. To submit the information the following tag is used:

```
<INPUT TYPE=SUBMIT>
```

When the web visitor has completed the form they can submit its content to the URL specified by the form's ACTION attribute when the user clicks on the *Submit* button. When the content of the form is sent, the browser encodes the information before uploading it to the server and the CGI application. Once the user enters the values for every field, the symbolic names are passed with the following specifications:

- Spaces are replaced with pluses (+). Fields are separated by an ampersand (&).

- Name and values are separated by equal signs (=), name on left, value on right.

- All "abnormal" characters are also replaced with a percent sign (%) followed by the two-digit hexadecimal character code.

An encoded string will result in this output:

```
name1=value1&name2=value2&name3=value3...
```

This is a sample of a very simple form:

```
<html> <head>
<title> Name, Age and Gender</title>
</head>
<body><form action="/cgi-bin/profile.cgi" method=POST>
Please provide us your name: <input type=text name="name"><p>Please
    provide us your age: <input type=text name="age"><p>
Please provide us your gender: <input type=text name="gender"><p><input
    type=submit>
</form>
</body></html>
```

If your website visitor enters his name as Joe Blow, age 34 and gender Male, the input will be encoded into the following string:

```
name=Joe+Blow&age=34&gender=Male
```

Form data consists of a list of name/value pairs. Before the browser transmits data to a server and a CGI program it encodes the information using a scheme called URL encoding.

```
name        Joe Blow
e-mail      jblow@doc1.com
```

First all non-alphanumeric characters (@) gets encoded to (%40):

```
name        Joe Blow
e-mail      jblow%40doc1.com
```

Next, it replace all spaces with plus signs:

```
name        Joe+Blow
e-mail      jblow%40doc1.com
```

Then, each name and value get paired with an equal sign:

```
name=Joe+Blowe-mail=jblow%40doc1.com
```

With the final encoded string of pairs separated by an ampersand:

```
name=Joe+Blow&e-mail=jblow%40doc1.com
```

After a CGI program receives the encoded form input, it parses the string and stores it so that you can use the data, which is in the structure of name/value pairs. This string can be manipulated so that, for example, pluses (+) can be replaced with spaces, commas, or tabs. URL-encoded characters can be translated back to their original char-

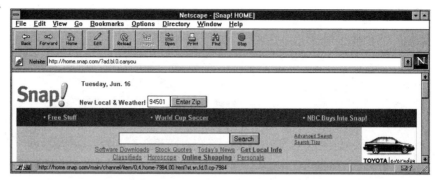

Figure 6–6
A simple one line form can provide targeted information to website visitors.

acters. The purpose of doing this of course is so that the encoded strings can be in a format suitable for merging with other internal and demographic databases and subsequently mined. Most of today's data mining tools are able to import text files delimited by commas or tabs.

```
name=Joe+Blow&age=34&gender=Male&jblow%40doc1.com
```

can become a comma delimited flat-file:

```
Joe Blow,34,Male,jblow@doc1.com
```

which is a format readily importable into most data mining tools.

A simple one-field form requesting your visitors' ZIP code for purposes of providing links to local classifieds, news, services, and weather can also be used to collect the all-important ZIP code (Figure 6–6). A ZIP code can be used to not only localize a website to meet the need of its visitors, but for matching with demographic and psychographic databases for subsequent data mining analysis.

Common Gateway Interface

The CGI is the most popular protocol by which browsers interact with web servers. It is a robust and versatile method by which visitors and customers communicate with online stores and other providers of products and services. CGI is a method by which web servers are able to interpret input from browsers and in some cases return information based on their input. The protocol defines a standard way for programs to communicate with the web server. CGI communications is handled over the standard input and output using any programming language, although Perl is the most common.

Perl is a high-level language that excels at parsing text, which is what most CGI scripts do. CGI programs usually involve getting

Figure 6–7
A form used to capture website visitor information for personalized content delivery.

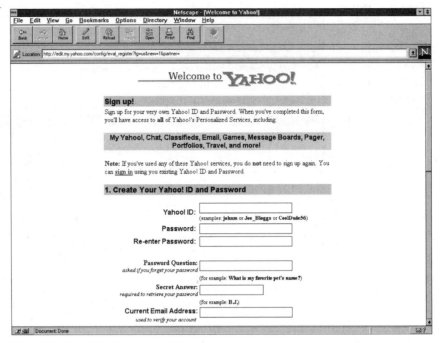

information from the browser and sending it to the server. CGI programming can be reduced to (1) getting input from the browser, (2) processing that input at the server, and (3) sending that output back to the browser. The most common method of doing this is, as we discussed, through HTML Forms, which for data mining is an important component because unlike logs or cookies they are being provided by the website visitor or customer themselves. Often, the website visitor or customer is presented with a form to complete, such as their ZIP code, age, gender, preferences, and so forth (Figure 6–7).

Once the visitor or customer fills out the form and submits it, the information is sent to a CGI program, which processes the input, such as appending it to a database. Next the program will acknowledge or send something back to the browser, like a user identification or password. For example, in exchange for customer information you may want your CGI program to provide a code for accessing a special location in your website, or you may want to grant a special discount. The point is that via the use of CGI and the forms that they support, you are able to interact with your visitors and customers. More importantly you are also able to capture important information about who they are and what they want and need.

CGI programs can read and write to files and databases, allowing the capturing of important customer information at the server level. How you accomplish this can be done either by server side processing of compiled programs or scripts executed by an interpreter. Most commonly this is done using a scripting language such as Perl, although C and C++ can also be used as well as JavaScript or Java. The problem with using C and C++ is that the administration requirements increase in complexity. Programs need to be recompiled any time a modification is made. In a highly dynamic environment, such as a large website, this can be a problem.

Java and JavaScript provide an option to using forms to capture customer information with just the traditional CGI. Java is an object-oriented programming language, while JavaScript is an object-based scripting language with a set of built-in objects. JavaScript is an extension of HTML and allows for some of the processing to be shifted from the server to the client, thus reducing processing time and server load. Because JavaScripts are embedded in HTML pages, web visitors do not have to wait for servers to respond because when pages are received by the client the scripts immediately execute for faster response time. JavaScript can also be used on the server side with Microsoft's Active Server Pages and Netscape's LiveWire.

Assembling the Components

To take advantage of each of these data components you likely will need to use both log and cookie files in combination with forms. A possible method for doing this involves using both server-side CGI scripts along with client-side JavaScript. The basic JavaScript used to set a cookie for both Netscape Navigator and Microsoft Explorer can be embedded in an HTML file, and it may look something like this:

```
document.cookie = "myCookie=A Value; expires=Tuesday, 06-Jul-199908:00:00 GMT"
```

When a visitor accesses your website, their browser will load the cookie set forth in the document .cookie object as one long string. When you assign a value to this object, the browser updates the named cookie if it exists, or creates the named cookie if it does not exist. The name of this particular cookie is myCookie, the value being stored is set to "A Value," with an expiration date of July 6, 1999 at 8 am. In order to store a website visitor's name, age, and gender when they submit a form along with a cookie you can write a JavaScript to look something like this:

```
data = document.FormName.visitor_name+"|"+
    document.FormName.visitor_age+"|"+
      document.FormName.visitor_gender;
document.cookie =cookie_name+"="+data+
      "; expires="+expiration_date;
```

Through the use of CGI, Java, and/or JavaScript, you can link the tracking ability of cookies with the important customer-provided demographic information captured with a form to gain an understanding of *who* is going *where*. In incremental steps you can begin to assemble a composite of who your website visitors and customers are:

```
Log File Information:
ntt.com.jp - - [08/Jul/1999:16:44:14 -0744] "GET /webminer/index.html
    HTTP/1.0" 200 5898
    "http://search.yahoo.com/bin/search?p=data+mining+websites"
    "Mozilla/3.01 (Macintosh; I; PPC)"
plus Cookie File Information
Session_ID=1BABV317MEN
plus Form Information
Joe Blow,34,Male,94502,jblow@doc1.com
equals Visitor/Customer Record String
ntt.com.jp - - [08/Jul/1999:16:44:14 -0744] "GET /webminer/index.html
    HTTP/1.0" 200 5898
    "http://search.yahoo.com/bin/search?p=data+mining+websites"
    "Mozilla/3.01 (Macintosh; I; PPC)", Session_ID=1BABV317MEN, Joe
    Blow,34,Male,94502,jblow@doc1.com
```

This comma-delimited string can easily be imported into a database such as Access for pre-processing and preparation for data mining (Figure 6–8).

One of the key strategies for capturing customer information at your website is to identify certain demographic features from their ZIP, which can be commingled with commercial consumer and census data. Analysis of both external and internal patterns can provide you an insight into the type of consumers that you are attracting to your website. These market clusters are individuals who have a propensity to buy your products and services. Your analysis of the type of individuals attracted to your website can reveal some common psychographical profiles with common behavior and values. Through the analysis of your website data you will be able to identify individuals with an interest in what you are selling.

You may in fact discover different types of market segments for different parts of your website, especially if you have a large website. Because of the dynamic nature of the Web you can create and test different content and marketing campaigns and promotions almost on the fly. The testing of offers and marketing concepts on the Web flows

Figure 6–8
A customer database can be constructed from several web data components.

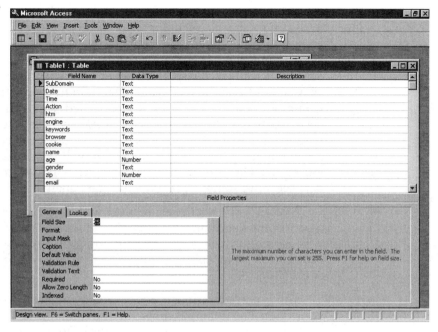

Figure 6–9
Your customer profiles will range in detail based on the components you use.

very quickly and works very effectively—without expensive focus groups and delays. In fact, through the use and creation of dynamic content today you can very easily test different product descriptions, offers and promotions and then do quantitative comparisons to see which work best.

Components Considerations

You need to consider the location of the data you want mined, that is, its storage, prior to analysis. Will you store it on the same server? Probably not. Like other types of data mining projects, issues over data variables you want to capture and convert as well as sample size need to be considered. Additional issues include the intervals of these analyses and what type of customer attributes you need to capture for sales, marketing, strategic planning, etc. For example, do you want to mine your data on a daily basis, or will a weekly sample of 10 percent of your online transactions suffice? Keep in mind that irrelevant, redundant, or covariant variables in a database constitute noise to any data analysis and can weaken your data mining predictive models. The Common Log Format was not designed for data mining; it was designed to measure server traffic, and as such it contains a lot of redundant and useless information that can be discarded from the mining analysis. In some instances you will need to append or merge log or database information created from registration forms into a data set more suitable for inductive data analysis (mining).

Another issue you need to deal with is dirty data. You must fix inconsistent data whenever possible including deciding how to deal with missing values. Some data mining tools provide the options and utilities for fixing spotty databases and some do not, so be prepared to do some cleaning.

Lastly, consideration must be given on how you will represent your data. For example, how do you want to deal with categorical attributes such as gender or ZIP codes? Do you want to group them into classes? How do you want to deal with continuous value variables? Do you need to create ratios from them? Compounded by all of these issues is the fact that data from a website is highly dynamic. Keep in mind that these elements are not set in stone, and that their customization is the norm rather than the exception. The data components generated from your website are only the starting point in the data mining process, for their value increases exponentially when merged with your data warehouse and third party information.

7

The Providers

In this chapter we will discuss several *external* sources of information that can be linked or appended to your website data for additional insight into the identity, attributes, lifestyle, and behavior of your visitors and customers (Figure 7–1). These sources of information fall into two general categories: the traditional marketing database vendors and a new breed of web-based software and network service providers. The first group represents the traditional marketing packagers and resellers of demographic, consumer and household information. The second group, on the other hand, represents a whole new genre of web companies offering software and services (sometimes both) designed to capture and generate "webographic" data about Internet users' behavior and preferences. These new players use a myriad of solutions to track and profile visitors and shoppers, everything from collaborative filtering technology, to proprietary software and the commingling of cookies via server networks.

Figure 7–1
Your website data can be enhanced by linking it to offline and online external sources.

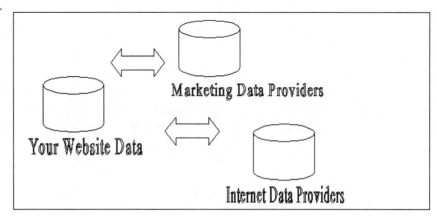

Marketing Data Providers

There is an entire industry of information resellers who accumulate, organize, and package data for companies and marketers wishing to improve their sales, retain their customers, and enhance their relationships with their clients. The use of demographics, household, income, and consumer data can also be used to add value to the vast amount of customer and transactional information already being captured at your website. Through the appending of this third party data you can gain a new insight about your online customers.

A common methodology in data warehousing is the merging of various internal company data with external commercial information. Data warehousing is the process of bringing together disparate data from various business units scattered throughout an organization for purposes of providing decision-support. A key strategy is often to use data mining technology to identify likely customers for products and services by integrating customer information with external demographic and lifestyle data. Similarly, in database marketing it is quite common to "append" household information from such companies as Acxiom, Equifax, Experian, and others in order to understand what type of individuals are responding to mail campaigns or other promotions and sales incentives.

The merging of server-based data with external demographic, psychographic, and household information can provide an electronic retailing site important insight into the identity of its online visitors and customers. As with the data warehousing and database marketing applications, this additional information can assist a website position, communicate, relate, and retain profitable online customers.

Several firms specialize in aggregating public, census, public records, directory, and consumer information and repackaging it in a format that companies and marketers can use with their own internal data. These data providers sell various levels of information about consumers and households. The following is a description on some of the largest data integrators and providers in the United States—all of which you can use to enrich your perception of your website customers. This can be accomplished by using either the ZIP code or physical address as completed by visitors and customers in your website's registration and purchase forms.

Applied Geographic Solutions

Applied Geographic Solutions provides current year demographic estimates, five- and ten-year projections, consumer expenditure estimates, and the MOSAIC neighborhood segmentation system. Data is provided for all standard geographic levels including Block Group, Tract, and ZIP codes, including:

- Basic population and household data, including group quarters population
- Labor force status, employment by industry and occupation
- Household and family income distributions and averages
- Income distributions by age of head of household
- Household size and age of head of household
- Population by age, sex, and race
- Educational attainment
- Vehicles available
- Marital status

The AGS consumer expenditure database covers 340 base variables, arranged in a hierarchical structure to permit ready cross-category and cross-geographic analysis and is available at the block group and higher level. The CEX database is available for the current year and both five- and ten-year projection periods. The main expenditure groups included in the AGS database are:

- Household Furnishings
- Household Equipment
- Food and Beverage Personal Services
- Transportation
- Entertainment Contributions
- Apparel Shelter
- Gifts

www.appliedgeographic.com

Acxiom

Sequestered in the Ozark hills of Arkansas, Acxiom is a company with more information on Americans than the Internal Revenue Service. It certainly has the information better organized and in a more usable format for such tasks as marketing, risk management, fraud prevention, and other knowledge-based applications. Acxiom provides consumer information it has gathered through acquisitions, alliances, and partnerships to verify, identify, and segment customers and prospects on nearly every American today. Acxiom also compiles a variety of public file data from such sources as telephone directories and county recorder and assessors' offices. Axiom acquired DataQuick, one of the largest compilers and resellers of real estate information in the country; thus, they can identify home ownership and related transactions.

Acxiom's Consumer InfoBase is one of the largest multi-sourced database in the United States. It contains:

- property information such as age of the structure, size, and physical characteristics
- household characteristics such as marital status and type of vehicles owned
- individual characteristics such as gender, occupation, and education
- lifestyle information such as interests, hobbies, and activities
- geographic characteristics such as census demographics
- address information including full mailing address
- contact information including telephone number

Consumer InfoBase lists combine consumer data and public record data with information from other sources to create a database of over 150 million individuals residing in over 100 million households. Acxiom also contains data on consumers from Europe, Asia, and South America. The company has also moved to make their vast information available via the Web through their Acxiom Data Network (ADN) system (Figure 7–2).

ADN provides household demographics such as marital status, occupation, and estimated income ranges, as well as other useful

Figure 7–2
ADN provides consumer data on demand on the Web.

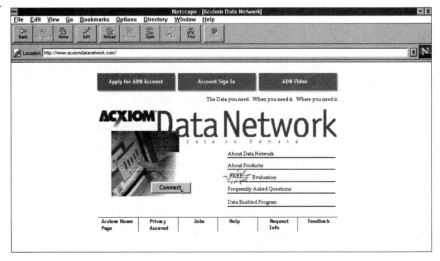

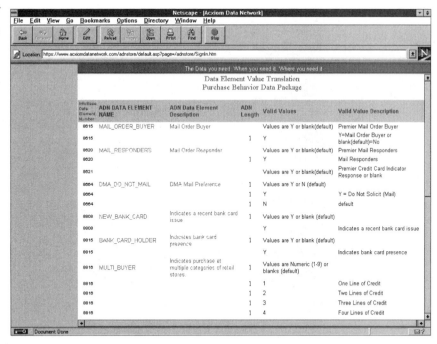

Figure 7–3
Various types of behavior indicators are available for profiling your web customers.

information such as details on vehicles, some retail buying habits, and home rental and ownership (Figure 7–3). For example, real property information can be used by home improvement, real estate, and insurance websites to more accurately market their services based on their visitors' and customers' home's age, size, and value. Financial online lenders, like e-loan.com or e-card.com, can also benefit from this type of real estate information for making timely and focused messages based on home equity and loan-to-value information based on a website visitor's length of residence and purchase date.

Auto information from Acxiom can also be used to identify potential prospects for the sale and leasing of cars and trucks for such national sites as autotel.com, carpoint.com, auto.com, and local auto dealership websites. This same type of information can be used by websites selling related products and services, such as auto alarms, stereo systems, painting services, tires or anything else that relates to cars, trucks, and sport utility vehicles. By knowing their website visitors' vehicles, whether they buy used or new vehicles, and what type of vehicles they purchase (compact, convertible, SUV, etc.), they can position the appropriate offers and banners and serve and deliver the appropriate message, product, and service to their site's visitors.

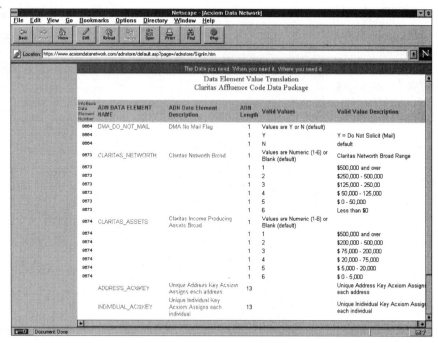

Figure 7–4
Detailed consumer income information is available from the Acxiom system.

Extensive consumer buying information is available from Acxiom and their ADN system including the indication of prior mail-order purchases. A propensity to buy from catalogs can be a signal to an electronic retailer that a specific visitor to their site is a consumer who is pressed for time and may favor buying during their spare time, rather than trekking to the neighborhood mall. ADN also contains the Claritas Affluence Code. Claritas is one of the largest providers of marketing data. The affluence code analyzes a variety of economic factors to provide an accepted means of determining relative wealth. This information can be used to identify upscale website visitors who are likely to be interested in luxury items, or for an environmental organization, a possible contributor or supporter.

ADN provides online access to marketing information on U.S. consumers on the basis of demographic, geo-demographic, and personal interest information (Figure 7–4). Axiom does not provide confidential data on individuals, such as credit or medical information. Credit consumer information is protected by federal law and is generally available from the three major credit companies: Equifax, Experian, and TransUnion.

www.acxiom.com

CACI (ACORN)

CACI's ACORN neighborhood segmentation system is one of the oldest consumer classification systems. ACORN segments consumers according to ZIP code; thus, if your site is capturing this information in your forms you can use it. For example, suppose you're an electronic retailer of snow boards, and you are looking to expand and grow your online sales. One of the best ways to find new customers is to determine the makeup of your current website visitors and customers and then find others that are similar. Using ACORN to analyze your current website customer base, you may find that a large percentage of your online customers are "Twentysomethings" and "Young Frequent Movers," two of ACORN's 43 clusters, or neighborhood segments.

With this information in hand, you can now seek out other web visitors with ZIP codes with a high percentage concentration from these two clusters. By narrowing your selection of possible customers in this manner, you can now concentrate and focus your incentives or offers to these visitors and shoppers. You can position your ads or banner in websites known to be frequented by these two market clusters. For example, "Twentysomething" consumers are the second ranked market for fast food, while "Young Frequent Movers" are the top ranked market for pet ownership. Armed with this intelligence you may want to position your banner with search engines when keywords such as "dog training" or "pizza" are entered.

ACORN's neighborhood segments are broken up into 43 clusters, which are collected in 9 general categories (groups). The following are some of their key traits:

GROUP 1: AFFLUENT FAMILIES

1A Top One Percent	These are the wealthiest neighborhoods in the United States. This highly educated type is the top-ranked group for investments, drinking wine, and ordering by phone, a key indicator they are also likely to buy via the Web from such sites like Virtual Vineyards *virtualvin.com.*
1B Wealthy Seaboard Suburbs	This type is located along the eastern seaboard and in California. They rank among the highest for auto club memberships and travel extensively, a key indicator for travel-related websites like *travelocity.com.*

1C Upper Income Empty Nesters	These are business owners and managers who are distributed throughout the country. Home furnishings and improvements rank high among their expenditures. Office supplier retailers like *officemax.com* and *officedepot.com* may want to identify, attract, and retain these visitors.
1D Successful Suburbanites	Essentially suburban, they drive new cars and spend money on sports, exercise equipment, and personal computers. These consumers are seasoned online shoppers and will likely continue to buy products and services on the Web. They have a particularly high lifetime value LTV ranking. These are savvy consumers and likely to shop at *compare.net*.
1E Prosperous Baby Boomers	They participate in sports, but do not invest or save in proportion to their income. *espn.com* and sport equipment retailers will want to recognize these visitors.
1F Semirural Lifestyle	They maintain their livelihood by self-employment—many of them working at home. They are interested in reading, needlework, and cooking. Home office workers, these consumers have come to use the Web for browsing and shopping. They are likely to be the most loyal and profitable customers of *amazon.com*.

GROUP 2: UPSCALE HOUSEHOLDS

2A Urban Professional Couples	Taking domestic vacations, they spend on theater and concerts and dining out rather than cooking in. These are *geocities.com* browsers and shoppers.
2B Baby Boomers with Children	This is a homogeneous type who spends their time and money on home and family-oriented activities and goods. These are the *disney.com, etoy.com,* and *ty.com* consumers.
2C Thriving Immigrants	Owning 2+ cars, they neither invest nor save. Activities include casino gambling and ordering take-out while watching the NFL on TV. This is the *WebTv.com* crowd.

2D Pacific Heights	Living in high-rent districts, located primarily in California and Hawaii, these residents are predominantly Asians and Pacific Islanders who are slightly older, urban, and upscale. These visitors are location and ethnicity-specific and may warrant ads and incentives geared to their area and interests, such as *sfgate.com* the San Francisco local newspaper website.
2E Older Settled Married Couples	Spending is home-oriented; almost 20 percent draw retirement incomes. These visitors are age- and income-driven and may be primarily interested in bargains such as those found in *ebay.com*.

GROUP 3: UP & COMING SINGLES

3A High Rise Renters	They use credit cards extensively and are top-ranked for ATM use. These consumers should be of interest to card issuers and banks such as *wellsfargo.com* and *e-card.com*.
3B Enterprising Young Singles	They tend to rent videos and use PCs at work and at home. These consumers are savvy users of the Web and would be of interest to such sites as *reel.com* and *movies.go.com*.

GROUP 4: RETIREMENT STYLES

4A Retirement Communities	Luxury cars, outdoor gardening, attending sporting events, using vitamins, and ordering by mail and phone are popular. Increasingly consumers over 50 are beginning to make online purchases; as such, these consumers may be of interest to such sites as *gardenweb.com* and *classicar.com*.
4B Active Senior Singles	They tend to use coupons and spend money on specialty food items, romance, mystery books, and lottery tickets. These coupon hunters are likely to be of interest to *www.qpons.com*, a site that not only dispenses coupons online but also e-mails them to visitors when new coupons become available in their area.

4C Prosperous Older Couples	Home-oriented, they do take domestic trips and participate in sports such as fitness walking and playing golf. A site of interest to these consumers might well be *golfweb.com*.
4D Wealthiest Seniors	They rank first in domestic/foreign travel, fitness walking, coffee drinking, subscribing to cable, and mail/phone order. These consumers are likely to step up to *walking.org* and *cnn.com*.
4E Rural Resort Dwellers	Four-wheel drive vehicles, camping equipment, and domestic trips reflect their lifestyle. Top-ranked for gardening equipment, owning large dogs, and taking vitamins. These consumers will be of interest to *camping.org* and *4wd.com*.
4F Senior Sun Seekers	They are the top-ranked market for mail/phone orders of audio tapes and the purchase of lottery tickets, and are the second-ranked market for book club membership. Sites, which could benefit from these consumers, include *audiosource.com* and *audiobookclub.com*.

GROUP 5: YOUNG MOBILE ADULTS

5A Twentysomethings	This is the second-ranked market for fast food and they are also dieters. What else but *mtv.com* and *pizzaclub.com*.
5B College Campuses	Top-ranked for take-out fast food, having ATM cards, and making long-distance calls using calling cards, they rank highest for watching sports on TV: *abc.com, nfl.com,* and *nba.com*.
5C Military Proximity	They are top-ranked for Bible purchases, disposable diapers, and watching rented videos: *gospelcom.net*.

GROUP 6: CITY DWELLERS

6A East Coast Immigrants	They spend on foreign travel, furniture, and household goods: *furniturefind.com*.
6B Working Class Families	They buy apparel, are top-ranked for owning 4+ televisions and for drinking wine coolers and cola sodas: *foxnetwork.com*.

6C Newly Formed Households	Most drive older cars and use coupons for groceries: *hotcoupons.com*.
6D Southwestern Families	Their lifestyle is both urban and rural with spending being family-oriented purchases: *hispanic.com*.
6E West Coast Immigrants	Their budgets include heavy expenditures on groceries, baby products, and movie attendance: *fox.com*.
6F Low Income: Young & Old	They purchase infant toys, toy cars and trucks, jewelry, and household items such as flatware and washing machines: *toysrus.com*.

GROUP 7: FACTORY & FARM COMMUNITIES

7A Middle America	Their budget priorities are home-oriented (improvement, children's apparel, lawn equipment) with leisure activities including hunting, fishing, and needlework: *build.com, hometime.com,* and *yarntree.com*.
7B Young Frequent Movers	This is the top-ranked market for pet ownership and sites like *petquarters.com* and *petco.com*.
7C Rural Industrial Workers	Most own 3+ vehicles: *ford.com* and *chevy.com*.
7D Prairie Farmers	Their top-ranked activity is hunting and fishing and they are likely to own pets: *fbnews.com* and *sportsmensweb.com*.
7E Small Town Working Families	Active in their communities, they are top-ranked for buying preschool toys and reading *Country Home* magazine: *countryliving.com*.
7F Rustbelt Neighborhoods	They tend to drive used cars, splurge on lottery tickets, and are top-ranked for using coupons for beauty and household cleaning products: *ausedcar.com* and *valupage.com*.
7G Heartland Communities	They are top-ranked for outdoor vegetable gardening, flower gardening, and buying videos at discount stores: *wal-mart.com*.

GROUP 8: DOWNTOWN RESIDENTS

8A Young Immigrant Families	They tend to spend their money on major household appliances, athletic and dress shoes, and baby products: *nike.com.*
8B Social Security Dependents	They spend money on mail and phone order items and are the number one market for having personal loans: *hfc.com.*
8C Distressed Neighborhoods	They are top-ranked for shopping at malls and buying children's items. Admittedly, these consumers will not likely be online shoppers, as they prefer the physical malls.
8D Hard Times	They are top-ranked for buying major household appliances and baby products and they tend to purchase fast food and takeout food: *sears.com.*
8E Urban Working Families	They are top-ranked for purchases of grills and climate control machines, and buying educational toys: *grategrills.com.*

GROUP 9: NONRESIDENTIAL NEIGHBORHOODS

9A Business Districts	Business Districts have a residential population of less than 100 and a significant daytime business population.
9B Institutional Populations	These neighborhoods are home to institutional group quarters, including prisons, juvenile detention homes, and mental hospitals.
9C Unpopulated Areas	These areas are unpopulated and include developed acreage such as parks, cemeteries, golf courses, or undeveloped land.

www.caci.com

Claritas

Claritas introduced the original lifestyle segmentation system in the early 1970s called PRIZM. The system segments all the neighborhoods in the United States in terms of 62 demographically and behaviorally distinct types, or "clusters." In doing so Claritas developed a marketing tool that can be used to identify, understand, and target consumers based on their locale and lifestyles. Currently PRIZM links with virtually every major marketing database, consumer survey, and direct mail list in the United States.

Claritas also provides information on consumer expenditure databases, which allow the user to segment markets by age and income, and isolate consumers by revenue potential. Claritas uses a network of over 1,600 local government and private sources to create this information. Claritas' Dimensions database incorporates household- or individual-level data from file enhancement vendors (Experian, Infobase, etc.) or actual client files with neighborhood clusters and demographic distributions to produce industry- or company-specific segmentations.

Claritas also has a database for financial services targeting called P$YCLE, a system created expressly to differentiate households in terms of financial behavior. It predicts which types of households will use which types of financial products and services. It is used by leading financial institutions for prospective cross-selling, branch evaluation, product planning and development, advertising, and media planning. Potentially P$YCLE could be used by stock trading sites and other investment and financial related sites, such as *quote.com, etrade.com, ameritrade.com,* etc.

LifeP$YCLE is a household-level segmentation system that groups customers in terms of 57 distinct types of life insurance customers. LifeP$YCLE is optimized to predict who is most likely to buy insurance products based on actual usage patterns of asset accumulation and income protection products. Claritas' Market Audit is the largest syndicated database of consumer financial behavior. Data is compiled annually using comprehensive, random-dialed phone interviews with over 100,000 households. The Market Audit covers household use of specific financial products, accounts and account balances, and where accounts are held. This database will likely interest insurance-related sites, such as *insweb.com.*

www.claritas.com

Equifax

The San Diego-based Equifax National Decision Systems (ENDS) is another consumer segmentation system. To see how the ENDS segments a neighborhood go to the "LifeQuiz" application on their website at *http://www.natdecsys.com* and input your ZIP code (Figures 7–5 and 7–6).

Equifax provides MicroVision reports, which uses demographic data and aggregated consumer demand data at the ZIP+4 level to classify every U.S. household into unique market segments. Each segment consists of households that share similar interests, purchasing

Figure 7–5
*Input your ZIP
code here.*

Figure 7–6
*And see the
demographic
profile of your
neighborhood
here.*

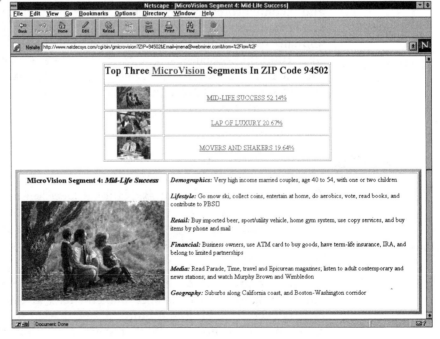

patterns, financial behavior and demand for products and services. The MicroVision reports cluster each U.S. household into one of 50 segments based on census demographics, interests, purchasing patterns, and financial behaviors.

MicroVision also classifies every U.S. household into one of 95 unique and homogeneous sub-cluster codes. The codes are assigned at the Zip+4 level—it is assumed that all households within that Zip+4 share the same characteristics. These sub-cluster codes are the building blocks for industry-specific systems such as Micro-Vision Insurance. Equifax creates MicroVision reports for businesses in the real estate, retail, restaurant, banking, insurance, investments, cable, telecommunications, utilities, consumer products, publishing, and other industries.

www.equifax.com

Experian

Experian, formerly known as TRW, provides the MOSAIC targeting system, which identifies consumers according to the type of neighborhood in which they live. The MOSAIC system is international and is available in 16 countries; an estimated 779 million people are classified by Experian, which may be of interest to large online directories and major portals who attract visitors from around the world. In an effort to enhance MOSAIC, Experian acquired Direct Marketing Technology Inc. also known as *Direct Tech*, a company that processes billions of direct mailings in the United States.

Experian generates approximately 50 percent of all the prospect names for pre-approved credit offers, using the financial and demographic information held in their large consumer databases. Their geodemographic segmentation system, MOSAIC is one of the world's most widely used systems for classifying consumers. Their Global MOSAIC enables Experian to perform analysis of consumers worldwide. Experian also uses their psychographic systems for developing behavioral analyses for cross-selling among existing customers and risk-based scorecards for minimizing the likelihood of future financial loss when targeting new customers.

Experian has one of the world's largest databases of demographic and financial information. Supported by this core data they provide a wide range of data processing services. These include merging client files with new prospect lists, segmenting their files into more refined prospect groups using Experian's own profiling techniques, and enhancing information through deduplication and the addition of full address details.

Experian's lifestyle database in the U.K., called Chorus, is compiled from large-scale surveys to build a comprehensive picture of the way consumers live, together with their demographics and purchasing behavior. In the United States, they have developed a shared database of individual-level transaction information from more than 150 catalog clients. Called Z-24, the database helps contributing members make major improvements in their prospect targeting. Experian also manages customer databases for some major organizations.

www.experian.com

Polk

Polk is the oldest consumer marketing information company in the country. It compiles lifestyle and other demographic data on more than 100 million consumer households across the United States and Canada. It provides annual statistics on nearly 200 million cars and supplies detailed consumer analysis to more than 100 major consumer goods companies. Polk also provides geographic data covering more than 12 million addressed street segments in the United States as well as nationwide census and current postal boundary products. Among the consumer lists they provide are the following:

The Lifestyle Selector®. The Lifestyle Selector is a comprehensive consumer database made up of buyers who complete and mail detailed questionnaires regarding their lifestyle interests and the purchases they have made. It details such products as automotive accessories, consumer electronics, furniture, small and major appliances, outdoor recreation and others. This is the list count for computer hardware, which most likely was culled from warranty cards for each product type:

CD-ROM Owners	2,968,000
Fax Modem Owners	89,000
Laptop Computer Owners	137,000
On-Line/Internet Service Subscribers	92,000
Personal/Home Computers Enthusiasts	14,210,000
Personal Home Computer Owners	7,861,000
Personal Home Computer Users	9,205,000
PC Compatible Owners/Users	6,447,000
Apple/Macintosh Owners/Users	1,525,000

Buyer Beware

Although these data resellers are very good at providing timely and accurate demographics, the density of their coverage, or "file penetration," is not always 100 percent. To give you an idea of just how accurate their information is the following table reflects the actual coverage of a household database provider by individual attributes and file density:

Attribute	Inferred	File Density (Accuracy)
Head of Household Age	yes	98% (Exact—YOB)
Income	yes	98%
Marital Status	yes	25–76%
Number of Children	no	22%
Gender	yes	100%
Mail Order Responsive	no	70% (26 categories)
Ethnicity	yes	25%
Education	no	4–100%
Wealth	no	100%
Employment Type	no	11%
Length of Residence	yes	88%
Age of Children	no	15%
Lifestyle	no	12%
Phone	no	80%
Loan to Value	no	48%
Dwelling Type	yes	100%
Available Equity	yes	48%
Home Value	yes	88%
Presence of 1st Mortgage	no	88%
Presence of 2nd Mortgage	no	26%
Credit Cards by type and #	no	6%
Installment Products	no	4%
Savings Accounts	no	2%
Home Age	yes	88%
Lender Type	no	30%
Loan Type	no	28%

Keep in mind that this is a household file, not a consumer credit file, and as such does not contain detailed information on loans and other financial account activity. This type of information is available by simply providing a matching address. You should be aware that the density of the file that you purchase is likely to vary depending on the vendor you select and the type of attributes you desire.

Business-to-Business Intelligence

There are also data providers who sell information on companies and corporations. For a business-to-business site doing electronic commerce this type of company intelligence can enable it to improve its sales and evaluate the credit-worthiness of its trading partners and clients.

The data providers of business information are totally different from those providing consumer demographics. These data resellers provide timely and accurate company data gleaned and assembled from regulatory and licensing federal, state, and local agencies. One major provider of public records is Information America, which makes its database available on its site KnowX (Figures 7–7 and 7–8). Through KnowX, Information America provides access to public records including real estate transactions, lawsuits, judgments, and professional license information from states, counties, and cities.

As with the profiling of online consumers, the profiling of companies can enable a website involved in electronic commerce to gain an insight about its clients. Through the same processes of warehousing and mining a business-to-business electronic commerce site can model and improve its sales and its competitive status by constructing composites of trading partners and its most profitable accounts.

```
http://knowx.com
```

Lexis-Nexis is another firm that offers legal, legislative, regulatory, news, business, and public record information by subscription:

```
http://lexis-nexis.com
```

Dunn & Bradstreet also provides to U.S.-based companies credit, collections, and marketing reports:

```
www.dnb.com
```

High Tech Connect®. Of special interest to web administrators and marketers is this Polk list of home computer consumers. The High-Tech database has 45 high-tech data elements, falling into the following five categories:

- Software Users and Buyers (including Mail-Order Buyers)
- High-Tech Product Owners and Users
- Online/Internet Service Subscribers
- Online/Internet Service Intenders
- High-Tech Product Intenders

This is a 36 million-name database self-reported by consumers themselves, which can be segmented by 11 demographic and more than 65 lifestyle characteristics. This is a partial section of this file:

Figure 7–7
KnowX provides legal and business information.

CENTRAL
Register Now!
Subscribers Log In
QUICK & EASY Search
PROFESSIONAL Search
Pricing & Billing Info
Other Resources
Public Records & Privacy FAQs
Help
Click to win two months' free rent.
@ GetSmart.com
The Ultimate Business Finder
Select One Database & Enter an Individual or Business Name. Guests may search only one database.
State Corporate Records
DBA Records
Business Yellow Pages
Sales Tax Permits (CA / TX only)
FEIN Locator
Tip: Click above for Database & Price Info.
Name:
State:
Alabama
Search Tips!
To search for Owners & Officers click here.
To try D&B Business Records Plus NEW click here. TRY IT!
Search

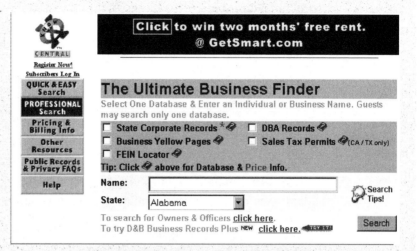

Figure 7–8
Multiple and single searches of company information are available.

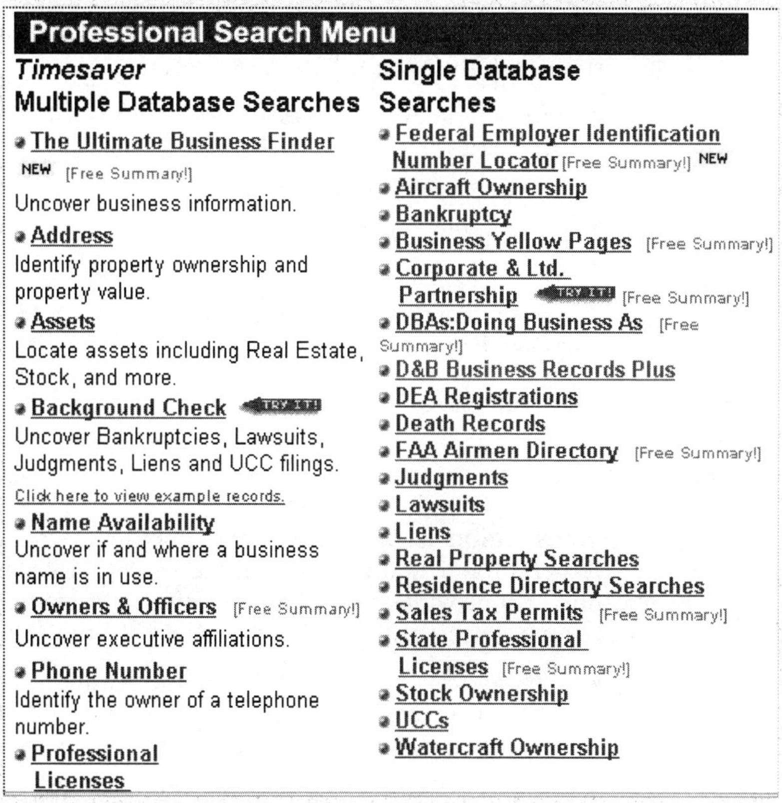

Professional Search Menu
Timesaver
Multiple Database Searches
The Ultimate Business Finder
NEW [Free Summary!]
Uncover business information.
Address
Identify property ownership and property value.
Assets
Locate assets including Real Estate, Stock, and more.
Background Check TRY IT!
Uncover Bankruptcies, Lawsuits, Judgments, Liens and UCC filings.
Click here to view example records.
Name Availability
Uncover if and where a business name is in use.
Owners & Officers [Free Summary!]
Uncover executive affiliations.
Phone Number
Identify the owner of a telephone number.
Professional Licenses
Single Database Searches
Federal Employer Identification Number Locator [Free Summary!] NEW
Aircraft Ownership
Bankruptcy
Business Yellow Pages [Free Summary!]
Corporate & Ltd. Partnership TRY IT! [Free Summary!]
DBAs:Doing Business As [Free Summary!]
D&B Business Records Plus
DEA Registrations
Death Records
FAA Airmen Directory [Free Summary!]
Judgments
Lawsuits
Liens
Real Property Searches
Residence Directory Searches
Sales Tax Permits [Free Summary!]
State Professional Licenses [Free Summary!]
Stock Ownership
UCCs
Watercraft Ownership

Online Subscribers	
Any Online Service	266,000
America Online	151,000
CompuServe	41,000
Microsoft Network	25,000
Prodigy	35,000
Other Internet Provider	48,000

TotaList. Polk's TotaList database is one of the largest consumer databases on the market today. With information on more than 95 million U.S. households and over 180 million individuals, the TotaList database delivers a combination of automotive ownership data, lifestyles, interests, and activities. The file is continuously updated with new sources and processed against ZIP+4 from nearly 30 sources of data, and it has more than 100 individual selection features including the following sectors:

- Household Automotive Finance selects General Household characteristics
- Household Member information
- Household Automotive selects
- Specific Motor Vehicle selects Housing/Property information

Other Polk files include the *Vehicle Databases* and the *Auto Purchase Predictor Database.*

www.polk.com

Trans Union

Trans Union is the third credit bureau in the country along with Experian and Equifax, which like the other credit reporting companies also provides several information management products. Among the marketing products lines it offers are the following:

- *Silhouette,* a market segmentation product that groups consumers into one of 25 clusters according to their individual credit lifestyle. Demographics are included. Permissible purpose is required.
- *Facets,* a risk-based clustering system, uses individual-level credit information to segment accounts into one of 13 clusters. Trans Union claims Facets is optimized when used in conjunction with a risk score, because it improves the risk-prediction of these scores.

- *Sentry* is an attrition model that predicts the likelihood of an account voluntarily closing within 3–5 months.
- *Revenue Projection Model* rank orders individuals by the relative amount of revenue they are likely to produce on a revolving credit account during the next twelve months.

www.tuc.com

Web Services and Software Providers

The Web is a highly competitive and expanding marketplace that doubles every hundred days. As the general content of the Web gets broader, visitors and shoppers will cease to browse aimlessly and will instead gravitate toward sites that deliver products and services customized to their consumer needs. It is more important than ever to provide customers with an interactive, personal web experience. Retailing sites must plan now to respond to this expectation or risk being left behind as the Web changes to a personal medium. These web vendors concentrate on providing webographic information, which allows sites to tailor content to a visitor's preferences.

The following group of webographics providers is a relatively new breed of Internet companies, who are in the business of selling software or services for collaborative filtering, relational marketing, and customer profiling. They provide detailed information on visitor behavior, preferences, and profiles.

These vendors differ dramatically in how they approach these tasks. Most use proprietary technology on the server-side for capturing some of this customer information, while others concentrate on monitoring the behavior of users and then predicting what type of products or incentives they are likely to purchase and what ads or banners they will respond to. Almost all provide the products and services exclusively on the Internet for electronic retailers and marketers.

It is a very new industry with few standards and clear winners; a highly dynamic market sector with many novel approaches to the main electronic retailing questions: *who are my customers and what kind of products and services are they likely to purchase from me?*

Some of these services and products track and log every web page displayed to every user so you can develop a "clickstream" view of what they saw, when they saw it, and for how long. This type of data can be stored and mined for a complete understanding of their usage, behavior, and preference. A few of these firms provide audience measurements and advertising services, which may not provide additional data for mining, but they may provide additional insight about your visitors and customers.

Art Technology Group

The Art Technology Group (ATG) started as a web design group and is now providing a suite of Java-based electronic commerce products, collectively referred to as *Dynamo Product Suite,* which is designed to provide highly scalable, multi-platform, business-to-consumer capabilities. The suite consists of the following discrete products and two components, the Personalization Server and Commerce Application:

The first part of the Dynamo Personalization Server is made up of the Dynamo Application Server, a web application server (WAS) that provides the runtime engine for all of the three electronic commerce products. It supplies native interfaces for Oracle, Sybase, and Microsoft databases, and runs on Java Virtual Machines of the major variants of Unix as well as Windows NT. The other part is the Dynamo Personalization Station, which was designed to dynamically track user behavior. It also provides user survey capabilities that predict user behavior. These usage tracking and survey tools are often referred to as "personalization" features. This is the key customization component: it combines information from demographic databases and user behavior to dynamically display personalized content. Open Content Adapters are used for integration to financial data systems and other system repositories. Business rules can also be specified regarding the presentation of content to visitors.

The Dynamo Commerce Application is also made up of two parts. The first is the Ad Station, an advertising management product that targets delivery of the entire media range of Web-based ads based on user profiles and behavioral information. Ad Station includes ad response measurement and reporting and audience analysis features, in addition to core ad server functions. The other part is the Retail Station, which provides catalog, storefront, site design, and shopping-cart build and management capabilities for commerce site developers. Retail Station also offers ongoing administration applications for store management, inventory, and sales personnel.

Although buyers may purchase any of the products individually, ATG designed the products to work in concert as a total business-to-consumer "relationship commerce" solution. In addition, ATG offers design and related services in support of its relationship commerce product line. ATG provides turnkey customization of this Java-based electronic commerce system.

www.atg.com

Aptex

Aptex is a subsidiary of HNC, a neural network company and a world leader in monitoring for credit card fraud. Aptex is a company using both proprietary real-time content analysis techniques coupled with neural networks to predict web user behavior; they call it Content Mining technology. Aptex's two core products are *SelectCast* and *SelectResponse*. Both products are designed to enhance customer relationships, personalize one-to-one marketing, and attract potential customers by engaging their interests and motivating them to make online purchases.

SelectCast is designed to assist online publishers and retailers by attracting and retaining customers, delivering targeted one-to-one product recommendations, promotions, content, and advertising based on real-time behavior. SelectCast customers include Advanta, Excite, Infoseek, MatchLogic, and Cendant. Aptex claims SelectCast for Ad Servers is able to boost ad clickthrough over other targeting methods by making each ad an independent, intelligent agent that continuously seeks out interested users. The "agents" make decisions based on real-time user behavior, reacting instantly to serve more impressions to groups of users that demonstrate interest based on the content of current and recent page views, queries, clicks, and ad impressions.

SelectResponse is designed to enhance and personalize customer interactions through automating online e-mail, web, chat, and call-center responses to real-time customer inquiries. SelectResponse reads the content of customer inquiries and either responds, using FAQ documents and corporate knowledgebases, or it can route messages to the appropriate customer service agent with a suggested response.

One of the unique features of the Aptex profiling technology is that it doesn't store personal customer information. It instead uses a neural network to profile users based exclusively on their real-time actions and observed user behavior. Aptex claims their system can learn continuously a user's interests based on the content they browse on, the promotions they click on, and the products they eventually purchase. Among the features claimed by Aptex are the ability to target specific behavioral audiences and the delivery of designated promotional content. The ability to identify new audiences automatically as they emerge and to act as an "intelligent observer"—mining the context and content of all actions—including queries, page views, promotional impressions and clicks, and purchases.

Aptex's Content Mining technology uses a patented mathematical modeling technique it developed under a four-year U.S.-government contract and proprietary neural network algorithms derived from their parent company HNC. Aptex's Context Vector data modeling technique is supposed to "read" and "understand" unstructured text. This learning provides the basis for both interactive and automated decision-making based on the text and its internal relationships and for predictive modeling of future patterns, trends, and behaviors.

www.aptex.com

Autonomy

Autonomy sells a suite of Agent software products for commercial websites, ISPs, and information providers. The Agentware technology provides the ability to categorize, hyperlink, and present large volumes of text-based content automatically, without the need for manual input. Autonomy also claims the unique ability to automatically create "user profiles," which monitor and encode each individual's specific areas of interest and to deliver personalized information in real time. Autonomy is supposed to monitor the activities of site visitors and recognize their areas of interest, from which it develops individual interest-profiles.

Agentware Content Server is the nucleus of the Autonomy's products. Autonomy's Adaptive Probabilistic Concept Modeling (APCM) technology enables the Agentware software to identify and encode the unique "signature" of key concepts within text documents. APCM then uses this signature of the concept, a Concept Agent, to seek out and uncover the presence of similar concepts in volumes of content such as a set of similar products, pages, or websites. Autonomy's technology is based in part on neural networks and Bayesian statistics. Autonomy technology allows for collaborative filtering, eliminating the use of forms at websites—it instead makes recommendations based on the preferences of users with similar tastes and allows for the creation of user profiles.

www.agentware.com

BroadVision

BroadVision One-To-One is a server software application system. It incorporates a suite of management tools that allow a web adminis-

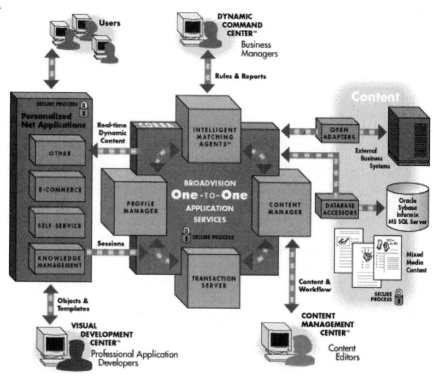

trator to dynamically control multiple server applications. The suite of tools includes:

- Intelligent Matching Agents, which are tools that dynamically match user profiles with content. (The intelligent matching feature can be driven by business managers, users, or agents.)
- Content/Data, which includes BroadVision content that is stored in relational databases plus content/data from any existing business system, host, or legacy database. (See Figure 7–9.)
- Transaction Server provides end-to-end, secure management of transactions that can be customized to meet business needs.
- Profile Manager, which manages user-profiles including information supplied by the user, observed during sessions, or derived from existing customer databases.

Personalized Net Applications deliver individualized content in real time and provide secure interactions and transactions for consumers and business users.

BroadVision was issued a patent on a database system, which creates a "customer monitoring object" for each visitor. Referencing information relating to that visitor creates the object, which is stored in the customer information database and accessed when the visitor selects a product, makes a purchase, or requests information. The customer information database, which the BroadVision system creates, can be mined to uncover important hidden patterns about activity in that website. BroadVision stresses the marketing concepts of one-to-one marketing espoused by Rogers and Pepper and has designed their software to provide the type of retailing model their popular marketing books describe.

www.broadvision.com

DoubleClick

DoubleClick is a provider of targeted ads over a group of large networked commercial websites. The DoubleClick system tracks user movements between various member websites run by clients on their advertising networks. DoubleClick is able to serve up a unique ad for each user, depending upon a user's interests as expressed via their selections in the websites that are part of the DoubleClick network (Figure 7–10). The DoubleClick Network consists of a collection of over 60 highly trafficked sites that commingle their cookies in order to place the appropriate ad to visitors. The Network of sites use

Figure 7–10
DoubleClick is in the business of putting the "right" ad in front of the "right" visitor.

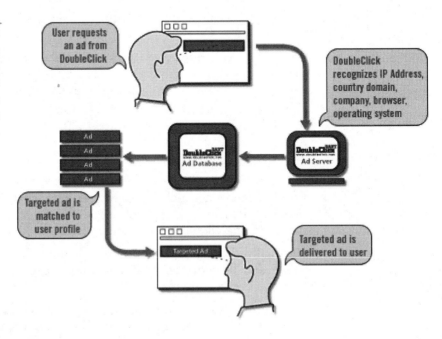

DoubleClick's proprietary DART targeting technology that allows advertisers to target their best prospects based on the most precise profiling criteria available.

DoubleClick uses its network of sites to collect information on where users have gone and what they are likely to respond to positively. DoubleClick also uses a feature that allows clients to deliver demographically targeted ads based on the site's own database of user registration information. DART, which is DoubleClick's proprietary ad targeting and reporting technology, was once available only to affiliate sites of the DoubleClick Network. However, the company recently began providing its DART Service to other sites. The newly enhanced DART technology aggregates information, voluntarily offered by the user, in a website's database against DoubleClick's other targeting criteria, such as company name and geographic location. The DART data that is being captured may be used in conjunction with a website's own data. This aggregated data may also be mined to extract customer profiles and additional insight.

www.doubleclick.com

Engage Technologies

Engage Technologies sells software that is designed to enable sites to distinguish anonymous and registered visitors and customers. Engage Technologies products include the Engage Suite, which is made up of:

- Engage.Journal, for website data collection and visitor individualization.
- Engage.Portrait, for customizable website registration management system.
- Engage.Discover, for customizable usage analysis, reporting, and iterative querying against website data.
- Engage.Link, for high-performance API leveraging user profile data for personalized content generation.
- Engage.Knowledge services allow website members who are "Engage-Enabled" to access their proprietary database of millions of Internet user profiles, which include historic and multi-site views of anonymous, individual users' interests, experiences and usage patterns.
- Engage.Knowledge Real-Time Visitor Intelligence is a usage-based subscription service that provides immediate access to the world's

largest database of behavior-based profiles of anonymous Website visitors. By accessing this database, members can use multi-site interest profiles of their visitors for use in real-time personalization applications and ad targeting.

- Engage.Journal, which offers organizations a standardized method of automating the capture, integration, and management of website visitor data.

Engage.Journal identifies individual website visitors using global and local "certificates." These certificates link visitor identifications to anonymous log statistics, including page requests, the domain from which they originate, and interest classifications based on the content they view. Certificate information can also be transmitted to a global server, housed either at Engage Technologies or at an organization's site, which allows visitor information to be captured and correlated across multiple websites and Internet domains.

Engage.Journal works with Netscape's NSAPITM and Microsoft's ISAPITM to log user actions and issue certificates. When a customer or prospect first visits your website, Engage.Journal automatically issues that user a unique local certificate that identifies the user anonymously during the current session and all future sessions. This process provides a standardized method for identifying and observing unique visitors within a single website or across a network of websites and allows for profiling, analysis, and personalized marketing activities to anonymous individuals.

Engage.Journal can be used separately or in partnership with the Engage.Portrait, Engage.Link, and Engage.Discover products. Engage.Portrait is a complete, customizable website registration system that records and leverages demographic and psychographic information about visitors to an organization's website. Engage.Portrait includes a wide array of demographic and psychographic categories to choose from when designing registration forms. These categories range from personal information, such as name, address, and marital status, to professional information including business interests, job function, industry, and size of company. Engage.Portrait includes affinity information that allows you to build profiles of your website customers and prospects based on general and specific areas of interest. The Engage system uses declared data from registration forms or observed behavior either globally or site-specific, as well as overlaid demographic and lifestyle data to suggest propensity to action. This data of course can also be mined for clustering, segmentation, classification, and prediction of customer behavior.

www.engagetech.com

Firefly

Firefly started as an application based on "agent" technology, a collaborative filtering engine that runs on a server and provides advice to website visitors based on their own tastes and on others with similar preferences. Pattie Maes from the MIT Media Lab developed Firefly as an intelligent, active, and personalized agent collaborator. The idea behind collaborative filtering or agents is that instead of user-initiated interaction via commands of direct queries, the visitor is engaged in a cooperative process in which the software initiates communication, monitors events, and performs tasks. The concept of the original Firefly "agent" was that it would become gradually more effective as it learned a visitor's interests, habits, and preferences. Firefly was one of the first collaborative filtering firms, having started at the MIT Media Lab. It was subsequently purchased by Microsoft.

In the core technology of Firefly, an agent memorizes which books, CDs, or other consumer items a visitor or customer has evaluated and purchased. Then it compares these preferences with other agents, correlating them with similar items and values—correlating them and assigning a value of "similarity" which it uses to recommend future books, CDs, etc. The important concept hidden in the application is that the agent gradually "learns" how to better assist the client, much like the corner store clerk who has observed your preferences. An agent learns by observing and imitating the customer, receiving feedback and instructions from the customer, and asking advice from other agents.

Firefly's flagship product, called Firefly Passport, is used to collect user preferences anonymously, recommend Internet content, and send appropriate advertising. Passport, makes it possible for sites to register visitors and exchange user profiles with other Firefly-enabled sites. The company's one-time goal was to build a network of such sites and deliver personalized content and community services to registered users.

The Firefly Navigator Catalog lets sites steer users toward products by creating personalized lists of recommendations and connecting users with similar interests. The Firefly Network Hub allows for the network administration with affiliated sites. The data that Firefly aggregates can also be merged with your own transactional data for subsequent mining, giving you the ability to tailor your offers and presentations to fit your visitors' and customers' needs.

www.firefly.net

GuestTrack

GuestTrack is another personalization and tracking software system designed to gather and store information about each visitor and personalize content "on the fly." GuestTrack uses a profile database to ask users questions on practically any Web page, and store the information in their personal profile. The GuestTrack ID is stored in the user's bookmark file, and most GuestTrack personalization is done with special tags in the HTML file. GuestTrack logs every web page displayed to every user so you can develop a "clickstream" view of what they saw, when they saw it, and for how long. Included in the GuestTrack system is an export module that creates a standard comma-delimited file that is compatible with most major database and spreadsheet programs. This provides the ability to sort, select, tabulate, report, and mine the data. The log contains the date and time in both traditional and Unix formats, as well as the individual's GuestTrack ID and the web page displayed. This data is exportable to data mining software for in-depth analysis.

With GuestTrack, companies can customize a guest book that allows users to store profile information and "tag" each user with a unique ID that is recalled each time they visit their Website. A feature of GuestTrack is the "include" function that allows sites to modify one file and have it instantly affect all HTML files that included that changed file. One of the frequent uses for the "include" function involves the navigation links that are repeated on practically every file within the website. Since an include file can use any GuestTrack personalization function, the included file can display profile information, modify links, or decide which piece of information to display. The feature allows for the customization of a site for every unique visitor. This is also very rich information, which can be culled and mined for insightful analysis via data mining.

GuestTrack also sells GT/Catalog, an interactive catalog system that builds upon the GuestTrack tracking and personalization software. GT/Catalog allows organizations to create web catalogs from scratch or use existing catalog product database. In addition to providing a full-featured catalog-shopping environment, the tracking and personalization features of GuestTrack allow businesses to display customized catalog pages by marrying product information with a customer's profile.

www.guestTrack.com

Gustos

Gustos Software develops and markets collaborative filtering Java software products and tool kits. The products are designed to integrate into existing websites to enable presentation of product recommendations or content that is personalized to each individual user. Gustos is designed to allow users to find the things they like and avoid those they don't. As with most collaborative "agent" software, Gustos is designed to be trained on visitor tastes and preferences.

The core of the system is the ability to find relationships between users, items, and ratings using collaborative filtering technology for making recommendations or predictions that can be derived by comparing a specific user's ratings to those of "like-minded" individuals. To benefit from Gustos, the user must entrust Gustos with certain information or it is impossible to get accurate results. To preserve anonymity, Gustos simply assigns a unique "cookie" ID to each visitor that chooses to enter ratings for items. Subsequent user ratings are tracked via this "cookie" so no user login is required.

The Gusto flagship product is StarRater. StarRater is a Java applet that a site can use to capture user ratings and give personalized recommendations to visitors. All data collected is stored and processed on central Gustos servers. StarRater provides several automatic functions such as "Recommended" and "Most Popular" item lists. "Gustos" is Spanish for preferences.

http://www.gustos.com

Internet Profiles Corporation (I/PRO)

I/PRO offers several auditing products to allow Websites and ad networks to deliver audited reports to their advertisers. Their flagship product is NetLine, an interactive measurement and analysis system. It automatically delivers a set of daily, weekly, and monthly reports designed to provide insight into the profile of a website's visitors and how they are using the site. Custom reports enable analysis of ad banner performance, activity of particular pages and files, and reports on domains that visit that site. NetLine is an outsourced solution and includes data management and storage, system support, and training. NetLine delivers pre-formatted presentation style reports through a user-friendly interface. Although this provider does not generate any content for mining, its reports may be of interest and provide additional insight to a large website.

www.ipro.com

IMGIS

The AdForce service from IMGIS is a full-service, end-to-end advertising management solution for ad networks and large websites (Figure 7–11). Like DoubleClick, IMGIS also uses cookies dispensed from member sites to positioned targeted banner ads.

AdForce is a service for the management and delivery of web advertising. Servicing the needs of agencies, websites, and ad sales networks, AdForce requires no hardware or software; it is an outsource service. AdForce provides advertisers the ability to target ads to all visitors by the type of content they are viewing, the time of day and day of the week, by keyword, by frequency (the number of times a visitor sees an ad), and by sequence (the order in which a series of ads are shown to a visitor).

AdForce Targeting Parameters

Content	Time of Day
Day of Week	Keywords
Frequency	Sequence Operating System
Browser Type	Internet Service
Provider Domain Name	Telephone Area Code
SIC Code	

Figure 7–11
The AdForce system from start to finish.

In addition, whenever an Internet visitor requests an advertisement (from AdForce or any other ad server), the request specifies the visitor's operating system (Windows, Macintosh, etc.), browser type (Microsoft Internet Explorer or Netscape Navigator), and IP address (e.g., 205.11.55.1). Using its database of IP addresses, AdForce is able to infer additional information about the visitor. For dial-up visitors, AdForce determines the visitor's Internet Service Provider. For corporate visitors, AdForce determines the visitor's domain name (e.g., .com or imgis.com), telephone area code, and SIC code.

www.imgis.com

InText

One of the products supplied by InText is WebInterests!, a software product that automatically watches for new information as it becomes available in a website, such as a news provider, then dynamically compares it to user interest profiles and delivers live via e-mails. WebInterests! allows for "Active Notification" providing website visitors with new information specifically of interest to them. It also allows users to describe their own interests by a few sentences or a set of concepts. Users can set relevance thresholds describing whether to route documents whose content closely matches their needs, or only touches on it. For lengthy documents, WebInterests! sends users automatically generated summaries. Of interest to data miners is the content of the profiles this product is able to create.

www.intext.com

LikeMinds

LikeMinds is another collaborative filtering tool able to assist websites to make personal recommendations and to offer direct marketing based on visitors' past behavior. Its *Preference Server* delivers personalized recommendations based on either preferences explicitly stated by the visitor or customer or implicitly determined by sales records, click throughs, or other user interactions within that site.

As with other collaborative filtering system, LikeMinds works by asking users to state their preferences about multiple topics. The software compares one user's preferences to others', finds people of similar tastes, then makes recommendations based on what similar users like. The software also can factor in preferences based on what a visitor buys or looks at on a site. LikeMinds tools also generate consumer data, which it calls "cybergraphics," that

Websites can use for direct marketing. Cybergraphics, LikeMinds claims, allows greater accuracy for targeting interested customers because it takes into account not just demographic data or psychographic data (based on what people say they like) but also the activity of site visitors.

LikeMinds is positioning itself against Firefly, which has the first collaborative filtering technology to hit the market. Firefly issues a "Firefly passport" that registrants can use on any site that licenses its tools. The data from all those sites is compiled in Firefly's database and used to make recommendations. In contrast, LikeMinds does not require its licensees to share their data, and it does not promote its own brand. Rather than offering a collaborative filtering service, LikeMinds delivers applications websites can use themselves.

LikeMinds recently merged with Andromedia, a website analysis software company. Demographic predictions can be incorporated into LikeMinds applications as "archetypes," allowing marketers to exploit existing databases of demographic information. LikeMinds generates data, which can be mined for additional insight and for profiling visitors. LikeMinds collaborative filtering technology can be used for personalizing based on consumer taste and behavior, while additional demographics and psychographics data coupled with machine learning and neural networks can enhance the overall performance of relational marketing.

www.likeminds.com

MatchLogic

MatchLogic is an online ad firm that integrates Internet advertising, database, and direct marketing into a single service company. Exclusively a service company, MatchLogic provides the management of ads. MatchLogic's core service is *TrueCount*, which tracks and manages banner ad impressions even on pages served from a cache on a proxy server (normally one of the chief stumbling blocks to effective online advertising management). MatchLogic developed the TrueCount technology at the request of General Motors in an effort to increase measurement standards as they relate to marketing on the Web. TrueCount is a very accurate method of counting and controlling all impression views that occur on a website, page, or advertising banner—even those normally hidden from counting by proxy servers and web browser caches. TrueCount not only counts, it also permits the optimization of the ads caught in proxy caches. It does this by controlling the rotation of the ads.

MatchLogic has five data centers in the United States and overseas, and currently serves ads on more than 2,500 sites. MatchLogic also has expanded to develop a marketing service. The new service, called DeliverE, currently has half a million users in its database, and MatchLogic expects that number to grow to five million. The basic premise behind DeliverE is one of sending e-mail to users who have opted in and soliciting information about their lifestyles and interests. MatchLogic offers a suite of services that enable advertisers and agencies to outsource their Internet advertising campaigns. It performs as an ad insertion network for advertisers and agencies, which pay up to $4 per thousand impressions for the company to place ads. It also measures their effectiveness and delivers real-time reports. This service may be of use in the data mining of your website since it can provide a more accurate view of what is actually happening at your server.

www.matchlogic.com

MicroMass

MicroMass sells software designed to develop and sustain unique individual customer relationships. MicroMass's proprietary IntelliWeb software assembles video, audio, text, and graphic images into individually tailored communication products at mass production levels. These communication products are based on individual profiles generated from customer database information. IntelliWeb personalizes messages by dynamically creating single web pages or entire websites based on information provided by each website visitor.

MicroMass links database information to individual content elements through the use of simple "if-then" statements. At runtime, the software pulls the appropriate content together based on an individual's database profile. Using this approach, messages can be sufficiently refined to provide each reader with a personal perspective. The IntelliWeb system can tie content databases to expert system-based rules/facts databases that are triggered when visitor's information is entered via a standard HTML form provided from a customer database or supplied by an individual's personal IntelliWeb Profile (Figure 7–12).

MicroMass claims it can create each web presence in real-time, based on the current *individual* profile of each website visitor. With the IntelliWeb Plug-In and IntelliWeb Profile Administrator, end-users can construct confidential profiles that automatically create personalized versions of an IntelliWebsite when the user enters. As more information is passed to the IntelliWeb Server, each message becomes increasingly more relevant and timely. MicroMass uses proprietary

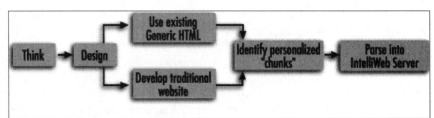

Figure 7–12
*MicroMass's
IntelliWeb links
web content to
web profiles.*

HTML tags to identify which areas to personalize, adding content as desired. This process breaks up a website into "chunks." When a user hits the site, IntelliWeb pulls together appropriate chunks in real-time based on that user's individual profile. The resulting content can also be mined in order to build lifetime value for each of these customers.

www.micromass.com

NetPerceptions

NetPerceptions is another software provider that allows for the profiling of website visitors based on real-time interaction and dynamically changes the contents of the website accordingly. NetPerceptions use strategies in which they ask customers to name favorite albums, for example, then predict other selections users might like. It is mining in real-time, based on purchase data customers provide and using that data to make recommendations.

The core technology of NetPerceptions' system is their GroupLens and Learning Intelligent software, which learns personal preferences about an individual. Working behind the scenes, GroupLens software observes what visitors actually do at a Website, rather than relying solely on what they may say about themselves in psychographic or demographic profiles. Preference information can be collected explicitly by directly asking individuals about their opinions on a particular subject. Information may be gathered implicitly, by inferring interest from specific actions and behaviors of visitors at a website using NetPerceptions software.

Learned personal information is used to predict how desirable a customer will find particular items. The information is matched up in real-time against a community of other individuals who have demonstrated similar purchase or preference behavior. This allows certain predictions to be formed about likes and dislikes. In addition, other prediction tools (e.g., expert reviews, market summaries) can be included in the GroupLens database and applied to the individuals for whom they add value.

Predictions are used to recommend products or services for consideration or promotion. The knowledge gathered by the GroupLens Recommendation Engine is presented to an online business for their further action. The business is then given the final opportunity to select only what it wishes to present or recommend to its customer. Obviously, the GroupLens database presents an excellent source of information that is ripe for data mining.

www.netperceptions.com

Vignette

Vignette Corporation provides software for sites who need to provide dynamic content-driven service applications, such as promotion, publishing, community, and customer support. Vignette flagship product is StoryServer4, which consists of four components to attract, engage, and retain website customers.

- *Lifecycle Personalization Services* is based on observed behavior and explicitly stated preferences. Three agents enable lifecycle personalization—Presentation Agent, Matching Agent, and Recommendation Agent. Each is useful at a particular stage of the customer relationship lifecycle, from arrival to the stage where the visitor becomes a trusting customer. The Recommendation Agent uses a collaborative-filtering technology based on Net Perceptions' GroupLens Express.

- *Open Profiling Services* has three key capabilities: content catalog, visitor registry, and the observation manager. These features manage and populate a centralized repository of visitor profile and content information. The observation manager gathers and stores information about visitor activity and behavior.

- *Advanced Content Management* provides advanced support for XML-based content, dynamic versioning of websites, and broad platform support for databases and Web servers.

- *Business Center.* This component provides an environment for managing and reporting on visitor profile and behavior data collected with the Open Profiling Services. A variety of reports can be created to gain a deep understanding of customer behavior and to fine tune the personalization capability of the website.

StoryServer 4 provides open access to a datamart of customer information for integration with other enterprise applications, including data mining analysis. The features of this product can be integrated with additional demographics and best of breed data mining tools.

www. vignette.com

Your Data Warehouse

Your company's data warehouse represents an additional source of information, which although it is not an external source, it can be linked to your website for data mining. Your data warehouse supports informational processing by providing a solid platform of integrated, historical data from which to do analysis, including of course customer profiling of online visitors and shoppers. One of the most valuable sources of customer information is that which is already in your own data warehouse. For this reason you should consider this as an additional resource that can be utilized for insight into the identity of your website visitors. For example, you may find certain inherent demographics in your existing clients which match those of certain visitors to your company's site.

A data warehouse provides the facility for integration of disparate application systems, from marketing, sales, operations, shipping—and now a company's website. A functional definition of data warehouse is that it must be a subject-oriented, integrated, and nonvolatile collection of data for decision support. One of the most important features of a data warehouse is that it is oriented toward the major subjects of the enterprise, such as its customers. A data warehouse is thus not only data-driven but subject orientated—in contrast to the classical data applications, which are organized around processes. For example, a bank's processing systems are built around such functions as loans, savings, bankcards, ATMs, marketing, real estate, sales, and investments. On the other hand, a bank's data warehouse is organized around a single major subject: its *customers*.

The differences between processing applications and subject applications show up quite differently in the content and detail of the data. A data warehouse contains very rich information about who its customers are and for this reason it can be used to match the demographics of website visitors. Data warehouse data is a long series of customer snapshots, which can be compared to those of your website visitors for similarities. For example, a bank can merge the data from its website with data from its warehouse to develop probability models and propensity profiles for one-to-one marketing of specific financial products, such as credit cards, bank loans, and CDs.

You should consider importing your web data into your data warehouse for enhancement with other customer files and mining. The linking of your data warehouse with your website represents the merging of the ultimate data depository with the ultimate marketing tool and delivery channel. On the Web your ability to target consumers leads to great efficiencies. You not only have the ability to reach only specific target audiences (avoiding waste), but also to learn more about your consumers so that you can service them more efficiently in the future. It is this process—the building of a one-to-one relationship—that can truly make your website a success.

Closing the Loop

The building of customer profiles comes not only from data mining but also from the data warehousing technique of constructing the object of your analysis from disparate components and sources. These customer attributes may well come from demographic providers as well as components created by collaborative software and finally your own warehouse. Your advertising, marketing, retailing, and business needs, as well as the products and services that you are providing, drive the components that you use in the profiling of your website visitors. For example, some information is slanted toward predicting financial behavior, such as Claritas' P$YCLE, while some is geared toward predicting online behavior, such as the content provided by Engage Technologies. Ideally you may want to assemble components from both types of providers to gain the optimum quality in your data for mining.

8

E-Retailing

Through data mining a company can synthesize website patterns into meaningful information, enabling it to individually distinguish, understand, and engage customers and prospects over the Web (Figure 8–1). The mining of transactional data and the vast flow of business intelligence it represents is the key to creating a lasting relation with online customers and establishing a productive website. The instant interactivity of web transactions breeds accelerated change in product design, delivery, and customer service. Make no mistake, electronic retailing is here to stay, and buying and selling will never be the same—for every transaction and "look" can now be digitized, aggregated, visualized, averaged, and (most importantly) mined.

In a networked environment with instantaneous connections, there is a huge premium on instant response and the ability to learn from and adapt to the marketplace in real-time. Winning electronic retailers accept this current culture of constant change and are willing to constantly break down and reconstruct their products and processes to evolve to their customers' expectations. Remember that data mining is about perception and learning; it is about artificial intelligence technologies being used to look for patterns in this fast changing business environment. Data mining is about using artificial intelligence technologies for business competitive intelligence. It is

Figure 8–1
Data mining is about recogniz-ing the signature of sales and the customer who made it.

```
1 "Number of Sales","Home Value","Vehicle Value","ZIP","Total Dollar Sales","Children","Gen
2 0,409490,"50000",90001,484,0,"0","30",8/29/97 0:00:00,0,0,0.00,0,0.00,0.00,0,0.00,0,0,0
3 3,409500,"50000",90003,541,2,"0","50",8/29/97 0:00:00,0,0,0.00,0,0.00,0.00,0,0.00,0,0,0
4 1,493590,"50000",90004,165,1,"0","44",9/13/97 0:00:00,3,0,0.00,0,0.00,0.00,1,14,0,
5 0,493600,"50000",90004,229,0,"0","40",9/15/97 0:00:00,3,0,0.00,0,0.00,0.00,1,14,0,
6 0,493610,"50000",90004,312,0,"0","44",9/13/97 0:00:00,3,0,0.00,0,0.00,0.00,1,14,0,
7 1,409510,"50000",90004,335,1,"0","35",8/29/97 0:00:00,3,0,0.00,0,0.00,0.00,1,14,0,
8 1,409530,"50000",90004,430,1,"0","40",8/29/97 0:00:00,3,0,0.00,0,0.00,0.00,1,14,0,
9 2,409520,"50000",90004,291,2,"0","40",8/29/97 0:00:00,3,0,0.00,0,0.00,0.00,1,14,0,
10 2,409550,"50000",90005,490,2,"0","44",8/29/97 0:00:00,2,0,0.00,0,0.00,0.00,0,13,0,
11 4,409560,"50000",90006,460,2,"0","44",8/29/97 0:00:00,0,0,0.00,0,0.00,0.00,0,3,0,0
12 1,409570,"50000",90008,214,1,"0","44",8/29/97 0:00:00,4,0,0.00,0,1.20,0.00,1,2,0,0
13 1,409630,"50000",90013,113,2,"0","40",8/29/97 0:00:00,0,0,0.00,0,0.00,0.00,0,0.9
14 1,409640,"50000",90016,493,1,"0","35",8/29/97 0:00:00,1,0,0.00,0,2.00,0.00,2,2,0,0
15 1,409650,"50000",90016,400,1,"0","50",8/29/97 0:00:00,1,0,0.00,0,2.00,0.00,2,2,0,0
16 1,409660,"50000",90016,520,1,"0","30",8/29/97 0:00:00,1,0,0.00,0,2.00,0.00,2,2,0,0
17 1,409670,"50000",90016,413,1,"0","30",8/29/97 0:00:00,1,0,0.00,0,2.00,0.00,2,2,0,0
18 0,409680,"50000",90016,141,0,"0","50",8/29/97 0:00:00,1,0,0.00,0,2.00,0.00,2,2,0,0
19 3,409690,"50000",90017,354,2,"0","44",8/29/97 0:00:00,0,0,0.00,0,0.00,0.00,0,0.0
20 2,409700,"50000",90017,170,2,"0","35",8/29/97 0:00:00,0,0,0.00,0,0.00,0.00,0,0.0
```

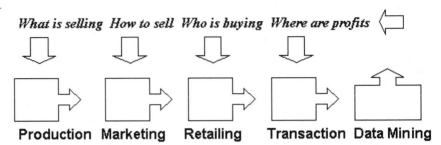

Figure 8–2
The cyclical relationship between data mining and electronic retailing.

also about evolving, and leveraging technologies and tools to quickly adapt to the flow of change of a digital networked marketplace that keeps expanding and accelerating.

The Web represents a unique retailing channel that by its very nature establishes a new type of foundation and structure for a close relation between the seller and the buyer. Electronic retailing enables the retailer to collect information about the consumer's tastes, rate of consumption, and preferences for products by quality, price, and volume—as they make their purchases. Unlike other retailing channels, the Web facilitates a one-to-one selling environment, allowing for tight interactions between retailers and consumers. Electronic retailing allows for two-way interaction, which feeds directly into a cycle of production, marketing, retailing, transaction, and mining (Figure 8–2). Data mining is an integral part of this retailing cycle, for it provides important insight into the consuming process, tendencies and attributes of customers. Data mining can answer the *what, how, who,* and *where* of electronic retailing:

The typical retailing distribution networks involving distributors, agents, and other middlemen are eroding. Already changes are starting to take affect in the buying and selling of airline tickets, stocks and mutual funds, car rentals, hardware and software, books, CDs, and a large range of digital products—everything from market reports to pornography. Electronic retailing changes not only the way products and services get distributed, it also impacts pricing—due in part to the customization of products and services—and the ability to use data mining technology in the analysis of consumer preferences. As the Web blurs the traditional concepts of retailing, the conventional relationships between consumers and retailers are gradually changing.

For example, I recently I purchased a sport utility vehicle, for which I had done some preliminary window shopping on the Web— some virtual tire kicking. By the time I walked into the physical auto dealership I knew more about that truck than the salesman did. I knew what engine options, colors, power features, and configurations the SUV came in, far more than the salesman did. I had already done some comparisons of several SUVs and knew exactly what I was buying. The Web makes consumers very informed buyers—more knowledgeable at times about product and services features, options, selections, and pricing than the traditional sales personnel.

The Product Is the Message

Unlike traditional retail channels, selling and buying on the Web truly take on the Marshall McLuhan adage, *"the medium is the message."* On the Web a digital product such as an e-mail message can contain as its content some digitized intelligence such as a company report, some market information or a stock quote, etc., and may be sold directly as a commodity or conversely used as a marketing component. On the Web "the message" can also be "the product" of the transaction or the medium for "the marketing offer." In the electronic retailing of digital products, the value of the transaction may well be in the content of the message. With the voluminous number of interactions that are occurring daily on the Web, McLuhan may well have seen it coming when he predicted that the only recourse to survival in our modern world would be pattern recognition.

Electronic retailing changes not only the distribution and marketing of products but more importantly it also alters the process of consumption and the related transactions of buying and selling. The data, which is an aftermath of every product and service purchased on the Web, is the ore that can be mined to develop customized products, forecast demand, profile customers, and improve relational marketing. Because of the interactive nature of electronic retailing, consumers not only order and buy products online, they also search for product specifications (thus revealing their preferences and criteria) and in some venues their willingness to pay.

The act of retailing on the Web is an interactive one in which the consumer can negotiate, exchange information, specify, and customize the product and services he or she wants from the retailer. For the electronic retailer it is of paramount importance that it analyze what consumers are doing and saying. Data mining can serve retailers by providing them the technology to understand how to sell more, learn what's working, and learn what's not. It can assist them in knowing how to personalize their storefront for repeat customers. As we discussed priorly, a data mining technology such as case-based reasoning (CBR) is similar to "collaborative filtering" software in that it can serve as a "recommendation engine" to suggests items that might interest a shopper, based on what similar shoppers are buying.

The potential for electronic commerce is immense due to the fact that a large number of services and products can be digitized. For example, all newspapers, magazines, articles, journals, and audio, video, and multimedia products can be sold online. This means you can use the Web to get stock quotes and buy movies, stamps, white papers, currency, concert tickets, hotel and airline reservations, and checks and other financial products. In fact products that require a minimum amount of descriptive information to advertise and of which there is a high number of different types and are cheap to ship are ideal for selling on the Web—books are the prime example.

In the traditional model of retailing, middlemen or bottlenecks controlled access to information between sellers and buyers. For example, insurance and travel agents typically control the access to information about claims, policies, and flights; they in turn processed inquiries and controlled pricing. However, this is changing today: with the advent of electronic commerce, the consumer is in control and can dictate the product they want to purchase and with what terms and conditions.

Data mining can be used to model patterns of behavior based on both the attributes of past web sessions and demographic information merged with the preference and customer data you gather at your website via your log files and registration forms. Propensity scores can be generated from the analysis of this data in order to predict the likelihood a visitor or customer will select an ad, banner, or a particular page in your website. Propensity to purchase the products and services on your website can also be modeled and scores can be generated in order to prioritize potential prospects for e-mail and special incentives and offers.

Figures 8–3 and 8–4 illustrate a sample session involving the development of a model designed to predict the selection of a specific page based on an analysis of thousands of sessions with demographic data matched against the website visitors' ZIP code as captured at a registration form. The data mining tool incorporates a neural network to construct a propensity to purchase model.

C code can then be generated from the data mining analysis for the scoring of propensity to buy for new unseen visitors and customers.

Figure 8–3
The network
begins to slowly
evaluate several
input variables.

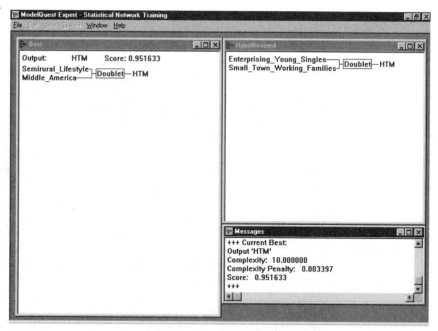

Figure 8–3
The network begins to slowly evaluate several input variables.

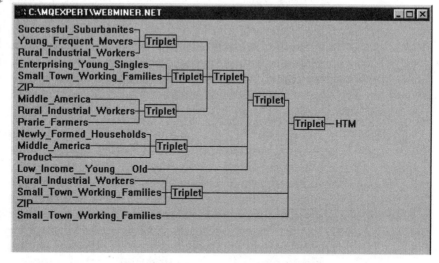

Figure 8–4
Eventually the data mining tool converges on a model.

```
double *webminer(double inarr[]){
double Successful_Suburbanites = inarr[4]; /* rename input for clarity */
double Product = inarr[45]; /* rename input for clarity */
static double outarr[1]; /* declare output array */
double HTM    ; /* rename output for clarity */
double node5  ; /* working variable */
/* node5—Successful_Suburbanites */
```

```
node5  = -1.19493 + 0.032543*LIMIT(Successful_Suburbanites,0,82.9);
 /* node5-Triplet */
node5  = 0 + 5.19459 + 15.1832*node14 - 61.5623*pow2(node14)
        + 15.62*pow3(node14) - 4.98188*node34
        - 13.6275*node14*node34 + 60.8895*pow2(node14)*node34
        + 0.0592666*pow2(node34) + 0.00802485*pow3(node34)
        - 4.45746*node44 - 25.4388*node14*node44
        - 20.8693*pow2(node14)*node44 + 0.519106*node34*node44
+ 0.105443*pow2(node34)*node44 - 3.17381*pow2(node44)
     - 18.6362*node14*pow2(node44) + 0.408554*node34*pow2(node44)
        + 0.295813*pow3(node44) ;
HTM = 0 + 75.1651 + 2.7993*node48 ;  /* perform output limiting on HTM */
HTM = LIMIT( HTM, 69, 79 );  outarr[0] = HTM ;  /* output value */
return( outarr ); /* output array */}
```

Sale Segmentation

To establish a competitive presence on the Web today and in the future you need to design your site to interact with your visitors. Your website is an antenna for receiving, not just a medium for pushing products and data. Your retailing site needs to establish a dialogue with your clients to better position appropriate messages, products, and services. Your website increasingly assumes a mission critical role for your company—it provides not only a new marketing channel, but more importantly an opportunity for discovering who your current and potential new customers are. The combination of data mining technology in a networked environment totally changes the traditional concepts of marketing and commerce. This is because electronic retailing changes the fundamental buyer and seller relationship.

Online selling is not simply about dispensing products. It is also about providing an ongoing service to your customers. Electronic retailing is driven by relations marketing and data mining; it is about selling to a single customer as many products as possible over their consuming lifetime. Online commerce is also about learning about your customers' likes and dislikes with each sale. Subsequently, the content of online transactions matters more than in traditional retailing. Each interaction and purchase is an opportunity for the electronic retailer to capture data about its customers and learn about their preferences. Electronic retailing is about encouraging continuous contact with your customers and incrementally improving your relations with them. In a digitized networked environment anything that tightens your relation with a customer increases your revenue potential.

The size of firms doing electronic retailing is not a significant factor in this type of marketplace. What is most important is the ability of the smart retailer to personalize their responses to each of their customers' needs and desires. An electronic retailer of any size can be competitive in this marketplace as long as it is capturing important transactional and customer information and leveraging data mining to enhance the service and quality of communications it provides to its clients.

On the Web shoppers can search for product information and do side-by-side comparison in a completely open marketplace. Online buyers have a dramatic new power to barter, bid, and compare for the best prices on products and services. Consumers today are assisted by new services, websites, and software that can quite easily retrieve the best available prices. In this type of marketplace your competitor is always a mouse-click away.

To stay competitive and attract and retain customers, it is important to provide an extra-added service along with low costs. You must personalize your products and services, making it difficult for customers to leave. Those firms that rely on physical barriers or traditional brand advertising and retailing channels to combat competition will eventually fail in this fast evolving environment. The winners will be those merchants who recognize the value of transactional data and mine it for all it's worth.

Monitoring the relationships with your customers in a digitized environment involves the mining of your data. This entails an analysis of all repeat visitors as well as those who have made purchases but have stopped buying from you. Periodically you may need to do a data mining analysis of your dormant customer accounts to investigate why they have stopped buying from you. In order to ascertain what kind of product they may be interested in, do a clustering analysis of products purchased by visitors with similar demographics. Make a special offer to encourage dormant customers to take the time to answer your "please come back" e-mail. Send a "we missed you" e-mail message, and ask them why they have not returned since their last purchase of "Product Z." Tell them of a special offer for a similar product they may be interested in based on your data mining analysis.

Cultivating existing customers is the most cost-effective strategy you can pursue in retailing on the Web. They represent visitors who appreciate your products and services, and you need to establish a strategy for retaining them. Do this via e-mail informing them of products they are likely to be interested in based on prior purchases and the interests they have indicated on their registration forms or through their prior interactions. Of course, data mining can also reveal what product they are likely to be interested in based on affinity analysis using association and segmentation tools. Cultivate your

Figure 8–5
*This decision
tree analysis
reveals no sales
for visitors with
Last Visit over
90 days.*

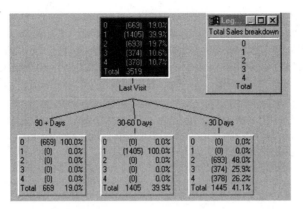

current customers, prize them, and reward them for buying from you again and again. A data mining analysis of your interaction with your customers can reveal those clients who represent most of your sales as well as those who are effectively dormant and who you may want to e-mail for purposes of making them profitable again (Figure 8–5).

This data mining analysis used a segmentation tool to generate a decision tree view of customers by the number of sales they have made in relation to the number of days since they last visited this website. For example, this decision tree found that:

IF   Last Visit = –30 Days

THEN

      Total Sales = 2   48.0%

      Total Sales = 3   25.9%

      Total Sales = 4   26.2%

The propensity to buy deteriorates quite quickly on the Web when interactivity drops, which can be remedied via an e-mail campaign. Effective e-mail interaction, however, should not be perceived as intrusive and you should ask for permission from your customers prior to sending them any e-mail. Offer legitimate incentives and send only quick personal messages. Ensure that you allow customers the option to discontinue receiving messages and include your address in the body of the message for single click access to your website. Lastly, don't keep sending messages to nonrespondents and don't send the same message more than once. There are several mass mail systems that can help you automate some of this process.

The Digital Marketplace

In the digital marketplace the buyers come to the retailer, and advertising is iterative with the consumer interacting with the ad and participating in the content of the message. Because of the digital nature of the banner or ad on the Web, selection of the audience and measurement of the participants of the advertisement are relatively easy. One of the unique abilities for shopping in this marketplace is the ability to automate the indexing and cataloging of product information. Queries for product information generate a trail of information about consumer demand and tastes, which can be mined. Data mining of this product and preferences information can result in the refining of your inventory and product development. It enables electronic retailers to eliminate waste and provide targeted products designed to meet specific consumer preferences. Measurement of clickthroughs or the requests for additional product information via a form can be stored for data mining analysis.

The mode of shopping in this marketplace is driven by "keyword" searches, which the retailer may use to position itself and its advertisements at the major directories like Lycos. Search engines such as Infoseek are positioned to not only guide consumers toward retailers, but more importantly they can monitor visitor activity and preferences. These engines can monitor consumer preferences based on keyword searches they make and associate them with the visitor information they provide in the personalization of their news, weather, stocks, etc., especially at such popular websites as my.yahoo.com, my.excite.com, or my.whatever.com (Figures 8–6 and 8–7). These search engines can become great sources of cross-reference information about consumers. The engines not only can customize products for the consumer, but by revealing their preferences consumers can drive the design of products and pricing.

The essence of targeted marketing on the Web lies in the ability for consumers to interact with retailers and the search engines that they use to browse the marketplace. Advertising on the Web can be driven by the consumers' choice of search keywords, allowing for real-time targeting which can in turn be linked to data mining, market research, distribution, and sales. Data mining can be used to analyze the consumer information gathered by these engines in order to customize the services and content they provided to their visitors. Retailers are better able to provide customized products and services based on specific preferences, rather than average tastes. As the Web grows in size and complexity, consumers will increasingly reveal their preferences

Figure 8–6
*The personaliza-
tion of the Web
can target the
content you
receive.*

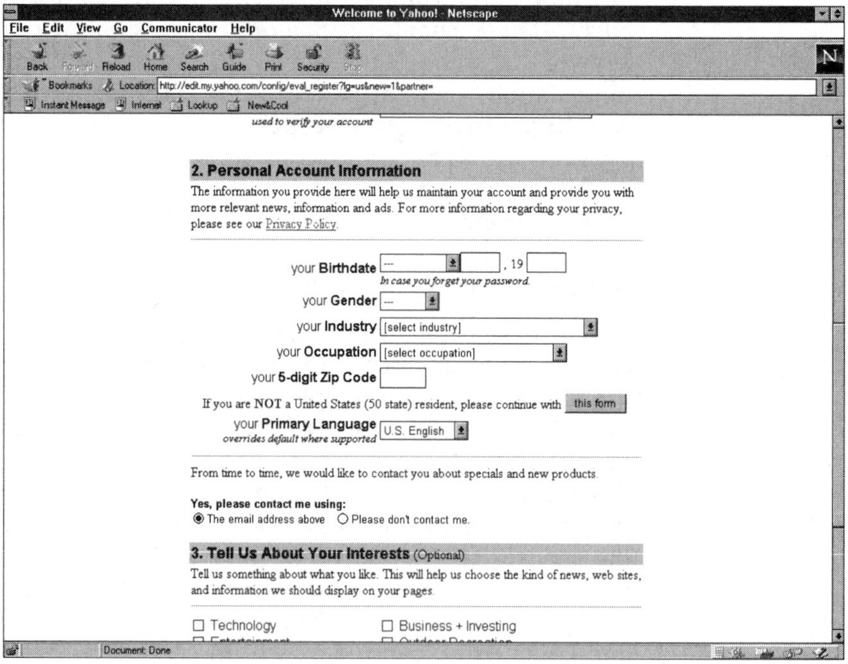

Figure 8–7
*The information
you provide
about yourself
can be mined.*

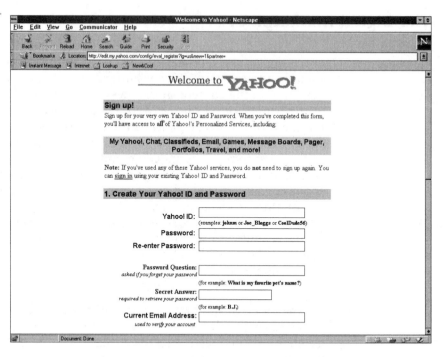

in order to get above-average quality in their products and services quickly and efficiently and in order to dictate selection and pricing.

This type of marketplace enables consumers to deal directly with manufacturers of products and services, eliminating middlemen. The Web reduces the number of intermediary steps necessary for doing business and trade. The Web hardwires the topography in which the buyers and retailers exchange goods directly instead of through intermediaries, creating a more efficient market. In this type of marketplace the creator and seller of products and services is able to deal directly with consumers and thus know who they are and what their preferences are. Electronic retailing radically changes the manner in which products are distributed, sold, and priced. The costs associated with the production of personalized digital products, such as for reports, news, or quotes, can vary for each customer.

This type of networked market in which buyers can deal directly with sellers seriously threatens traditional distributors and agents. But a new brand of middleman software or search agents may be created as the Web continues to expand and electronic retailing grows. As the amount of information clutter increases, new forms of agent software or specialists using special data mining technology will evolve to sift and sort through massive amounts of data into usable consumer information, or to negotiate pricing. These new agents or rovers will offer aggregated services, or intelligent customer assistance using data mining technology to provide product-based searches based on pre-arranged prices or consumer conditions. These new middlemen will sift through the ever-expanding digital marketplace in search for the products and services their clients have commissioned them to locate at the price they are willing to pay.

Product Customization

Because products and services can be customized to meet the specific needs of consumers a high degree of satisfaction can be obtained in this type of marketplace. In turn, the consumers obtain a high amount of value from customized products than traditional off-the-shelf products. Data mining can be used to converge on consumer preferences and assist in the customization of product design. Products can be manufactured to match the specific demands of specific consumers, which in turn leads to a high degree of customer retention and loyalty.

A high degree of product customization discourages customer attrition or churn. Customization of products and services discour-

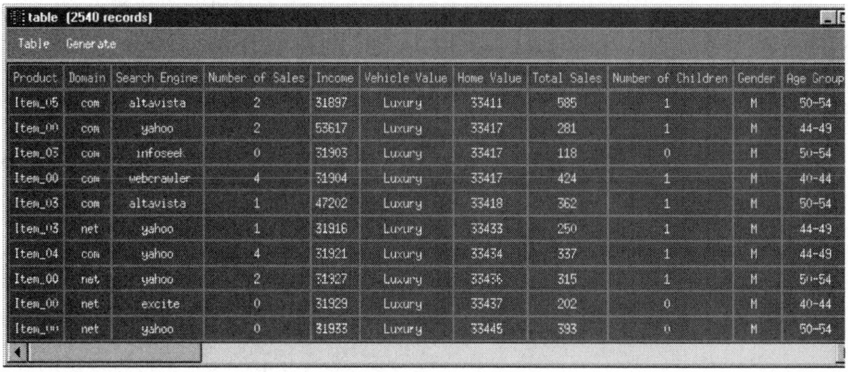

Figure 8–8
*Your web server
data can be
merged with
demographic
information for
mining.*

Product	Domain	Search Engine	Number of Sales	Income	Vehicle Value	Home Value	Total Sales	Number of Children	Gender	Age Group
Item_05	com	altavista	2	31897	Luxury	33411	585	1	M	50–54
Item_00	com	yahoo	2	53617	Luxury	33417	281	1	M	44–49
Item_03	com	infoseek	0	31903	Luxury	33417	118	0	M	50–54
Item_00	com	webcrawler	4	31904	Luxury	33417	424	1	M	40–44
Item_03	com	altavista	1	47202	Luxury	33418	362	1	M	50–54
Item_03	net	yahoo	1	31916	Luxury	33433	250	1	M	44–49
Item_04	com	yahoo	4	31921	Luxury	33434	337	1	M	44–49
Item_00	net	yahoo	2	31927	Luxury	33436	315	1	M	50–54
Item_00	net	excite	0	31929	Luxury	33437	202	0	M	40–44
Item_00	net	yahoo	0	31933	Luxury	33445	393	0	M	50–54

ages consumers from reselling or sharing of products, which they have developed, based on their unique needs. For example, my interests in music or books is not likely to be the same as yours. This is especially advantageous for real-time digital products, such as stock reports, which can be produced easily by the retailer—allowing for the pricing to be set on the basis of the consumers' willingness to pay. However, in order to effectively customize products and charge individualized prices, the retailer is required to have detailed knowledge about the consumers' preferences. This type of consumer knowledge and customer profiling can be obtained through the strategic use of data mining technology and techniques.

The economic impact of personalization and customization on the Web is accelerated when data mining technology is used. It's a one-on-one game. Information is easier to customize than hard goods. The information portion of any good or service is becoming a larger part of its total value. Thus, suppliers and retailers will find it easier and more profitable to customize products. In this type of electronic marketplace consumers will gradually begin to demand this type of customized tailoring from the products they consume. With increased customization of products and services, homogeneous pricing will no longer be practical or applicable. It will also mean that consumers will come to accept the fact that in order to receive premiere service and custom products, they will need to share personal preference information with their trusted retailers—personal customer information which can be mined in order to maximize the efficiency and value of the products and services being sold online.

In a traditional marketplace where products and services are sold by various competitors, they tend to be similar in functionality with the only difference between them being their price. However, if products and services are customized then the retailer can negotiate a price with each consumer. Customization also means product differentiation is based on the degree of dissimilarity. Customization means retailers differentiate products and services by adding extra value and thus reducing customer attrition. Time, for example, can be a function by which a product is priced. A product's timeliness in a networked environment and its detail level or response time can be used to determine its value to the consumer. All of these pricing and customization factors can best be achieved by the use of data mining to calibrate their degrees of detail, value, and time.

In a digitized marketplace retailers are able to gain detailed information about their customers' attributes and preferences in order to customize products and services without much added cost. In addition, since products are custom built, customers can be billed independently, which in the traditional marketplace would be difficult if not impossible to do, due to product variation and elaborate billing costs. However, in a digitized marketplace, transaction costs are low and the retailer has information about each consumer valuation and is easily able to negotiate prices independently on a one-to-one basis. In a digitized marketplace it is easy for the retailer to gather information, which can be mined in order to learn about the consumers' purchasing behavior. In the end, marketing, retailing, and data mining in a networked and digitized environment mean that the emphasis is on the interaction between the retailer and the consumer.

Consumer Profiling

Database marketing has always relied on the use of consumer information to target offers via mail. Consumers are often required to disclose and provide some form of personal data in most transactions involving the extension of credit or the use of noncash payment, both of which leave a trail of personal information that is often used and then re-sold to third parties who dissect, cross reference, and aggregate the data evolving into secondary consumer information often sold again by such companies as Experian and Polk. Usually this information is aggregated at the household level, which can vary in detail, but may contain the value of your home, the type of auto you drive, and the number of children that you have.

Yet another type of profiling involves the granting of credit, in which case a financial transaction is involved which legally allows the retailer, such as a renter or auto dealership, the right to obtain an individual's credit consumer report. There are several types of reports assembled by Trans Union, Equifax, and Experian (formerly TRW), which aggregate and assemble this information in different formats:

- *An individual identity profile:* This includes names and aliases used, as well as current and associated addresses (multiple), date of birth, marital status, and social security numbers used.

- *An employment profile:* Present position description, length of employment, and previous positions.

- *A public record profile:* A record of every civil suit, judgment, tax lien, bankruptcy, and legal proceeding recorded in a local, state, and federal court involving a monetary obligation.

- *A credit history profile:* This will list every grantor account you have including credit cards, debit cards, revolving accounts, auto loans, mortgages, etc. This section will detail when the accounts were established, how much you owe, and how much you pay on a monthly basis. It will contain account activity information detailing when you were late for any payment. It will also contain a trail of inquiries made by grantors and government agencies who have requested and paid to see your credit report.

These three national credit bureaus gather extensive credit and financial data on virtually every adult in the nation, for use by banks, mortgage companies, and credit-card issuers that need the information when deciding whether to make a loan or issue a credit card. The law prohibits the release of credit data in most circumstances, unless a consumer authorizes it—explicitly by signing a release, or implicitly by applying for a loan or credit.

The electronic marketplace allows for a different type of profiling. This type of profiling is based on user preferences and online behavior, much of which is captured from log files, cookies, registration forms, collaborative software, and server networks. This type of information is used to position the appropriate ad and messages based on observed behavior and explicit selections and preferences. Electronic retailing and consumer profiling deal with digital products, which are fundamentally different from other type of consumer items. Retailers and consumers in a digitized marketplace actively interact to influence each other to determine the product specifications, quality, volume, and price.

One of the functions of digitized products and services is that of their filtering features. This would be in the form of customizing news, reports, and information feeds, or the monitoring of markets, events, or stock activity, all based on personal profiles. The ability to effectively customize products and services has always depended on the ability of the retailer or marketer to know something about the likes and dislikes of the targeted consumer. If consumer tastes vary greatly, as can be the case with such products as software or books, then these products benefit from being highly differentiated. In traditional marketplaces this used to be done in part through warranty cards and market surveys. However, in today's digitized marketplace, the consumer information is hardwired to the retailer since not only does the buyer reveal the methods of distribution they require but also the type of products they want, the rate they want them at, and how much they are willing to pay for them. All are values that can be mined for the refinement and delivery of products and services by retailer.

Consider your customers and the data, which you are mining as the basis for the evolution and development of your website. Solicit feedback via e-mail from first-time buyers. Did they find what they wanted? How long did it take? What else should you be doing at your website in order to get your first-time buyers to return and buy again and again. How do you transform first-time buyers into loyal customers? Asking them is one way; another is doing an analysis of your website data. Use data mining tools such as decision trees and rule generators to segment your visitors and develop profiles of your existing customers. Use these analyses to find out what your visitor information requirements are. How did they arrive at your site? Are they looking for a leisurely browsing experience or the fastest path to a specific product or service at your site?

Your data mining analysis may identify several different market segments that are attracted to your website, which may impact how you organize your site. For example, a travel site may find that it is attracting travel agent professionals, people who do not travel much, die-hard travelers, and investors. This may point out the need to design different website sections in the home page targeted to these four different types of visitors. Data mining may also uncover what visitors are browsing for by analyzing the keywords they are using in their quest for product information. Poring over log files, registration forms, and e-mail can uncover some hints; however, using a data mining tool can accelerate this process and point out hidden patterns manual inspection may not detect, especially for a heavily visited site with thousands of daily visitors.

Electronic retailing is really about linking your back-end inventory database to the browsers of your visitors and customers. In the process, however, you have the opportunity to observe the interactions and patterns which can evolve over time. Data mining can assist you in uncovering these patterns and assist you in improving your retailing efforts and your relationship with your customers. With so much choice on the Web, the key differentiation is personalization. The mining of your customer preference information is the key to improving your relationships and personalizing your products, services, and communications with your visitors. Your data mining analysis can assist you in developing new insights into your visitors' behavior and your website's performance in meeting their needs.

Real-Time Buying

A large percentage of Americans have purchased something online, so that despite the fact that people see security concerns as a drawback to shopping on the Web, these concerns are evidently not enough to halt the wheels of commerce or hinder the growth of electronic retailing. For those who do buy online, benefits like not having to go to the store and around-the-clock shopping outweigh the disadvantages or concerns about privacy and security. There is also a new business model, which is prompting online transactions: online bidding auctions. The stimulating forces of greed, cheap prices, and getting something for less are driving this model of online retailing.

Single-click convenience and choice make up yet another business model driving the increasing prominence of small retailing products, such as book and music purveyors like Amazon.com. Electronic retailers continue to address security issues, since consumers who haven't bought through the Web say the primary reason is concern about giving out their credit card number. However, consumers are beginning to realize the advantages of electronic commerce, that is, that every product is available everywhere. The gap between desire and purchase has closed. The shelf space of the Web is unlike any other in that it has no bounds.

Artificial constraints on choice are replaced by the ability to purchase the precise product you desire, anytime, anywhere. The impulse to buy and the purchase itself used to be separated by a combination of physical and mental barriers. No more with the Web. Today you can discover the "right" product you desire and hit the "buy" button and the product will be FedExed to you that day. The entire retailing processes for marketing, sales, and fulfillment are merging into a single digitized transaction, which is recorded, stored, and made ready for data mining.

The ability to greet former customers with a personalized message or offer is possible with the utilization of a multitude of techniques and tools. These components include your website log files, server, and browser site cookies, and registration forms. The data in your website can further be enhanced by merging or appending it with household and demographic databases, or by the use of collaborative software and the networking with other websites. Of course, to gain the most value from all of this customer information the use of powerful pattern-recognition tools can allow you to know your client at a one-to-one level.

The more customized and personalized your website is, the more products and services you are likely to sell. For example, a bank may mine the data from its website and data warehouse and discover a correlation between high account balance customers and specific pages for products such as investment services or other types of bank accounts. This analysis may also reveal higher-than-average click-throughs for certain ads and banners with such messages as "Make your money work for you." Through the analysis of current and recent user behavior—that is, the content visitors are looking for as well as the content they use in their e-mail or registration forms—you can make some subtle adjustments in your website. For example, are visitors using certain keywords indicating an interest in investments, such as "investment for retirement," "good stocks," or "mutual funds"? The web designer of this banking site may want to make changes or provide the type of information on planning for retirement and investments—courting to the specific interests of these visitors.

Data mining this type of information can lead you to select the appropriate advertising, product, offer, section, incentive, coupon, banner, or wording. For example, an analysis using a data mining tool incorporating a rule-generating algorithm may uncover the following pattern:

IF KEYWORD	"camping"	
OR KEYWORD	"hiking"	
OR KEYWORD	"mountain"	
AND AGE	42	
AND ZIP	94502	
AND GENDER	MALE	
THEN	Sports Utility Vehicle Ad	89%
	Sedan Ad	11%

The demographics breakdown for this ZIP code reveals that the following type of consumers populate it:

52.14% *are very high-income married couples, age 40 to 54, with one or two children, who snow ski, collect coins, entertain at home, do aerobics, vote, read books, and contribute to PBS. They tend to buy imported beer, sport/utility vehicles, home gym systems, use copy services, and buy items by phone, mail, and the Web. They are business owners, use ATM cards to buy goods, have term-life insurance, IRAs, and belong to limited partnerships. They live in suburbs along the California coast, and the Boston-Washington corridor.*

20.67% *are very high-income married couples, age 40 to 54, with two or more children, who go to movies, visit zoos, go swimming and to the beach, engage in fundraising, and eat at fast-food restaurants. They buy "big ticket" furniture items, tennis equipment, video games, toys, jewelry, and boats. They have money market funds, savings bonds, passbook accounts, overdraft protection, group life insurance, and bank near work. They read business, computer, and sports magazines; listen to soft contemporary radio during commute hours; and watch NCAA basketball tournaments.*

19.64% *also have very high income and are between 25 and 54, with no children. They recycle products, phone radio stations, do fund-raisers, participate in environmental causes, and lift weights. They also order flowers by wire, purchase greeting cards, soft contact lenses, laptop PCs, and light beer. They have asset management accounts, VISA cards, accidental D&D, use financial planners, and have publicly held stock. They read* Money, Consumer Reports, *and* Epicurean *magazines; and listen to album-oriented rock stations.*

The above is a description from one consumer psychographic company; the following is a description from another demographic database provider. Note the similarities:

37.4% *live in suburbs located along the eastern seaboard and in California. They are married, middle-aged professionals at the peak of their lifetime earnings. They are more likely to belong to a health club than a country club. They pursue physical fitness through court and winter sports and golf and are heavy users of vitamins. The proportion of householders between 45 and 64 is 40 percent higher than the national average. They are predominantly white but include foreign-born residents, particularly Asians. They are well educated and have high incomes. They live in neighborhoods with single-family homes with values twice the national average.*

62.6% have achieved success and are homeowners. They drive SUVs and are sports active. They have loans and use credit cards to buy home furnishings, apparel, toys, and travel. The average household is 3.1, most householders are between 35 and 54, and have school age children. They have dual incomes and investments. Almost a third commute across county or state lines to work.

Given the demographics of this ZIP code, think of what other ads or banners a visitor might be shown. These consumers would probably be interested in financial products such as IRAs, travel services, and business supplies, as well as sports equipment and toys. All of these ads and banners would be driven by the combined "keywords," age, and other information available to the Web analyst professional, which as we have discussed can be gleamed from external data sources, as well as internal customer files and a company's own data warehouse.

Customer Service

Data mining can also be used to provide after-sale service, to ensure your customers are satisfied and become long-term loyal clients. An AI technology known as case-based reasoning (CBR), for example, can be used to provide customer service support in order to answer trouble report questions your customer may have on a product they have purchased from you. The basic idea in CBR is really quite simple: *adapt solutions that were used to solve old problems to solve new problems.*

A CBR software engine finds those cases in memory that solved problems similar to the current problem, and adapts the previous solution or solutions to fit the current problem, taking into account any difference between the current and previous situation. Finding relevant cases, such as trouble tickets, involves characterizing the input problem by assigning the appropriate features to it, retrieving the cases from memory with those features, and picking the case or cases that match the input best. CBR software engines are learning systems that use experience to

adapt their behavior to the requirements of a particular situation or a particular user. The detailed behavior of such a system, such as a help desk or customer support site, need not be completely defined in advance by a programmer or engineer.

A CBR system can be trained through the presentation of examples to adapt to the particular cases that are essential for an application, such as a product support help desk. The idea is that as a learning system, a CBR engine is much more flexible and can dynamically react to changing problems. Any new solutions not contained in the index of a CBR engine are added so that, it gradually *learns* these new solutions. So that, for example, if your customers encounter a problem with a printer they recently purchased from you, an interactive area at your website can be provided so that a "trouble ticket" session can be had with a CBR expert engine on your website. In the session shown in Figures 8–9 through 8–11, the CBR engine would prompt the visitor for certain trouble symptoms, in order to narrow down the possible solutions.

Customer Service *(continued)*

CBR is an index-based memory technology able to provide comprehensive knowledge management capabilities, coupled with an intuitive dialogue-based interaction. It allows your customers to solve technical problems as if they were talking with an expert. The technology provides after-sales customer care solutions, which you can use to significantly reduce your support costs and increase customer satisfaction. This type of automated customer support can translate into increased customer loyalty.

The CBR engine provides an extra-added benefit in that it can point out glitches and problems with products and services. Recurring problems that the CBR engine is time and again asked to solve can be incorporated into product enhancements and improvements. Not unlike reverse engineering, gradual product improvements can occur from the CBR process, impacting the help desk and customer service processes the technology supports.

One of the key aspects of a CBR software engine is that if it does not find a solution to a problem, it adds the new solution to its index, thus evolving and improving over time, as other data mining technologies from the field of AI tend to do. Of course, one of the beauties of the Web is that you can gradually accumulate a database of carefully written responses to common problems and gradually become more efficient in providing online customer support.

Figure 8–9
A customer service section in your website provides your clients automated support.

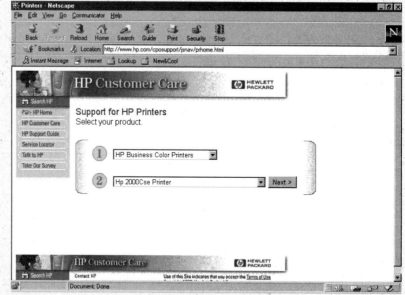

Figure 8–10
Common problems are dealt with quickly and inexpensively.

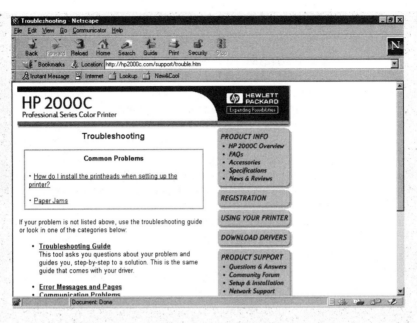

Figure 8–11
A CBR system learns common problems and solutions.

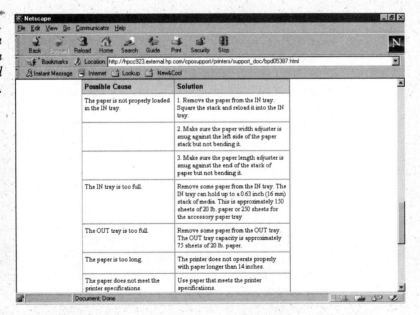

Organize Your Storefront

An electronic commerce strategy should include a clear view on your company's plans on entering and using the electronic marketplace. Since the electronic channel is destined to become the primary vehicle to conduct business in the future, your firm must learn how to attract and engage customers in it. It must plan on how it will process online orders and payments, how it will distribute products and services, and how it will support your online customers, suppliers, and partners in this new business environment. You need to consider how you will transform internal business processes into the requirements imposed by the new types of electronic interactions. As with your datamart and data warehouse, you need to plan ahead and consider what kind of decision support tools you will use to analyze your data and for what end products and processes.

Your company needs to plan and develop a strategy for doing business in a new type of neighborhood: the nonphysical marketplace. Consider how electronic commerce is going to impact your industry, your relationship with your distributors, your partners and customers, and eventually, your business. Consider what business opportunities are being created by electronic commerce in your market sector. Consider how your firm can take advantage of new electronic access to current and new customers and suppliers. What distributors and other intermediaries can be eliminated by electronic commerce? Decide what and how you want to conduct your electronic retailing, how you plan to organize your products in a database for quick browsing by your visitors, how shopping carts will be positioned, how payments will be processed, how you will facilitate one-to-one, one-stop shopping. Above all, how and what visitor information will you be capturing for subsequent data mining in order to foster a stronger relationship with them and a better shopping experience on their return?

To establish stronger relationships, offer special incentives to your online visitors. Offer them your latest product or service developments or some other unique method of benefiting your visitors that cannot be replicated via other retailing channels. How is your company prepared for processing and analyzing more and more customers as you migrate toward electronic retailing? Are you prepared to link your website to your other company databases, such as your customer information file and data warehouse? Consider what benefits such linkage can provide.

Microsoft's Intelligent Cross-Sell

Microsoft is incorporating data mining technology into its electronic-commerce server software, Microsoft's Site Server 3.0 Commerce edition, with a component called Intelligent Cross-Sell. ICS incorporates a data mining algorithm that can be used to analyze the activity of shoppers on a website and automatically adapt the site to that user's preferences. It's the first time Microsoft has made data mining a standard feature in one of its products. The vision for this product is that it will observe visitor patterns and use the information to completely optimize a website and reorganize the appearance of the online store to serve the customer better.

The Intelligent Cross-Sell component is based on historical sales baskets in stores, the browsing behavior of shoppers, and the contents of current shopper baskets.

The ICS module is designed to try and predict the ranking of products in electronic retailer sites most likely to be of interest to shoppers. The data mining component can be installed from a wizard in the NT Site Server. To keep online customers coming back time and time again, Site Server offers personalization and promotion features that help companies create targeted advertising campaigns and promotions according to preferences and past purchase patterns.

If you already have an inventory database, a call site, automated ordering process, financial back end, or lead tracker, consider how you can integrate it with your website. For example, if you are committed already to an IBM, Oracle, or Microsoft database for some of these operations, consider their web retailing products for faster integration within your company. Ensure the database software you plan to implement for your electronic retailing site is compatible with your central company database or data warehouse as well. A discussion with your database administrator over the compatibility benefits versus overall cost for linking your existing company databases and the planned website should take place before selecting your system. Include in your discussion the existing procedures for decision support of your existing legacy systems, such as your datamarts and customer database.

As your company moves toward electronic commerce, how will it change the nature of your products and services? Just as you monitor your marketing efforts and ad campaigns, you likewise need to plan how you will measure the efficiency of your website. Make sure you are prepared to mine your online data as you currently are mining your offline data. If you are not mining your website data, or planning on doing so, you will lose both time and money, especially when retailing your products and services on the Web. In this retailing channel, marketing ads, banners, offers, incentives and other methods of selling, provide you *immediate* feedback. The type of instantaneous feedback—in a digitized format which can be data mined, which is not possible with other media such as mail, radio, or television. Finally, consider how your company plans to manage and measure the evolution of your electronic commerce strategy.

Retailing and Mining

With the rapid advent of electronic commerce, retailing transactions are rapidly migrating to the Web. As the numbers of web transactions continue to increase, electronic retailers will be faced with the same dilemma as physical retailers—to recognize the patterns of opportunity and threats to their survival. As browsers turn into shoppers on the websites, companies will realize that customers can be lost with a mouse click; the ability to decipher purchasing patterns will increasingly become a critical factor to their survival. In the daily ebb and flow of online interactions, patterns are evolving about shopper tendencies, preferences, features, and behavior. By taking advantage of both server and client side programs to monitor, identify, and track the activity of your website visitors, you can gain the ability to capture important customer information for mining.

The primary objective of a data mining analysis of your website is to identify the characteristics of those visitors and customers who make purchases. To mine your website data you will need something much more powerful than the existing server traffic analysis tools. You will require software incorporating multiple pattern-recognition technologies, such as neural networks and machine-learning algorithms. The mining of your website data should provide you with an insight into the identity of your online customers in order that you may improve your relationship with them. Through e-mining, you may discover that a relatively small percentage of your customers account for most of your sites' profits.

The key to electronic retailing revolves around providing premiere services, customized products, and convenience. For the customer, convenience is not having to tell the retailer what it is you want or need in the products and services you are purchasing. For the retailer, this means being able to figure out what the customer wants before they ask. This is accomplished through to use of cookies, CGI forms, a customer database, and data mining analyses. It also involves using the preference information provided by the visitors as they register or make their purchases, and sending targeted reminders via e-mail or providing them special lists of services or products on their return to your site. Data mining is the missing link in providing the connection and relationship between consumers and the Web—a relationship that can be leveraged to serve them in a timely, efficient, and personal manner.

Although some consumers are concerned about privacy and security, many continue to register at websites and fill out surveys and sign up for one-click credit card ordering. The fact is that personal information is more secure online than offline. Consider how many people look at your credit card number when it is taken away by a waiter you have never seen before. In addition, personal preferences of products are already routinely captured every time you use your credit card—to the level that these companies know whether you use room service or not. Supermarket retailers, who encourage you to use their discount cards, already know the number of apples you consume in a week.

Customer preference information about what you like and consume is already out there and is being used to position the right products, services, and messages in front of you. Convenience drives the sales on the Web for individuals who on the average have higher-than-average incomes and education levels and tend to be very busy. On the whole, more and more consumers will come to accept that by providing some personal information, services will improve and products will be better suited to their unique needs. By providing personal preferences, consumers will find that the "right" products, services, and information will flow to them, rather than their having to go out and search for them in the ever-expanding Web.

To demonstrate how data mining can be used to improve online sales, an analysis was performed on a small sample of visitors who had made purchases of computer hardware. The objective is to discover what attributes constitute good prospects for this website. We begin the analysis by selecting our desired output, in this case "total number of sales" (Figure 8–12).

The total number of customer account records for the analysis was 1200, and the total number of errors was 66. The success rate for predicting when more than one sale was going to be made was .943. The following are some of the rules generated from the analysis:

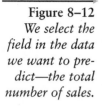

Figure 8–12
We select the field in the data we want to pre-dict—the total number of sales.

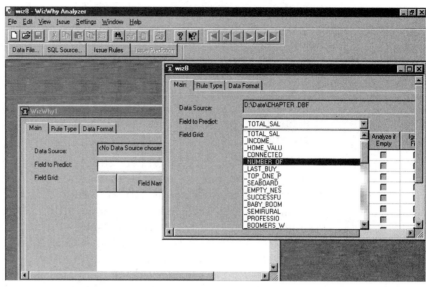

```
If      Number of Children is 2.00
Then    Predicted # of Sales is more than 1.00
        Rule's probability: 1.000
        The rule exists in 391 records.
        Significance Level: Error probability <    0.01
```

This rule, or condition, is indicating that visitors to this website who have more than two children have a very high probability of making more than one purchase. This is a very important pattern since it occurs in nearly one-third of the sample data set: 0.32583. It may indicate the fact that a family will likely buy a PC for the kids along with a second purchase such as a printer for those school reports.

On the other hand another rule was generated, which found that customer income level coupled with the number of children indicated the propensity to make no more than one purchase:

```
If      Customer Income_ is 47,807.00 ± 205.00
and     Number of Children is 1.00
Then    Predicted # of Sales is not more than 1.00
        Rule's probability: 1.000
        The rule exists in 109 records.
        Significance Level: Error probability <    0.1
```

Still another rule found a relationship between the number of children and the search engine used to find this website: it found it limited the number of sales to no more than one:

```
If      Number of Children is 1.00
and     Search Engine_ is Excite
Then    Predicted # of Sales is not more than 1.00
        Rule's probability: 0.908
        The rule exists in 99 records.
        Significance Level: Error probability <    0.1
```

This rule found a relationship between the keyword used and gender and the propensity to buy more than one item:

```
If      KEYWORD_ is desktop
and     Gender is MALE
Then    Predicted # of Sales is more than 2.00
        Rule's probability: 0.930
        The rule exists in 66 records.
        Significance Level: Error probability <    0.1
```

This rule found a relationship between the visitor's age and their ZIP code, which in this case are those of a consumer class classified as Young Frequent Movers with a percentage between 71 and 92 percent:

```
If      AGE_ is 33.00
and     YOUNG_FREQUENT_MOVERS_ZIP is 71.00-92%
Then    Predicted # of Sales is more than 3.00 Rule's probability: 1.000
        The rule exists in 22 records. Significance Level:  Error
        probability <    0.1
```

The Young Frequent Movers consumers are young families with children. Typical of this population is their mobility: they tend to live in the South, with some concentrations in Nevada, New Mexico, and Wyoming. The data mining analysis found that when the visitors come from a ZIP code with these demographics, with a concentration between 71 and 92 percent and their age is 33, then their propensity to purchase multiple products is very, very good.

An analysis such as this can provide executive management and marketing and Internet teams the insight they need to know who their visitors and consumers are. It can tell them what consumer class they represent, their median age, how they found the website, what portals they use, their income level, and a bit about their family makeup. All of this intelligence can assist this retailer in how and where to advertise and where to position links to their website. It can also assist them in knowing what types of incentives they can use to increase their sales, what banners and wording to use. In the end it will help them in improving their relationships with their customers. For example, this website seems to make sales to visitors with children. This fact may indicate that marketing campaigns geared to these consumers, such as discounted kids' software, may be a good strategy.

Electronic Commerce

Despite modest growth, electronic commerce revenue is expected to hit $400 billion by 2002, according to a study by the research firm International Data Corporation. The figure was estimated in a study predicting global Internet and e-commerce growth from 1997 to 2002. An overall increase in Web users around the world will be the main stimulus for the robust electronic commerce revenues expected over the next few years. The IDC predicts that the global number of Web users will jump to 320 million by 2002. During this same period, the percentage of Web users making purchases online will grow to 40 percent by 2002. The same study predicts that actual number of Web users who will purchase goods online will shoot to 128 million in 2002. Another research firm, Forrester Research, Inc., places much higher estimates for e-commerce; they project $3.2 trillion by 2003! These are promising figures for electronic retailers.

Electronic commerce is changing the way all companies do business. Electronic commerce impacts all aspects of retailing: business-to-business as well as business-to-consumers. However, the core of electronic retailing means more than the buying and paying for products and services over the Web. Electronic retailing also ushers in a new method of doing online transactions and market research and data mining. Electronic commerce is pervasive, encompassing such tasks as electronic mail, peer networking, order processing and tracking, customer support, inventory management, and distribution. It impacts the monitoring of manufacturing processes, marketing, and pricing. At the core, however, is the ability to digitize, store, and analyze all aspects of marketing, retailing, delivery, and after-sales servicing.

Products and services sold and purchased over the Web can be both the traditional (physical) type as well as virtual (digital), with the latter being produced and delivered exclusively via this new retailing channel. Retailers of digital products and services have an inherent advantage over traditional ones, in that manufacturing, marketing, ordering, advertising, customer service, and all other aspects of doing business leave a digital trail of transactions which can be mined for insight, competitive intelligence, and targeted marketing. Thus the digital retailer is more responsive to the whims and preferences of his or her customers.

Consumers of physical and digital products also behave differently in this type of networked environment. They are instantly converted into experts and given the powerful ability to window shop the worldwide mall that the Web represents. The efficiency of these online shoppers will over time impact product choices, pricing strategies, and competitive efforts, which will include the aggressive use of data mining strategies, tools, and techniques. Companies and their relationships with their customers will also be affected as transactions migrate to the Web, removing the spatial and temporal limitations of the traditional modes of retailing. New costs, network efficiencies, product customization, relational marketing, models of interaction, and data mining on the Web will evolve. Vertical preference-based territories will supersede the traditional markets, which in the past were bound by national or physical regions.

In an electronic retailing environment, consumers have higher control over product specification, quality, and price because of the shorter delivery cycle from design, production, and delivery. In this type of digital economy, physical products are superseded by digital ones, innovations to product design and delivery are accelerated, and there is a convergence in products, markets, and the infrastructure in which they exist. In this type of marketplace, information becomes a product commodity with value coming from knowledge-based processes such as data mining. It is a fluid and hardwired economy where marketing and retailing processes are interactive and digitized.

Consider Priceline.com, which sells airline tickets over the Web. Priceline.com lets consumers post prices they want to pay for trips, and the first airline to accept that offer gets the business. This business model has been so successful that Priceline.com has patented the process and is moving to include other retail items such as rental cars and hotels. Now consumers have control over the pricing for specific trips they want to take, challenging the retailers to meet the best possible product. Priceline.com has introduced one-to-one interaction between consumer and retailers. For the consumers it means they have control over pricing of the trip they want to purchase. For the retailer the challenge is making the sale while still making a profit. For the electronic retailers it means arriving at the right profit margin and having the ability to do some powerful analyses of sale transactions via data mining.

The same type of data analysis is required by other types of electronic retailers in which price is of paramount importance: online auctioneers. As bids and sales occur on specific retail items, patterns on prices will evolve which lend themselves to predictive modeling via data mining tools and technologies. Because every bid amount can be captured and digitized across such factors as wholesale price, how

OptiMark: The AI Middleman

OptiMark is a new AI electronic retailing model changing the rules in securities trading at the Pacific Stock Exchange. OptiMark lets investors buy or sell in large volumes without telegraphing their moves to other traders, which helps keep the market from moving against them.

OptiMark automates buying and selling at Internet speed and efficiency. The core technology of OptiMark is that of fuzzy logic, which looks for a matching price between what the retailer wants to sell for and what the consumer wants to buy at. The OptiMark system could very well be one of the electronic retailing models of the future.

The basis of fuzzy logic, if you recall, is that of shades of memberships, with nothing being a crisp black or white. Fuzzy logic is a departure from classical two-valued sets and logic, that uses "soft" linguistic (e.g., large, hot, tall) system variables and a continuous range of truth values in the interval [0,1], rather than strict binary (True or False) decisions and assignments. Fuzzy logic is a structured, model-free estimator that approximates a function through linguistic input/output associations. Fuzzy rule-based systems apply these methods to solve many types of "real-world" problems, especially where a system is difficult to model, or where ambiguity or vagueness is common. A typical fuzzy system consists of a rule base, membership functions, and an inference procedure.

OptiMark uses fuzzy logic technology to play the role of the ultimate AI middleman. First, it allows buyers and sellers to express hypothetical trading preferences along a range of prices and volumes. Secondly, it conducts a search of all buyers' and sellers' interests at that instant. Thirdly, in less than two seconds it returns with a mutually satisfying trade at the optimal available price and volume. The OptiMark system allows for complete anonymity, nondisclosure, and the ability to express "degrees of willingness" to trade over a range of prices and volume. Using a supercomputer and fuzzy logic algorithms, OptiMark conducts an exhaustive search of all possible trades in its network, completing up to several billion calculations per stock in one or two seconds. And rather than simply matching buyers and sellers, OptiMark discovers the "sweet spot," or best possible price.

The OptiMark system is currently being used for trading in the Pacific Stock Exchange, but its developers are already looking at consumer markets on the Web for selling everything from airline and stadium tickets to insurance, energy, and diamonds—at real-time trading marts. With the Web as the conduit, consumers using the OptiMark trading system could specify what they'd be willing to pay and let the AI

Figure 8–13 *OptiMark uses a fuzzy logic engine to facilitate buying and selling on the Web*

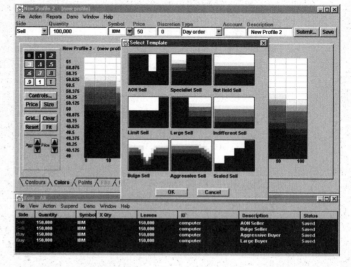

OptiMark: The AI Middleman *(continued)*

middleman find the right deal. The system would seek to match consumers and retailers wherever they can be matched, creating a compromise with the best possible trade.

The OptiMark vision: all trading interests and requests are processed via an AI system instantly and continuously via the Web, making all the mathematically and logically possible matches between consumers and retailers. No consumer would ever pay more than they wanted and retailers would never undercut themselves unnecessarily.

long the bid has been open, what the starting bid was, the number of prior bids made, how many other retail items this bidder has bought, etc., all of these factors can be analyzed. Online bid websites can use such modeling tools as neural networks to model starting prices for their items. Through the strategic use of data mining technology, the electronic auctioneer can edge their profit margins on consumer items they put up on the electronic block for bid.

The Web represents a seamless marketplace combining pattern-recognition technology, telecommunications, and commerce. In this fluid marketplace, structural changes will impact retailing, transforming marketing methods by hardwiring consumer demands directly to product design, manufacturing, quality, performance, and pricing. Competitive strategies will impact entire industries and consumers will drive the changes to the marketplace. Consumers will select content and interact with producers and retailers in the design of their own products. The voluminous nature of digitized transactions in this type of networked environment leads to the prevalent use of data mining software enabling retailers to interact with customers and to create and process digitized products.

Today, money is nothing but a type of data moving from one system to another, with data mining being nothing more than a technique of trying to recognize and anticipate these evolving patterns. Electronic retailing represents a growing exchange of this type of data over the Internet—where consumers and retailers create an evolving process—much as an organism develops a nervous system. In this type of networked marketplace the processing and analysis of these digitized transactions will allow companies to know who their customers are. It will allow them to leverage human-emulating technologies for recognizing and calibrating their customers' loyalty and value.

9

E-Mining

Mining Your Site

E-mining is the iterative process of analyzing the patterns of your online transactions and extracting knowledge about who is buying what, when, and, most importantly, why from your website. It is about extracting previously unknown, actionable intelligence from your website interactions. It is about using pattern-recognition technologies to answer such bottom-line questions as:

- How do I optimize my website inventory and design?
- What strategic partnerships should I be developing?
- How do I increase my share of my customers?
- What cross-selling opportunities do I have?
- Who is visiting and buying at my website?
- What ads and banners should I be using?
- Who are my most profitable customers?
- How do I increase my online sales?

Websites of all sizes are currently experiencing an explosive growth in their capabilities to generate massive amounts of server data. However, few administrators are leveraging data mining technology to transform this web data into the type of competitive intelligence that can improve their e-commerce efforts. E-mining is a powerful method of "recalling" the daily contacts your company's website had with your visitors and customers and "seeing" their behavior. Of course, memory and observation are human functions which data mining tools and techniques, based on AI technologies, are designed to emulate in the processing and analysis of large data sets. This type of inductive data analysis can answer questions you hadn't thought of asking, because it can discover relationships you were not aware existed and in the process uncover hidden patterns in thousands of visitor interactions in your website.

E-mining can assist you in figuring out exactly what customers want and deliver just that. It can assist you in improving your profit margins, in gaining control over your back-end inventory, and in the end, in improving the design and sequencing of your web pages. Most of all it can assist you in keeping your online customer satisfied by allowing you to profile them, through the mapping of their online behavior and demographics. E-mining removes a lot of the guesswork from doing business on the Web. Through the mining of your transactional data you can become more responsive to your online customers, making it hard for them to go elsewhere. Above all, e-mining is a business process with a specific goal: *to extract a competitive insight from your online interactions.*

Beyond providing your customers the right product and service options, e-mining can also guide you in creating a strong relationship with your online clients. If your website provides a product or service that succeeds in your customers' eyes, and you are responsive to their needs again and again, then their investment in your company can create a lasting loyalty, helping you increase your market share of that client. In the following example, we will demonstrate how several data mining techniques can be used to gain this type of insight through an analysis of visitor site behavior, which in turn can provide you a composite profile of who they are.

However, as with all other data mining projects, we must first start with the basics: the data and its various components. For these analyses we start with some basic server log files coupled with some customer information culled from a registration form database. We then merged this website data with our own data warehouse and some external demographic and household database sources. Several data mining analyses will then be performed to demonstrate the different insight and output each of the technologies and tools can provide to web, marketing, and business teams involved in e-commerce. The e-mining process breaks down as follows:

Data Analysis	Technology	Goal
Association	Visualization	Discover product and consumer relations.
Clustering	Self-Organizing Map	Discover cross-selling opportunities.
Segmentation	Decision Tree	Discover key market segments.
Classification	Neural Network	Predict propensity to purchase.

Data Analysis	Technology	Goal
Optimization	Genetic Algorithm	Maximize overall website design.
Mapping	Geographic Information System	View purchasing patterns.
Integration		Combine clustering, segmentation, and classification to gain an overview.

Figure 9–1 illustrates the entire e-mining process.

Figure 9–1
The e-mining process.

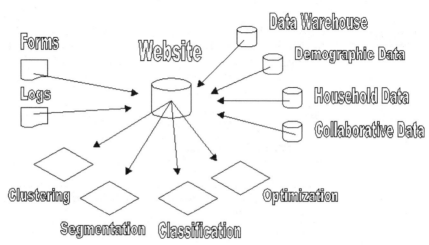

Capturing the Look

At this very moment your future customers are accessing your website. Do you know who they are, where they live, what they make, how they live, what they buy, or what they like? In the preceding chapters we have discussed a rather diverse number of topics, everything from relational marketing, to neural networks and machine-learning algorithms, to cookies and collaborative filtering. Most importantly we have tried to emphasize the glue which binds them all together: *data mining*. In this chapter we put these concepts in practice through a series of examples using several data mining techniques, technologies, and tools.

We begin by reviewing the process involved in capturing visitor and customer data at the server level and then using those components to append additional household and demographic information. The resulting data set is then mined using a variety of tools. The final results of these analyses are varied, although all of them are designed to provide you a new insight into who your website visitors are, where they came from, what they like, and most importantly, how you can gain and retain a relationship with them over their consumer life.

When it comes to your website, the one concept you need to be clear about, especially in a networked environment, is that it's not just a transmitter—more importantly it's a receiver. What it receives is visitor behavior information: Information about who your visitors are, what they are searching for, how and what information, services, and products they want, and which offers they most likely will respond to. Start thinking of your site as a magnifying glass, capable of discovering the features and characteristics of its many visitors and potential new online customers. To gain an insight into the behavior and features of these visitors to your website, multiple techniques can be used to perform such tasks as:

Sequencing: If they buy Product A, will they buy Product C or Product X and when?
Segmentation: What differentiates my most loyal clients from all the others?
Profiling: Who are my most profitable customers and how do I keep them?
Association: What relationship does visitor gender have to sales at my site?
Classification: How do I recognize high propensity to purchase visitors?
Clustering: What attributes describe high return visitors to my site?
Prediction: Who is likely to be my most loyal customer over time?
Optimization: How do I design my site to maximize my online sales?

Be aware that these analyses are not exclusive of each other or need to be done sequentially; your business needs will determine when you execute them. As we have discussed previously, most data mining tools are based on artificial intelligence technologies designed to emulate human perception and learning. Unlike database query programs, web analysis report generators, collaborative filtering software, or statistical packages, data mining tools are different in that they perform their analyses of patterns in an unbiased and autonomous manner; they are driven by the data contained in log files and web-generated databases rather than your personal hypothesis or interpretation of web traffic behavior. Data mining can be used to surmise and simplify the intricacies of thousands of website sessions and visitor patterns in the form of a score, a ratio, a rule, or a decision tree graph.

As with more traditional sources of data mining, the key to predicting the future lies in the analysis of historical transactional data. In the retailing industry, for example, this is usually in the form of bar code data. In the financial services sector, this may be in the analysis of prior loans, credit card accounts, portfolios, CDs, or other types of financial products. In both instances the key to the construction of predictive models starts with the modeling of past transactions and interactions with customers. In the data mining of your website, these building blocks are the components of online transactions captured at the server level. These data components, coupled with a collaborative filtering engine or external demographic and household information, allow you to profile your visitors and potential future customers and to discover their preferences by analyzing their online behavior and purchasing patterns.

A Sample Website Session

1. Website visit generates an entry in the server log file.

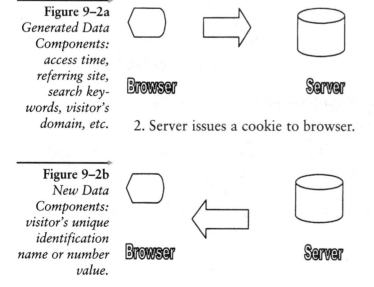

Figure 9–2a
Generated Data Components: access time, referring site, search keywords, visitor's domain, etc.

Browser   Server

2. Server issues a cookie to browser.

Figure 9–2b
New Data Components: visitor's unique identification name or number value.

Browser   Server

3. Website visitor completes a registration form.

Figure 9–2c
*New
Components:
visitor's age,
gender, ZIP
code, etc.*

4. Website data components are matched with other databases.

Figure 9–2d
*New
Components:
visitor's
consumer
behavior, value
of home and
auto, number of
children, etc.*

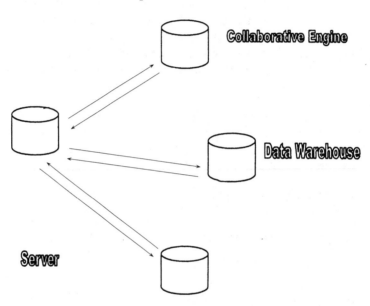

5. Finally, the enriched website data is mined.

Figure 9–2e
*New
Component:
insight about
your visitors/
customers.*

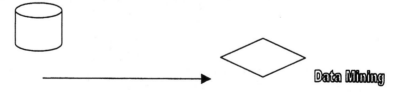

Interactive by Design

Prior to mining your website data, you first need to have a strategy for identifying who your visitors and customers are and what kind of information you want to capture through your logs, cookies, forms, and personalized or collaborative filtering software, or combination thereof. With incremental steps you can begin to assemble a composite of who your website visitors and customers are. This commonly starts with your:

Log Files, to find out where they came from, how they found you, and what they saw.

```
ntt.com.jp - - [08/Jul/1999:16:44:14 -0744] "GET /webminer/index.html
    HTTP/1.0" 200 5898
    "http://search.yahoo.com/bin/search?p=data+mining+websites"
    "Mozilla/3.01 (Macintosh; I; PPC)"
```

Cookies, to find out where they went and who returned.

```
Session_ID=1BABV317MEN
```

Forms, to find out who they are and how to contact them.

```
Joe Blow,34,Male,94502,jblow@doc1.com
```

This then is the *start* of a customer record for data mining:

```
ntt.com.jp - - [08/Jul/1999:16:44:14 -0744] "GET /webminer/index.html
    HTTP/1.0" 200 5898
    "http://search.yahoo.com/bin/search?p=data+mining+websites"
    "Mozilla/3.01 (Macintosh; I; PPC)", Session_ID=1BABV317MEN, Joe
    Blow,34,Male,94502,jblow@doc1.com
```

This comma-delimited string can easily be imported into a database for pre-processing and prepared for merging with other data for subsequent data mining. This is the genesis of the data mining analysis, because the true value of your website data is when it's merged with other personal customer information. True value is obtained once this enriched new data set is mined and "golden ore" is excavated. One of the key strategies is to merge this "stateless" Internet data with household, demographic, and your own company databases and in doing so convert it into a "solid state."

Solid State

The web and the data it generates are often referred to as being "stateless" due to the architectural design of TCP/IP. At times this makes the task of mining this type of server data quite difficult. However, certain data captured at the server level can be linked to lifestyle and consumer information in order to convert this data into a *solid state*. Through the strategic use of site-specific data merged with external data, you will be able to "profile" who your customers are. For example, the preparation of the data may involve the merging of your registration form database with a demographic data set using the ZIP code as the joining link. Or, it may involve merging your log files with a collaborative or personalization service provider using shared cookies, pooled over a network of websites. In both instances, a new and much richer data set will be created, which may be mined in order to discover specific features and behavior about your website visitors.

A common methodology for extracting features from customer information files and data warehouses, especially for highly competitive market sectors such as retailing, financial services, insurance, and telecommunications, involves the enrichment of internal customer data with external demographic and psychographic information. These types of commercial databases are usually based on census information, which has been enhanced by database marketing resellers. These data vendors usually sell information culled from such public record sources as:

- real estate deed recordings
- government publications
- motor vehicle records
- public record files
- tax assessor files
- warranty cards
- questionnaires
- birth records
- white pages
- direct mail
- the census

Detailed demographic information from these diverse sources not only helps you to determine the types of products and services your visitors are most receptive to purchasing, it can also assist you in choosing the types of ads, banners, links, and messages you present to them. E-commerce is highly driven by branding and the method by which a product is marketed. The lifestyle and values of your visitors can influence the overall design of your website and the method by which you market your product and services. Your visitors' demographics may also lead you to forge alliances or partnering with other firms and sites. In fact the level by which your website data can be enhanced by merging it with other information sources varies in relation to the activity which occurs with each visitor or customer. You can only link information to data, which is generated by the interactions that take place in your website:

Visitor Action	Data Captured	Data Can Be Linked To
Browse	Referrer log, cookie	Collaborative filtering, ad network
Register	ZIP, gender, age	Demographic database
Purchase	Customer address	Household file, data warehouse

With every interaction, website visitors provide more information about themselves that can be used to merge it with other sources of lifestyle and consumer preference databases. In addition, with every purchase a retailer can determine a consumer's preferences and rate of consumption. This data gathering starts at a very low level, where only server log information is being captured and where the only matching which can occur is that involving the matching with collaborative filters and the commingling of cookies, such as that of the DoubleClick DART ad network. At the next stage, when a visitor completes a registration form at your website, important information can be captured, such as their ZIP code, which can be used to match it against such demographic databases as those from the Claritas, CACI, and Acxiom systems.

Lastly, when a visitor becomes a customer and actually makes a purchase requiring that a product be mailed to them, their physical address is captured, which can be matched against an assortment of other sources of information. These sources include household information providers like Experian and Polk, which cull consumer information from warranty cards and other public records and consumer sources. All of these third party data providers vary in the amount of detail they can provide about consumers starting from the ZIP code, ZIP+4 and down to the track or single household level. It is recommended that you do some comparison shopping and testing to determine which vendors give you the highest file penetration for your particular customers. Ask for specific statistics on their information content and their percent of file coverage.

Website customer information can also be linked to your own data warehouse enabling you to do some additional data mining analysis, such as a clustering or segmentation analysis. One of the immediate benefits of linking your website and data warehouse is that you can match, compare, and mine the data in order to compare the features of your existing customers with potential new clients. You may uncover some similarities in their regional location, age, gender, or other demographic, income, or lifestyle features. An important side benefit is that you may find a new market segment or a completely new type of customer you did not have before.

The Data Set

As you interact with your visitors and customers you gradually capture more and more information about them. You begin by first finding out how they found your site and what keywords they used to find you, which you capture from your log files. Next, as they complete a form you find out what ZIP code they live in and other important information, such as their preferences and age or gender. Finally, should they make a purchase, you then have their physical address. All of these elements that you have captured can be used to match them against a collaborative engine or demographic and household information files in order to gain an additional understanding of their lifestyle and their preferences. More importantly the combined data set can be mined in order to segment and construct profiles about who they are. This composite can be constructed as a comma-delimited string, which can easily be imported into a series of data mining tools.

The Data Set Breakdown

A single customer record with server data and appended household and demographic values:

```
ntt.com.jp - - [08/Jul/1999:16:44:14 -
   0744] "GET /webminer/index.html
   HTTP/1.0" 200 5898 "http://search.
   yahoo.com/bin/search?p=data+mining+web
   sites" "Mozilla/3.01 (Macintosh; I;
   PPC)", Session_ID=1BABV317MEN, Joe
   Blow,34,Male,94502,jblow@doc1.com,
   4,$81,895, "Luxury",$153,408, $278,
   1, 1998-08-29, 3, 5, 10, 70,0,2,0,0,
   0,0,0,0,0,0,0,0,0,0,0,0,0,0,0,etc.
```

This is the information breakdown of this single customer record sample:

This contains the domain:	ntt.com.jp
The data and time:	[08/Jul/1999:16:44:14 -0744]
The requested page:	"GET /webminer/index.html
The version number:	HTTP/1.0
The status results:	200
The number of bytes sent:	5898"
The referring search engine website:	http://search.yahoo.com
The search keywords:	/bin/search?p=data+mining+websites
The browser used:	"Mozilla/3.01 (Macintosh; I; PPC)"

The cookie ID:	Session_ID =1BABV317MEN	The demographic breakdown by percentage of consumer classes for this visitor's ZIP code:	3,5,10,60,2,20,0,0, 0,0,0,0,0,0,0,0,0,0,0,0, 0,0,0,0,etc.
The visitor name:	Joe Blow		
The visitor's age:	34		
The visitor's gender:	Male		
The visitor's ZIP code:	94502		
The visitor's e-mail address:	jblow@doc1.com		
Number of prior sales:	4		
The visitor's estimated income:	$81,895		
The visitor's type of vehicle:	Luxury		
The visitor's estimated home value:	$153,408		
The total amount of online sales:	$278		
The estimated number of children for this household:	1		
The last date a purchase was made by this visitor:	1998-08-29		

These last fields are the percentages of consumer classes as provided by a demographic database and can be interpreted as: 3 percent of Top One Percent, 5 percent Seaboard Suburbs, 10 percent Empty Nesters, 60 percent Successful Suburbanites, 2 percent Prosperous Baby Boomers, 20 percent Semirural Lifestyle, etc. There are 40 possible consumer classes, each of which is represented as a percentage value.

For purposes of these analyses we used this single data set containing components from log files and a forms database, appended with customer information from a company data warehouse, and household and demographic information:

Attribute	Source	Data
Product	Form Database	"Item_03"
Domain	Log File	"com."
Search Engine	Log File	"yahoo"
Number of Sales	Data Warehouse	4
ZIP	Form Database	94502
Income	Household Database	$81,895
Vehicle Value	Household Database	"Luxury"
Home Value	Household Database	$153,408
Total Sales	Data Warehouse	$278
Number of Children	Household Database	1
Gender	Form Database	M
Age Group	Form Database	45–49
Last Buy Date	Data Warehouse	1998-08-29
Top One Percent ZIP Code	Demographic Database	3
Seaboard Suburbs ZIP Code	Demographic Database	5
Empty Nesters ZIP Code	Demographic Database	10
+37 other ZIP code percentage breakdowns		

Clustering (Association and Sequencing)

In order to discover possible associations and sequencing patterns in the data, the first analysis involves using a data mining tool incorporating a Self-Organizing Map (SOM), also known as a Kohonen neural network. This type of neural network is ideal for exploratory analyses and can be used to search for discrete clusters in the data. A k-nearest neighbor statistical algorithm can also be used to accomplish the same type of task. The purpose for doing this type of clustering analysis on your website data is to discover associations between visitor attributes, such as gender or age and the number of sales they make or the total amount of purchases they have made at your site.

Clustering is a good e-mining start—it is an exploratory method of discovering relationships, which you may find surprising and totally unexpected. An SOM network explores all the data that you have compiled and gradually constructs spatial clusters of data. This type of analysis is commonly done by retailers in "market basket analysis," where they search for patterns or relationships between the sale of certain products for cross-selling and mixed promotion opportunities.

This type of clustering analysis is also known as "unsupervised learning" because the neural network used to do the clustering is not instructed or provided a desired output. A SOM is instead designed to discover—on its own—specific clusters or classes within a given data set. For purposes of this example we will use an SOM to explore and discover clusters within a 10,000-sample data set. Hopefully it will find for us some cross-selling patterns and marketing opportunities. Using a data mining tool with a graphical programming interface we are able to import the comma-separated value (CSV) flat text file and partition a random sample of 50 percent of the records. We connect a table viewer to visually inspect the data and ensure the expected values are correct (Figure 9–3). Next, we connect a "type" node, which ensures the data types are correctly set prior to importing the data into the Kohonen (SOM) modeling node (Figure 9–4). The data mining tool will generate a graphical view from which the user can gradually begin to see the partitioning of the data into clusters identified by different shades of color and density, as shown in Figure 9–5.

After some time (this can vary from a few minutes to a few hours depending on your CPU, the size of the data set, and the complexity of the settings of the network), the SOM will construct some distinct data cubes, or clusters. The parameters for determining the distinctions between these clusters can be set or allowed to default to the software setting. Next, as shown in Figure 9–6, the results of the clus-

Figure 9–3
It is a good practice to visually inspect your data once imported into a data mining tool.

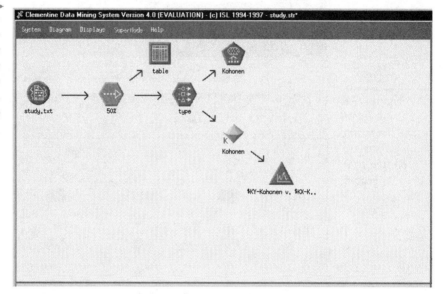

Product	Domain	Search Engine	Number of Sales	Income	Vehicle Value	Home Value	Total Sales	Number of Children	Gender	Age Group
Item_03	com	yahoo	3	45243	Luxury	99336	477	2	M	44-49
Item_00	edu	yahoo	4	45244	Luxury	99337	265	2	M	40-44
Item_03	net	excite	1	45246	Luxury	99337	343	1	M	44-49
Item_04	com	webcrawler	0	24715	Luxury	99352	413	0	M	30-34
Item_03	aol	infoseel	2	56836	Medium	99502	418	2	M	40-44
Item_01	net	yahoo	1	45260	Medium	99502	223	1	M	35-39
Item_02	edu	yahoo	0	50506	Medium	99503	567	0	M	35-39
Item_00	com	yahoo	2	45266	Medium	99504	292	2	M	55-50
Item_00	com	yahoo	1	45263	Medium	99504	390	1	M	44-49
Item_01	com	altavista	1	45275	Medium	99506	144	1	M	40-44

Figure 9–4
A random 50-percent sample of the data is passed through an SOM network to create clusters.

tering analysis can be plotted and the significant distributions of data can be "marked" for further "drilling" by simply marking them on the fly and generating a sub-segment from them for further analysis, using a rule-generating algorithm.

The marked clusters can now be generated as a derived class of the entire database, which represents the five clusters marked in Figure 9–6. This subset of the data is now passed through the rule-generating C5.0 machine-learning algorithm, which is used to extract a set of rules, or conditional statements, that describe the clusters discovered by the Kohonen neural network. This two-step process involves first generating an autonomous analysis of the data (clustering). Next the clusters are diagrammed and areas of interest are identified and

Figure 9–5
Gradually clusters begin to develop from the website data.

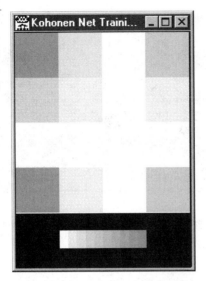

Figure 9–6
The results of the clustering analysis are plotted to a graph.

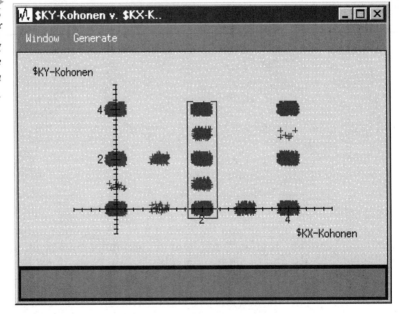

partitioned. These partitioned clusters are then evaluated using an algorithm, which describes the data further via the process of descriptive rules. These are rules that are easily understood by online retailers, webmasters, marketing, and business professionals. Figure 9–7 illustrates the steps taken to partition the data into clusters and link the output to a rule-generating algorithm.

Figure 9–7
*Rules can be
generated to
describe a region
in a cluster.*

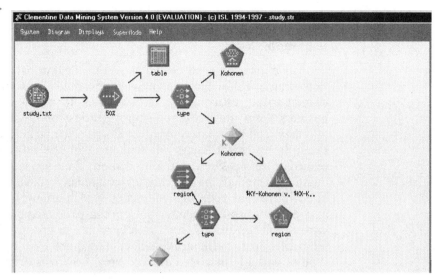

The following is a set of rules generated directly from the clusters created by the Kohonen SOM neural network. The mapping of the clusters represents the high concentration of accounts around region1 (the five-cluster area), which represents website customers who made two purchases:

```
Rule 1.
IF Search Engine excite
AND Domain [aol edu] -> THEN region1 (2 Sale Items)
```

Rule 1 relied solely on log file information to develop an association.

```
Rule 2.
IF Search Engine infoseek
AND Vehicle Value High -> THEN region1 (2 Sale Items)
```

Rule 2 uses components from the log file (the referrer section) and information culled from a household database to find an association with the number of sales.

```
Rule 3.
IF Search Engine webcrawler
AND Vehicle Value Luxury
AND Age Group 30-34 -> THEN region1 (2 Sale Items)
```

```
Rule 4.
IF Domain com
AND Vehicle Value Luxury
AND Age Group 40-44 -> THEN region1 (2 Sale Items)
```

Rules 3 and 4 found associations between log file and household information, and with the visitors' age, which was obtained from the registration form.

This clustering type of analysis is an ideal approach to take when exploring for associations between products and transactional and demographic information. It can reveal to the web marketing and business team undiscovered opportunities for cross- and up-selling, and may lead to the development of specific marketing strategies. For example, in this analysis ads will probably be most cost effective if placed at Infoseek rather than at Yahoo, since visitors from this search engine seemed to have a higher propensity to buy at this website. You'll note that visitors from other search engines, like Webcrawler and Excite, also made multiple purchases at this website, but it was with other conditions, such as a certain age group, vehicle value, or from certain sub-domains. In fact it is quite easy to zero in on any type of variable in your data and view how it is affected by the clus-

Figure 9–8
We select Search Engine as the variable to plot and view.

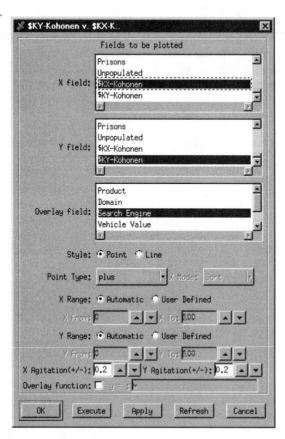

Figure 9–9
The clustering of website visitors based on the search engine they used.

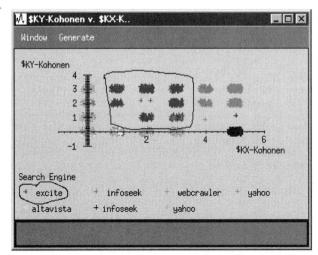

Figure 9–9
The clustering of website visitors based on the search engine they used.

ters uncovered in your data mining analysis. The fields to be plotted can be selected on the fly, as shown in Figures 9–8 and 9–9.

Note in Figures 9–8 and 9–9 that the predominant search engines for this website seem to be Excite and Infoseek. This clustering analysis concentrated on identifying the features of those visitors to this website who made two purchases and what search engine they used. However, similar analyses can be performed to identify other types of associations, such as those customers who have spent more than $50 or $100 in purchases.

Another clustering analysis was performed, this time with the intent of identifying associations between various product lines being sold at this website. For this example, there are five distinct categories of product types: Item_00, Item_01, Item_02, Item_03, Item_04, and Item_05. The graph in Figure 9–10 shows a high concentration on the right, which can be marked again, in order to create a derived data subset, which will be generated as product_region1.

As in the prior analysis, we next derive a subset of the data directly from the clustering graph by simply marking the area we are interested in exploring further, in this case, the clusters on the right. We next connect the derived data set to the rule-generating C5.0 algorithm, which will extract the following rules describing this particular grouping:

```
Domain com

Vehicle Value Luxury

    Product Item_00 (248.0, 1.0) -> product_region1

    Product Item_02
```

```
Working Class =< 0.5 (54.0, 0.796) -> product_region1

Product Item_04
Age Group 44-49 (10.0, 1.0) -> product_region1

Product Item_05
Age Group [21-24 60+](0.0, 1.0) ->product_region1
Age Group 25-29 (3.0, 0.667) -> product_region1
Age Group 35-39 (6.0, 0.833) -> product_region1
Age Group 40-44 (11.0, 1.0) -> product_region1
Age Group 44-49 (17.0, 1.0) -> product_region1
Age Group 30-34
Number of Sales > 1.5(3.0, 1.0) -> product_region1
Age Group 50-54
Number of Children > 1.5
Income =< 40518(2.0, 1.0) -> product_region1
Product Item_01
Number of Sales > 1.5
West Coast Immigrants =< 0.5 (6.0, 1.0) ->
product_region1
```

The most important rule generated from this clustering analysis is the first one at the very top:

```
IF
Visitor's domain is .com
AND Their Vehicle Value is Luxury
THEN Product Item_00 (this occurred with 248 customers with a probability
    of 100%)
```

All of the other rules for the other product items had relatively small number of occurrences. For example, the next highest rule is for product Item_02 with 54 observations and a probability of 0.79

Figure 9–10
Each sale item is represented by a different color in the graph.

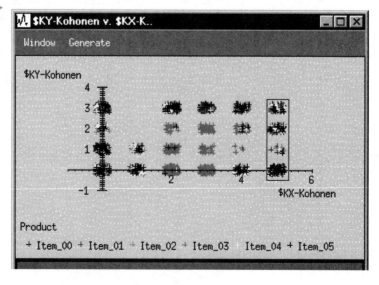

percent. The associations we discovered between the product lines may be of value in the overall design of the website and in the marketing strategies this website may want to take. For example, the analysis found that customers who purchased Item_00 had a stronger propensity to purchase Item_02 than Item_04 or Item_05 and Item_01. One marketing strategy might include notifying via e-mail all customers who have purchased Item_00 about a discounted offer for Item_02. Clustering and segmentation can also be used to do a similar type of analysis on other data components, such as the "keywords" in your log referrer file and those visitor sessions which resulted in actual sales.

Through this process you can select other clusters generated by the SOM network and extract rules to describe other segments which can provide conditions in the form of IF/THEN rules describing the relationships between website visitor attributes and the products you are selling. Through this clustering and rule-generation process you can select other products or dollar ranges to gain an insight about why certain items are purchased by some visitors while not by others. Still another form of clustering involves finding associations in time, which can be used to discover relationships between events. This type of clustering in time is sequencing, and can be used to uncover relationships in how a visitor moves through your website or if they purchase one item what is the probability they will buy another.

Figure 9–11 is a view of multiple product clusters that represent the html pages for various product lines. As you can see, some of the clusters overlap, while others do not. It is important to focus on those

Figure 9–11
A view of the distances between the key clusters uncovered.

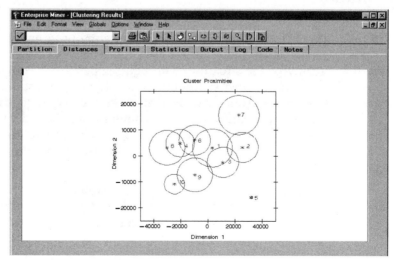

Figure 9–12
Clustering by product Item_01 and total number of sales.

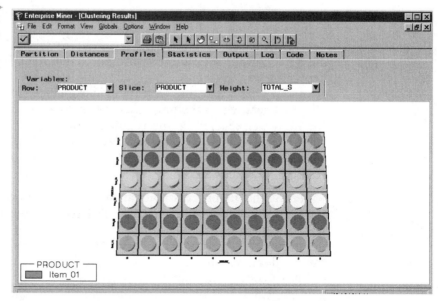

that show some closed distances or overlapping, for they are prime candidates for cross-selling. For example, cluster 4 (Product A) overlaps with cluster 6 (Product M) and cluster 8 (Product Z). This may indicate a sequencing order for navigating through this website, but it may also point out an interest by those visitors who purchased Product A to also purchase Products M and Z. Figure 9–12 is another view of the same data using a different format, by color, with each row being a different product and the height represented by total sales.

Segmentation

As is the case of any database marketing program, website segmentation enables you to adjust your retailing strategies and goals to fit the reality of the situation. Through segmentation you can narrow your focus on distinct sub-populations of your website visitors. Instead of marketing products to all customers and visitors in the same manner, you want to customize your communications and narrow your focus on each subgroup. You also want to market them on the basis of your "relations" with them and focus on providing them the products and services they prefer.

You can segment your website customers into distinct classes, such as High, Average, or Low, and modify your marketing messages accordingly. For High value clients, you want to concentrate on retaining them; as such, your marketing efforts will be to reward them. Conversely, with Low value clients, your strategy might be to educate them on your products and services, thus your marketing efforts will be geared toward informing them. In both instances, segmentation of your web customer data can drive the content of how your e-mail campaigns are geared to these separate and distinct customers: one to reward, the other to inform.

Through the mining of your website data and the discovery of the demographic features of your visitors your goal will most likely be to provide them with the type of information, product, and services they are most likely to want. You can also design your website to be more appealing to your visitors by knowing their lifestyles and the type of activities and products they prefer. For example, a website visited by consumers with kids should probably be designed differently from one visited by single males. One of the benefits of e-commerce is the flexibility to narrow your marketing messages based on lifestyle and preferences of your customers. Through the segmentation process you can begin to provide value-enhanced information and services based on the type of content your customers are most likely to be interested in.

To do this type of customer segmentation a data mining tool incorporating machine-learning and statistical algorithms, such as C5.0, ID3, CART, or CHAID, can be used to generate a graphical decision tree. A decision tree is a method of segmenting a data set on the basis of a desired output, such as the total number of purchases made by visitors. For example, a decision tree can be generated in order to explore the differences in the number of sales by such factors as your customers' income, which you can obtain from such household data providers as Polk or Experian. In the decision tree shown in Figure 9–13, an analysis of 10,000 online sales was conducted in order to discover what demographic and transactional factors impacted these online sales. The dependent variable, that is, the output we are segmenting the data on, is the total number of sales made at this website, which you can see varies between 0 (19.4%), 1 (39.4%), 2 (19.8%), 3–4 (20.6%), and 5+ (0.8%).

In this instance there were no significant differences in the total Number of Sales based on customer income levels. However, a common data mining technique is to sift through various customer attributes until you discover some meaningful "splits" in your data. This sifting process can be done with this type of data mining tool, providing you the flexibility to partition your data in various ways. You can split your data on the basis of the number of children a visitor

Figure 9–13
The propensity to purchase is very evenly distributed along income levels.

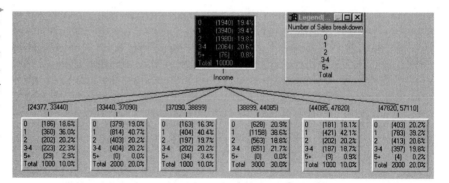

Figure 9–14
The number of children has a decided difference on the total number of sales.

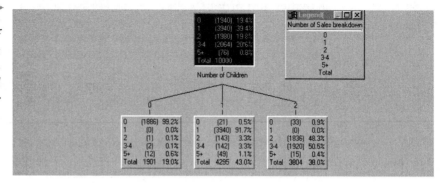

has, the search engine they used, the keywords they entered, their household income, or any other data attributes you have included in your data set. In Figure 9–14, for example, the decision tree revealed an interesting split: the number of children impacts the total number of sales.

Using this drill-down technique and this partitioning type of data mining tool, you can further focus on a particular profitable market segment in your website customer database. For example, in the decision tree in Figure 9–15, we drilled down on those individuals with two children in order to find that those residing in "Twentysomething" consumer class ZIP codes tended to make multiple purchases much more commonly than those of the general population.

Although the distributions to the "Twentysomethings" consumer class is very even there appears to be a higher number of sales of three or four items to visitors from ZIP codes where the demographic breakdown is between 46.2 and 83.9 percent for that consumer class.

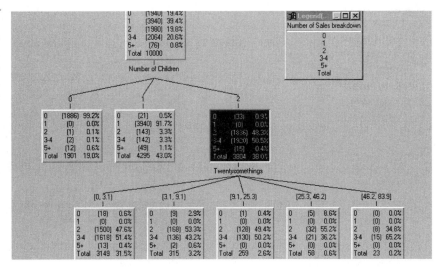

Figure 9–15
*The segmenta-
tion of sales to
the consumer
class "Twenty-
somethings"*

Using this type of segmentation tool we can easily explore and change customer attributes and see the impact and the resulting "splits" on the basis of other factors, such as the value of their cars, as shown in Figure 9–16.

The tree in Figure 9–16 can also be expressed in the form of IF/THEN rules, which can be easily generated in the following format:

RULE_1

IF   Vehicle Value = High, Medium or Unknown

AND Number of Children = 2

THEN

Number of Sales = 0	0.0%	
Number of Sales = 1	0.0%	
Number of Sales = 2	49.8%	<= High Probability
Number of Sales = 3–4	50.2%	<= High Probability
Number of Sales = 5+	0.0%	

These rules, generated via decision tree analyses, can enable web designers, analysts, administrators, and marketing managers to understand and surmise in concise statements thousands of online transactions. It is important to note that multiple rules can be generated for

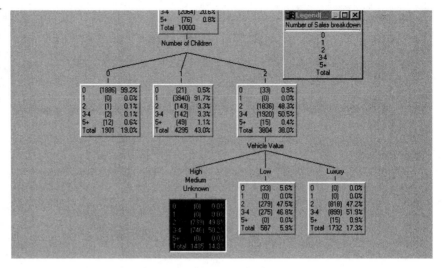

Figure 9–16
*A decision tree
converging on
product sales
based on multi-
ple consumer
attributes.*

each individual page (HTM) in your website, such as the following, which predicts the expected dollar amount in total sales:

IF	Income	=	[24377, 33441)
AND	Search Engine	=	Infoseek
AND	Domain	=	NET
AND	Vehicle Value	=	Luxury
AND	Middle American	=	[0, 10)
AND	Home Value	=	[43023, 70808)
THEN	Total Dollar Sales: Average $342.918		

Note that this type of rule is based on observed behavior consisting of past online transactions, which have been appended with demographic and psychographic information prior to being exposed to the machine-learning algorithm for segmentation. You can construct this type of segmentation analysis on the basis of product lines, specific sale items, or expected dollar sales. You can even do it on a visitor's propensity to click through on a banner, promo, ad, or any other expected online behavior at your website, as shown in Figure 9–17.

The segmentation of your website data can be done on the basis of age group, gender, income levels, etc. Most data mining tools give you the flexibility to partition your data on the basis of what you want to explore, or they can do their analysis on "automatic" mode with the core algorithm doing the statistical testing and partitioning on its own.

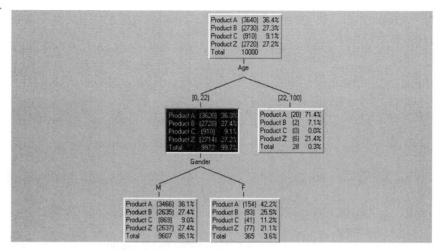

Figure 9–17
This tree is segmenting visitors under their propensities to purchase multiple products.

You should try to keep the decision trees you construct at a fairly high level, that is, avoid "bushy" trees with too many branches. The construction of overly complex trees with more than three or four levels can lead to a problem when you try to apply the results to new unseen data. A common problem is that of *overfitting*. This is a situation in which an overly bushy tree fits the data it is constructed with in such detail that it has a problem in generalizing when exposed to new cases or samples it has not seen before.

The core of the analysis can also be changed at any time. For example, rather than segmenting your data on the basis of projected "Number of Sales," you can change your analysis to mine something like "Total Amount of Sales" so that a dollar amount can be projected for each of your website customers, rather than the total number of online sales. Figures 9–18 and 9–19 illustrate such a segmentation.

In a large e-commerce site with thousands of session records and hundreds of pages, a data mining analysis such as this can assist it in determining the customer and transactional factors impacting its online sales. For example, at what point does it differentiate between "sporadic" and "occasional" website browsers, or "high" and "premium" customers? Does it do it on the basis of two or three purchases over the last six months, or five and eight transactions during the last thirty days? In short, how does it quantify customer loyalty, value, and profitability? Techniques and tools such as these are designed to autonomously segment a data set based on statistically significant intervals and attributes. These types of analysis can "interrogate" the data from a website and uncover market segments in an unbiased

Figure 9–18
*Income levels of
customers can
impact the
amount of dol-
lars they spend
at your website.*

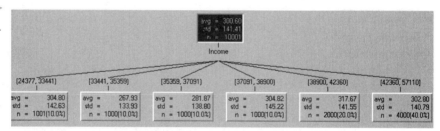

Figure 9–18
*Income levels of
customers can
impact the
amount of dol-
lars they spend
at your website.*

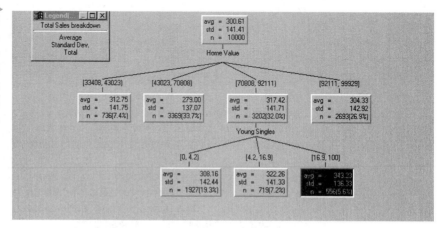

Figure 9–19
*A market seg-
ment is identi-
fied with a
higher than
average Total
Sales amount.*

manner and in the process answer some of the key business questions for the retailer about its visitors and customers.

Data mining technology can identify the factors and number of transactions that differentiate browsers from buyers. As demonstrated, this type of data mining analysis can segment your website customers into various classes, from which you can further calibrate their value and loyalty—enabling you to formulate unique ads and marketing strategies. Segmentation can generate rules that are especially effective not only in discovering patterns in your data but also in describing their findings in the form of concise statements that web, marketing, and business professionals can easily understand and use. The bottom line is that the data can be segmented and viewed via any attribute you desire. For example, in the tree in Figure 9–20 we wanted to view the relationship between Total Sales on the basis of the search engine used by the visitor, so we "forced" the split to get the view shown.

One of the advantages of segmentation is that it can be used to discover the analogous features of your website customers. After all, one of the most sought after "ores" of data mining are customer composites, which in these cases happen to be your profitable and loyal web-

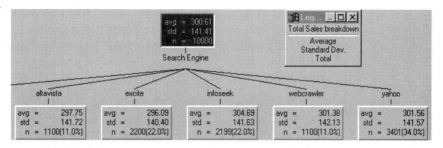

Figure 9–20
Infoseekers tend to spend more at this website than visitors from other search engines.

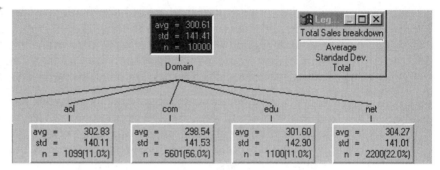

Figure 9–21
Visitors with NET domains tend to average higher sales at this website.

site visitors. Using this type of analysis a key question in your mind should be: who are my most profitable visitors and what are their features? These features may be in the form of their domain, keywords, age, income level, or other demographic attribute. Finally, segmentation of your website customers can be seen as your analysis of their lifetime value (LTV): i.e., the duration of their relationship with your website and the amount of money they have spent during that time (Figure 9–21).

Classification and Prediction

Another objective you may have for data mining your website is to be able to model the behavior of your visitors and assign a predictive score to them. This is commonly accomplished via data mining the patterns of priorly observed customer behavior. For example, credit card fraud detection neural network systems look at historical patterns of fraudulent schemes in order to detect new ones among thousands and even millions of daily transactions. Prediction via neural network modeling is commonly done in the credit card business sector as well as in banking and the insurance industry via such financial service applications as risk-analysis, portfolio management, and loan approval systems. They all use some form of neural network technology in an attempt to maximize their profits and minimize their costs. A similar situation arises with your website, in which you can model past online customer behavior in order to predict or anticipate how a new visitor is likely to behave.

For example, you may like to know whether a new visitor to your website is going to make a high number of purchases or spend a large amount of money. Using a neural network tool we can begin to train a model to recognize and predict the expected purchases for each website customer. To construct a predictive model you need to have a sample of customer sessions of both profitable and unprofitable customers. In this instance a neural network is being trained to recognize the features and actions of profitable customers, what they look like, where they come from, how they search, how long they stay, and more importantly, what they are likely to purchase.

As with a decision tree tool, a neural network looks at all the available attributes in your data in order to converge on a few important clues that communicate how visitors are likely to behave and respond to your marketing efforts and/or products or services. For classification we use a data mining tool incorporating a neural network to construct a model, which begins with a zero accuracy rate, in an attempt to predict the expected amount of purchases visitors are likely to make at a website (Figure 9–22).

At first a neural network cannot distinguish between customers who made purchases and those who did not and thus it cannot predict Total Sales. However, it gradually learns to distinguish between the examples as it recycles positive and negative samples of shoppers. Soon it begins to learn the attributes and behavior of each, and improves its accuracy in predicting Total Sales in just a few minutes of training time (Figure 9–23).

Eventually this neural network tool achieves an accuracy rate of 80 percent in predicting the total number of purchases a visitor is likely to make at this website. This particular tool, like almost all other data mining packages, allows the user to easily "split" their data into training and testing sets. The training data set is used to construct the neural network model, while the testing data set is used to evaluate the accuracy of the model. Once the user is satisfied with the accuracy of the model, C code can be generated from most of these tools which can be used to "score" new visitors to a website so that predictions can be made about their overall propensity to make purchases and their potential profitability.

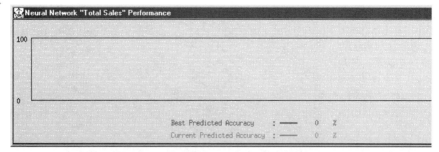

Figure 9–22
A neural network begins with a zero predicted accuracy rate.

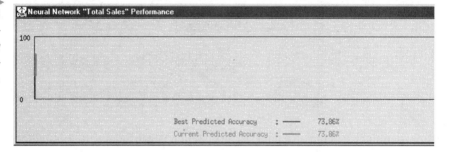

Figure 9–23
A training session generally takes a few minutes to learn.

Once a model has been constructed to predict the potential amount of purchases a visitor is likely to make, the data mining tool can be used to generate a sensitivity analysis report. This report describes the predicted accuracy of the test data set, which the model had not seen during its construction, so we know how accurate we can expect its predictions to be on unseen new visitor transactions. The sensitivity analysis report also prioritizes the customer attributes most important in predicting a visitor's potential amount of purchases. For example, Figure 9–24 shows that for this model the three top factors were the website visitor's vehicle value, their age group, and their membership of the "Upscale Asian" consumer class.

A neural network can be used to predict other factors, such as which ads and banners visitors are likely to click through or how many purchases a visitor is likely to make. One way an electronic retailer can use a predictive model is to score all new visitors on their propensity to purchase its products or services. Having daily scored all its new visitors it can next prioritize by scores these "potential buyers" and make specific offers via e-mail, starting of course with those with the highest probability of becoming loyal customers based on their characteristics.

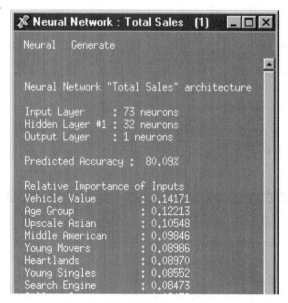

In order to construct a model with a back-propagation neural network you will need to "train" it with as many negative and positive samples as you can get. It is interesting to note that the factors affecting the outcome you are mining can vary in terms of the input variables values and their range. Ensure that your training data set contains examples of all conditions likely to occur once you deploy your model. One robust feature of neural networks is that they are able to perform even with spotty or missing values, so that, for example, if you don't have an input value, such as Age_Group, the model will still try to predict your desired output of Total_Sales.

It is important to construct small models rather than complex ones. For example, you may want to construct a separate model for every product on your website. This way you have the ability to generate propensity-to-purchase scores for every product or service you are selling, rather than a very general behavioral model. Of course for some retailers this will be impossible, such as a bookseller; however, you may want to construct models along product lines, such as a non-fiction model and a fiction model.

Models can be constructed to predict various factors including, for example, one that tries to predict the total number of purchases a new visitor is likely to make from your website. Using the same inputs or data we can construct this second model by simply changing the output from Total Sales to Number of Sales (Figure 9–25).

Figure 9–25
The data is again split and a new neural network model is created.

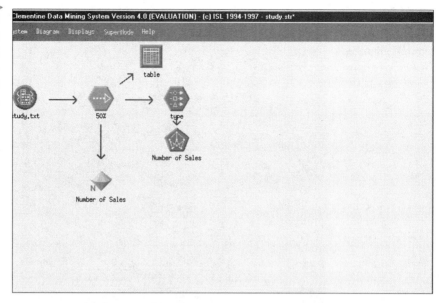

Figure 9–26
This model tends to be more accurate in predicting the number of sales.

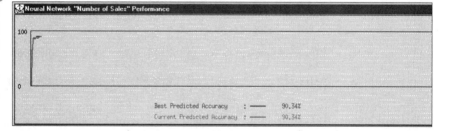

As with the prior model, the neural network starts to learn the patterns of these accounts by comparing those that represent a high number of purchases against those with a low number of sales. Gradually every attribute in the data is evaluated and the model begins to increase its accuracy, eventually becoming able to predict the number of purchases a visitor is likely to make at a rate of 90 percent (Figure 9–26).

Interestingly the factors impacting the prediction of total number of purchases are different from those attributes impacting the predicted total dollar sales. Even though these two models are being used to mine the data from the same website, different factors impact the values we are trying to predict. For example, as shown in Figure 9–27, for this second model the most important factor is not the value of the visitor's auto, but is instead—by far, the number of children a visitor has.

Figure 9–27
Factors impacting the predicted number of purchases at this website.

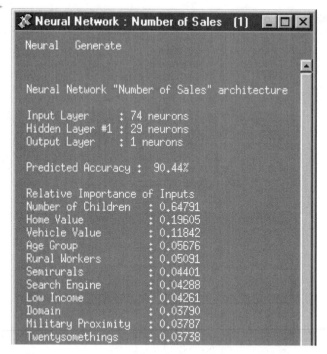

```
Neural Network : Number of Sales   (1)   [_][□][X]

Neural    Generate
                                                     [▲]

Neural Network "Number of Sales" architecture

Input Layer      : 74 neurons
Hidden Layer #1  : 29 neurons
Output Layer     : 1 neurons

Predicted Accuracy :  90.44%

Relative Importance of Inputs
Number of Children   : 0.64791
Home Value           : 0.19605
Vehicle Value        : 0.11842
Age Group            : 0.05676
Rural Workers        : 0.05091
Semirurals           : 0.04401
Search Engine        : 0.04288
Low Income           : 0.04261
Domain               : 0.03790
Military Proximity   : 0.03787
Twentysomethings     : 0.03738
```

Learning Propensity to Purchase Behavior

Through the analysis of your website's transactional server data—which has been commingled with household and demographic information—you can compile a profile of your potential future new clients. You can also begin to model and predict their expected behavior, and for a retailing website, their propensity to make online purchases. The process is based on an analysis of consumer features and behavior, and of course in the leveraging of (AI) technology.

For example, suppose Joe Blow buys "Product Z" and pays $46 via his Visa card.

1. *Observed Behavior.* The number of sales made to this visitor is recorded, as is the dollar amount, which is compiled and merged with other data from your web server, your data warehouse, and external household and demographic information, all of which will become a single string of data to be analyzed with thousands of other customer transactions by a data mining tool.

2. *Neural Network.* The data mining tool incorporating a back-propagation neural network analyzes the entire customer transactional process and the visitor attributes and behavior from a training data set, from which a signature gradually evolves. As the neural network trains itself on the relationships it gradually learns the

patterns distinguishing high sales customers from low or no sale visitors.

3. *Predictive Model.* This is the formula or set of weights written in code which classifies the observed behavior. It is the codified end product of the data mining process, which can be deployed at the server level to predict and classify new website visitors.

4. *New Visitors.* The behavior and attributes of new visitors are matched against the predictive model in order to ascertain their expected profitability and propensity to purchase your products and services. You may want to split your visitors into different classes based on their predicted outcome.

5. *Score.* The predictive model can be used to generate a "score" on each visitor and customer in order to classify and predict their online behavior and overall value to your website. You may want to prioritize your visitors based on their predicted profitability scores and probability to click through on ads or make a purchase of certain products and services.

6. *Marketing Action.* On the basis of the predicted classification or behavioral score of your new visitors you are able to present the appropriate ads, banners, and marketing messages. You may want to also make a targeted e-mail marketing campaign on the basis of what products or services they are likely to want to purchase.

Thus at the conclusion of this process, your marketing decision is: E-mail all the Joe Blow look-alikes about Product Z.

Figure 9–28 *The Store Clerk can be an AI*

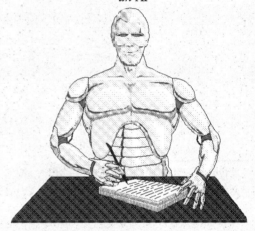

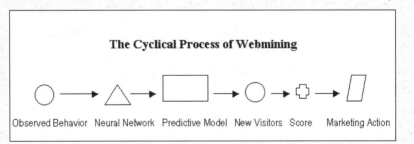

Figure 9–29 *E-mining is the process of evolving to meet your customer's demands and needs.*

The Cyclical Process of Webmining

Observed Behavior   Neural Network   Predictive Model   New Visitors   Score   Marketing Action

Optimization

One of the new ways data mining technologies such as genetic algorithms are being used by some forward-thinking physical retailers is in the overall design of their stores. Some retailers are beginning to use both neural networks and genetic algorithms to assist them in how they design their storefronts, how they arrange their shelves, how they position their products, and how they manage their entire inventory. Used primarily to assist them in this logistic problem, they are also using these technologies to evaluate the consumption patterns of their customers in order to maximize the efficiency of how and what inventory they deliver in order to minimize their overhead. Some retailers in fact are using this combination of nets and GAs to plan their entire stores, from the height of their shelves to the sizing of their parking lots (Figure 9–30).

As we have seen earlier, neural networks are excellent tools for analyzing patterns in data—large amounts of data. When combined with genetic algorithms their effectiveness improves, because GAs are primarily engines of optimization. When used in tandem, the GAs can work at the front end of a neural network to fine tune and recycle a number of architecture settings for a neural network, trying out mul-

Figure 9–30
A genetic algorithm tries thousands of combinations in tuning a neural network.

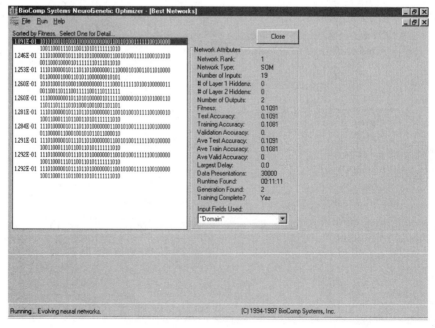

tiple models and gradually converging on the ideal solution to very complex problems.

You need to be aware about a couple of things regarding this data mining approach. First, it is very computationally intensive, meaning that it usually takes time to arrive at an optimum solution. Convergence on a model can often take several hours and, at times, several days. If you'll recall, a GA goes through several processes in its search for a solution including that of reproducing, crossover, and mutation in its random search for the optimum answer to problems. In this instance it is looking for the combined factors which affect the output you are trying to discover, such as "Total Number of Sales" or "Total Amount of Purchases."

This optimization process will recycle, mutate, and evolve until it reaches an optimum result as set by the user or to the tool default settings. As with a physical store, a website can also use a neural network and a genetic algorithm to increase its effectiveness by optimizing its overall design. The optimization of the storefront is done through a process of trial and error in order to improve overall online sales for the website. It is a process of evolutionary retailing. The particular data mining tool shown in Figure 9–31 provides the user with a wide range of instruments with which to observe the process of how the

Figure 9–31
Multiple views of the process of evolutionary retailing.

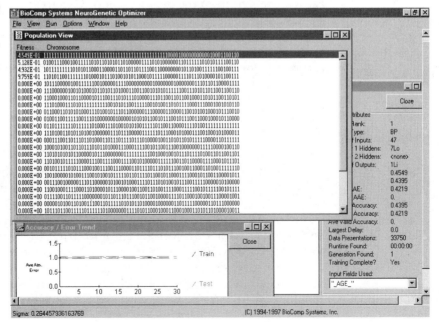

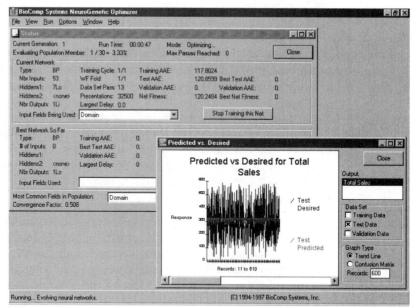

predicted outcome is eventually converged on—through a process of training, testing, and adjustment.

Similar to the optimization problem of physical storefronts, websites can also benefit from the deployment of GAs to assist them in the overall design of their products and services in their virtual stores. Just as physical retailers are using these data mining technologies to assist them in the design of their stores and the management of their inventory, so can web teams use GAs and nets to assist them in mining for the most effective website design for e-commerce. For example, what banners or offers and incentives should be paired up for each of your various product lines? What is the most revenue-effective sequence to arrange your pages? Which offers tend to maximize clickthroughs or ad views, or what product combinations tend to be optimized for improved sales?

As we have said from the beginning of the book, data mining technology is about perception and learning, which is what neural networks and genetic algorithms are designed to emulate. This evolutionary type of computing technologies can assist the designer and administrator of a website in optimizing their virtual storefront to ensure they are getting their biggest bang for their buck. Through the use of these data mining tools you can leverage the pattern recognition capabilities of the network to maximize your marketing and retailing efforts on the Web, with the GA being used to optimize the effectiveness of the network.

Visualization

Having the ability to get close to your data is very important. The ability to use one of the most powerful instruments of perception—the human eye—is critical in the mining of your website data. A data mining analysis using a machine-learning algorithm, which generates a decision tree, can offer you an insightful view of your website customer database. The tree illustrated in Figure 9–33 provides a segmented view of factors affecting the number of sales at this website.

This decision tree in Figure 9–33 revealed several interesting market segments impacting the number of sales at this website. It discovered that the number of children and additional household and demographic variables impacted the number of sales, which averaged 1.6. The most significant rules discovered were as follows:

IF	Number of Children is greater than or equal to 1.2
THEN	Number of Sales was 2.8 for 38% of the sample
IF	Number of Children is greater than or equal to 1.2
AND	Vehicle Value is Luxury or Unknown
THEN	Number of Sales was 2.8 for 23.8% of the sample
IF	Number of Children is greater than or equal to 1.2
AND	Vehicle Value is Luxury or Unknown
AND	Southwestern Families ZIP code is greater than or equal to 40%
THEN	Number of Sales was 3.4% for 0.6% of the sample

Figure 9–33
This view highlights the factors resulting in higher sales levels.

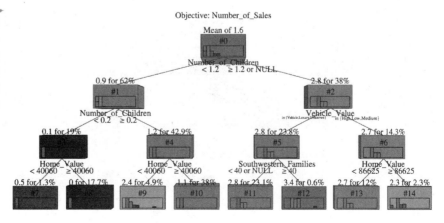

The identified consumer group of Southwestern Families is a small market, 2.8 percent of all households in the United States, with a small share (1.8 percent) of disposable income. They are a young population reflecting an emphasis on children and family. The average family size for this group is 3.8 which is 20 percent higher than the U.S. average. The spending of this consumer group is family-oriented, primarily baby products and children's apparel. Located in urbanized areas and smaller cities, 95 percent of these consumers can be found in New Mexico, Texas, Arizona, Colorado, and California, with the highest concentrations being found in communities like Wharton, TX, San Bernardino, CA, and Santa Rosa, NM.

Views of your website customers can be performed via multiple factors—for example, as shown in Figure 9–34, you can segment your website visitors on the basis of the total number of purchases by the types of products sold. Note that in Figure 9–34 for consumers of certain "Home Essential" products, the average number of purchases is extremely high: 101.7 orders, for a sample size of 4.8 percent of all customers. This three-dimensional decision tree generated from an analysis of a retailer website also found other products in combination which point to consumers with higher than average sales. This particular tool allows for the data to be viewed both in a decision tree format or as in a geographic map format. The map in Figure 9–35 is a view of the same website data displayed according to geographic state.

Figure 9–34
This decision tree is segmenting total sales on the basis of type of products purchased.

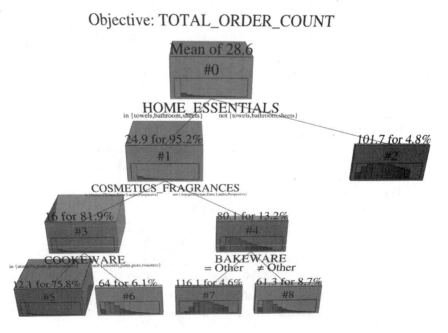

Objective: TOTAL_ORDER_COUNT

Figure 9–35
A map view of a website customer database.

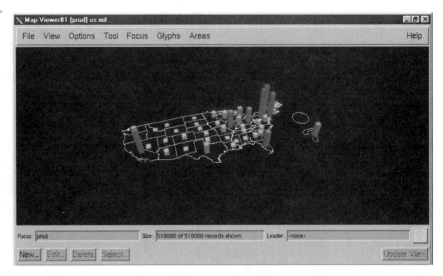

Figure 9–36
The view of the map can be made to follow that of the decision tree.

Using a linking feature within the data mining software, we can view specific market segments discovered via the decision tree component (Figure 9–36). The map in Figure 9–37 reflects a view of *only* those customers who were identified in the decision tree as having a higher than average number of sales, the consumers of HOME ESSENTIAL products. This market segment, identified by the previous decision tree, can be further visually analyzed using this data mining tool. Simply by selecting the state of California, additional insight can be gained at the county level, as shown in Figure 9–38.

Figure 9–37
This is a view of website customers who made a high number of purchases.

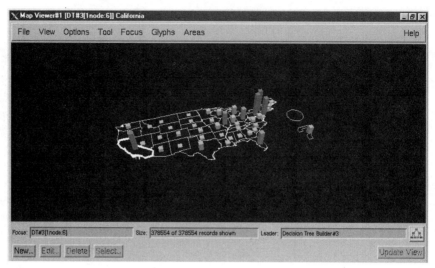

Figure 9–38
This view shows a concentration of customers who made a high number of purchases are mostly located around San Diego.

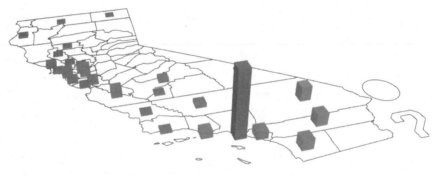

Using this visualization tool we can continue to drill down to the ZIP code level. This illustrates how an analysis using a machine-learning component can be used to segment your website customer data and then view the results not only in a decision tree format but also in a geographical map. This process transforms the segmentation of your stateless data into a geographical format so that you can visually see your online customers on a map. This data mining tool also allows you to drill down further to a more refined level so that you can literally see what states and cities your website visitors are coming from.

The same process can be applied to a cross distribution viewer so that you can do some exploratory analysis by which you compare the total number of purchases against other variables, such as the search engine a visitor used, or the type of product they purchased. This graphical output can be linked to either the decision tree or the geographical map components. Figure 9–39 is a view of the example

Figure 9–39
A view of product types by number of sales and search engine origins.

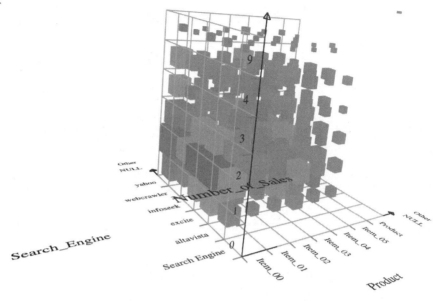

website's customer database by the dimensions of search engine, product lines, and number of sales in a three-dimensional cube.

The darker shading in this three-dimensional viewer represents a higher than average rate of sales. For example, the red cube on the lower left shows a high number of Yahoo! visitors are purchasing Item_00. Using this type of tool also allows the user to click on any object in order to drill down for additional information and to extract the SQL syntax, which generated it. A visual tool such as this allows the Web administrator to interact with the data from their website at a very close level. Visualization coupled with data mining algorithms and geographical mapping features enable the user to discover relations and explore them further in an interactive, three-dimensional environment.

It's an Integrated Iterative Process

Data mining your website is an iterative process very similar to an organic method of learning and adapting. It is a process of observation, mapping, modeling, and codifying your website visitors' online behavior. Every interaction at your website represents an opportunity for your company to learn something about your current customers and potential clients. Data mining software and techniques provide you a biological feed-forward method of observing your visitors'

Figure 9–40
An integrated
e-mining
workspace.

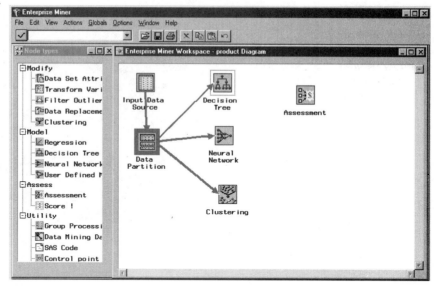

actions and reacting to those actions by providing them what they want in a customized and personalized manner.

As we have seen, there are various formats by which data mining techniques and tools can generate their results and benefits to a retailing website and the teams that are responsible for their maintenance. We have seen the clustering of data with inherent similarities. We have seen decision trees and IF/THEN rules, which can segment your data into significant subsets of website customer types. We have seen modeling via a neural network by itself and coupled with a genetic algorithm for optimization. We have seen how all of these results can be visualized in three-dimensional cubes and geographical maps.

Data mining provides web administrators and designers the ability to extend their customer service capabilities and enhance their perceptions about their markets and visitors. This type of inductive analysis is not like a query reporting statement in which the analyst poses a question. A data mining analysis is more along the lines of using an algorithm or network to discover a hidden signature in the data accumulating in your server. A signature or patterns which can be used to predict future visitor behavior, which a firm can use to:

- Design their website to maximize sales
- Anticipate demand on online inventory
- Attract more advertising to their site
- Predict website purchasing patterns

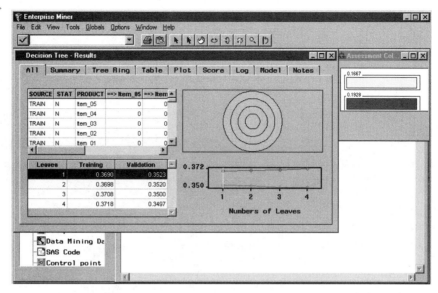

Figure 9–41
Multiple views of a website database.

- View evolving market developments
- Identify new website customers
- Be more competitive online

The e-commerce uses for data mining are many. The technology and techniques can help you discover the attributes of current customers in order to find new visitors who fit that profile. Conversely, data mining can be used to discover unprofitable customers. Data mining can produce an enterprise model that can be used for "what if" scenarios for website market segmentation. The tools can also be used to increase website visitor satisfaction and improve customer service by focusing on your online client relationship. Data mining can also be used to find quality problems, monitor improvements, and measure the success of cross-sales opportunities in your website. For example, Figure 9–41 shows how it is possible to generate a decision tree in order to segment and view the features of your website visitors and their attributes:

Data mining can be used to fine tune market demand with your product supply chain, reducing inventory carrying costs and cyclical inventory ups and downs, on the basis of purchasing patterns discovered through your analysis. It can mean the answer to such questions as:

- What characteristics make a new website visitor more responsive to a special offer?
- What affinity programs will generate the most interest and revenue sales?

- What kinds of online customers generate more transactions and revenue?
- How should your marketing and advertising be timed to maximize yield?

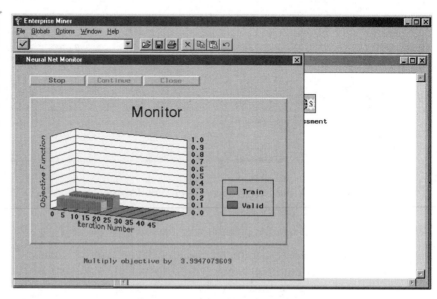

Figure 9–42
You can model on prior behavior in order to anticipate new visitors' propensity to buy.

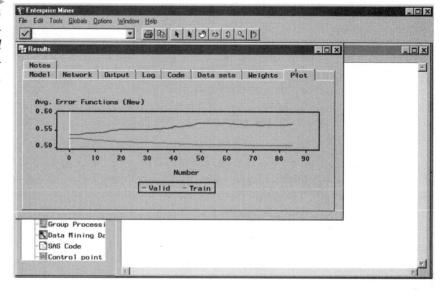

Figure 9–43
You can monitor, adjust, and refine your predictive models.

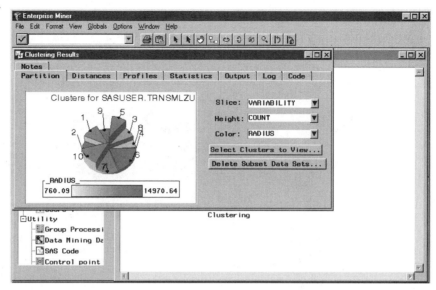

Figure 9–44
Multiple clusters can be extracted and viewed from your data.

A neural network can be used to train on the patterns of past website customers in order to predict the future behavior of new visitors (Figure 9–42).

A key advantage to data mining your website is that it will readily point out patterns of traffic, which will help you to improve the overall design of your site. For large commercial sites the discovery of common paths taken by thousands of visitors may point to some overlooked opportunities for cross-selling of related products. A data set from your website can be split into training, testing, and validating subsets, which can be used to measure and compare the accuracy of your predictive model (Figure 9–43). Using the same data from your website you can create clusters, market segments, and predictive models, as shown in Figure 9–44.

The demographics you discover, whether via ZIP code registration forms or other methods, will also assist you and your design team in the planning of your site. By knowing who visits and makes purchases at your website, you are able to know the type of products and services they are most receptive to purchasing. Figure 9–45 is a graphical view of the multiple clusters discovered from an analysis as they relate to such factors as search engines, gender, age groups, etc.

In the end, the benefits of data mining technologies lie in the ability to integrate all of these processes so that clustering can be linked to segmentation and segmentation be linked to a neural network, say,

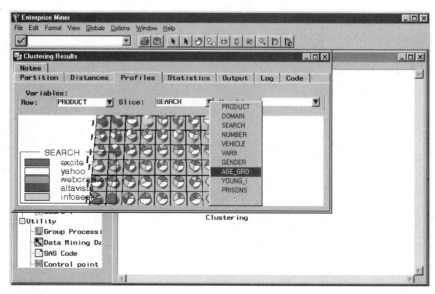

Figure 9–45
Cluster profiles can be viewed and altered on the fly by selecting the various attributes.

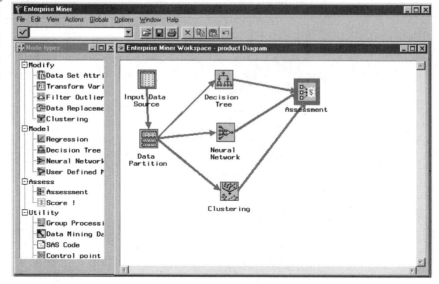

Figure 9–46
Clustering, segmentation, and classification can be done in parallel.

for a specific market segment. Where a neural network can be optimized by a genetic algorithm, with its results ported over to a three-dimensional viewer that can generate a geographic map, and so on. Having the ability to segment, cluster, and search for meaningful patterns in your data can be accomplished in parallel, allowing you to gain as much insight as possible about your website visitors and customers (Figure 9–46).

Data Mining Future

The data mining industry is a relatively new one. Most companies are recent startups. There are over a hundred companies providing an assortment of tools and services, consulting and seminars, and even specialized hardware. Surprisingly, almost all of them are concentrating their efforts exclusively in the area of datamarts and data warehouses; no company is looking at the Web as a potential market for mining (with the possible exception of Aptex, a spin-off from HNC). This is astonishing, in light of the explosive growth of electronic commerce and the Web as a marketing and retailing channel. As websites increasingly becomes the first point of contact between a company and its current and future customers the mining of this transactional data will grow in importance. So far most of these efforts have involved traffic reports, collaborative filtering, and the aggregate pooling of cookies. Few companies are looking at data mining technology to analyze the customer information being generated from their website.

Soon the core data mining technology will begin to be incorporated directly into web server systems in order to directly complement e-commerce activities. There is also considerable emerging research in the fields of databases, machine learning, applied statistics, visualization, and other fields relevant to data mining and knowledge discovery. Despite all the activities both in the market and in R&D laboratories, the field of data mining is still in its infancy. The data mining market is still in the early adoption phase, with most products and vendors still not fully matured. Many of the current commercial products do not yet have the robustness, scalability, and functionality that customers expect from other, more mature technologies. Various data-mining algorithms impose serious restrictions on their application. The process of data mining is far from automated, and is more an art than a science, and therefore quite difficult to use effectively. The field of data mining websites is also an interdisciplinary one, requiring cross-fertilization of several fields. It introduces new complexity involving logs, cookies, HTTP, CGI, and evolving new technologies from the field of electronic commerce like Java. Having said all of that, the benefits of e-mining can be staggering.

The Personalization of Self

In the new web-centric economy, customer expectations and demands will require that websites provide a new unprecedented level of customer service and product customization. It also means that consumers will grow to expect a new level of self-service and total customer control. It will be the age of the consumer who will require services and products via the Web tailor-made to their exact specifications, which demand that the retailer of the future be friendly, responsive, and above all, very knowledgeable about the demands of each of their customers. Data mining can assist the retailer of the future with this type of personalization.

Already we are beginning to see this with the personalization of certain search engine portals. By providing these portals with some personal information about yourself, such as the ZIP code you reside in, they are able to provide you targeted information about your city, state, time zone, latitude, and longitude. These portals can personalize the information you want so that you can customize your data feeds for:

Stock Portfolio	Headline News
Sports Scores	Sports Ticker
Home and Living Links	Favorite Links
Horoscope	Cartoons
Editorial Columns	Lottery
Search the Web	Weather
Sunrise/Sunset	Moon
Tides	TV Listings
Movie Listings	Video Releases
Upcoming Local Events	Reminders
Notepad	Holidays
Religious Holidays	U.S. Holidays/Events
Sports Reminders	Weather Reminders

However, the preference information you provide these portals can be mined and new and unique profiles about your likes and dislikes can be developed in order to personalize what information, ads, banners, links, and offers are presented to you. A future benefit of data mining is that it will filter information and prevent data overload, which is already at this early phase of the Web developing into a major problem. Data mining may well end up serving the function of content sifting and information filtering.

Right Turns, Hand Grenades, and Integrity

Consumer studies have found that 90 percent of the time, upon entering a store like a supermarket, shoppers turn right rather than left or straight. The question today of course is how do they behave in a virtual store, such as your website? Given thousands of visits, how do customers behave when they hit your site: do they go right or left? These are some of the questions technologies such as data mining are attempting to comprehend and synthesize about online customer behavior. This is the type of insight web teams and designers, marketers, and business units need to know about their visitors. They need to know also what these visitors want when they do turn left or right. Data mining in combination with other tools and technologies is all an effort to understand this type of online customer behavior.

Data mining can be compared to a hand grenade: you don't have to be perfect to be on target. As you mine your data you most likely will see incremental improvements, but this is OK. Soon you will see that data mining will provide you a more effective way of targeting your sales and marketing efforts.

Remember that the information that you capture and mine to enhance your relationship with your customers is the most valuable asset your website can have in a digitized networked economy. It provides your website the ability of distinguishing yourself from your competitors. It allows you to know what your customers want and what they like—and as such it gives you the leverage to provide it to them in your services and products. As we said in the beginning of the book, your customer information should be protected and guarded. Your integrity and customer relationship are riding on it.

There is an old joke about two campers who are surprised by a grizzly bear late at night. One of the campers stops to put his shoes on. The other one asks, "What are you doing? You know you can't outrun a bear!" To which the first camper replies, "I don't have to outrun the bear. All I have to do is outrun you!" Sometimes, being better than your competitor is good enough. Use data mining to serve your customers and to provide them the precise, personalized, prompt attention they cannot get anywhere else.

Appendix

Privacy Consortiums, Standards, and Legislation

With recent concerns over the gathering of personal information, privacy consortiums, software standards, and online legislation have evolved in an effort to regulate the Web. The following are a few of these privacy initiatives, which in the capturing and analysis of customer information you should be aware of.

TRUSTe

TRUSTe is a nonprofit web organization founded to promote online privacy. The TRUSTe "trustmark" is an online branded symbol that signifies a website that has made a commitment not to disclose its private practices by posting a privacy statement that is backed by TRUSTe's assurance process. All TRUSTe licensees display the trustmark either on their website with a link to the site's privacy statement or directly on the privacy statement. At a minimum, each privacy statement discloses:

- What type of information your site gathers
- How the information will be used
- Who the information will be shared with (if anyone)

TRUSTe member sites agree to disclose information management practices in privacy statements, display the trustmark, adhere to stated privacy practices, and cooperate with all reviews. The TRUSTe trustmarks labeling system tells the website visitors that the site they are shopping in adheres to a three-tier policy:

No Exchange. A website bearing the TRUSTe No Exchange trustmark lets website visitors know that no personal information is being collected or tracked.

Relational Exchange. This *trustmark* tells visitors that the personal information being collected from the website will be retained exclusively by that site and will not be shared, transferred, or sold to third parties.

Third Party Exchange. This trustmark alerts the Web visitor that this site will exchange their personal information with other parties. A privacy statement informs the visitor on what is being done with their personal information.

Direct Marketing Association

Not surprisingly, the DMA has also opted for self-regulation rather than government intervention. The DMA, however, has taken the initiative to issue guidelines on the collection of personal information alerting marketers to furnish individuals the opportunity to prohibit the disclosure of their personal information. The DMA has also issued specific guidelines regarding the collection of data from and about children, recommending that marketers be sensitive to parents' concerns and consent over the solicitation of children's name, address, and other personal information.

Internet Engineering Task Force

The IETF created a Request for Comments *RFC 2109 State Management Mechanism* in an attempt to set some cookie standards. The proposal sought to establish some industry guidelines on the use and control of how cookies are controlled by future versions of browsers. The proposal wanted to give web browsers the ability to block, reject, and delete cookies. New browser versions from Netscape and Microsoft did not implement the proposal, however.

Platform for Privacy Preference Project

Formed by the World Wide Web Consortium (W3C), the P3P seeks to ensure that there are standard privacy practices and protocols for the collection of personal information. It tries to give web visitors the right to informed consent. The P3P specifications will enable websites to express their privacy practices and users to exercise preferences over those practices. P3P products will allow users to be informed of site practices, to delegate decisions to their computer when possible, and allow users to tailor their relationship to specific sites. P3P gives users the ability to make informed decisions regarding their personal information.

The P3P seeks to establish protocols for providing the user the choice of whether personal data will be passed from the browser to the server and how that information will be used. It is also seeking to establish standards on cookies and the Open Profile Standard (OPS). P3P will support future digital certificate and digital signature capabilities, as they become available. P3P can be incorporated into browsers, servers, or proxy servers that sit between a client and server.

Open Profile Standard

The idea behind the Open Profiling Standard is that user information could be maintained in partitioned files, initially on users' hard disks. Separate areas would hold demographic information, web-specific information (such as e-mail addresses), and information specific to websites, such as content preferences or agent profiling keys. Users would choose which partitions a website's server could look behind and when and if websites could trade information, with the local resident profile as broker. Digital certificates from VeriSign would guarantee the user a measure of security on what was released, and the site a measure of accuracy that apparent users would be who they said they were.

The proposal, backed by more than sixty Internet vendors and the Federal Trade Commission, aims to form a universal system so that Internet users do not have to enter the same information at every site they visit. It calls for personal data such as age, gender, mailing address, hobbies, and phone number to be stored in a personal profile file that resides on the users' hard disks. With the user's permission, that profile can then be accessed by websites, who can tailor content for individuals based on individual preferences.

OPS builds upon two primary pieces of technology: vCards, or electronic business cards, that can pass information across multiple platforms, and digital certificates that ensure that parties on the Web are who they claim to be. The standard also calls for encryption so that personal information can only be viewed by those for whom it's intended. The OPS is a standard protocol proposed by Firefly, Netscape, and VeriSign which seeks to establish a way for the exchange, encryption, and storage of profile information from the browser to the server, the idea being that the website visitor would have final word on what profile information is passed to the requesting server. The OPS initiative proposes the following:

Permission Management: Protection of profile information, with constraints on access and modification.

Standard Attribute: A common standard for profile information, including identification, demographic, numeric, personal, contact, currency, and preference data.

Transaction Logging: Record of exchange of profile information between browser and server.

The personal preset profile would be completed once, much like other browser settings, when the software is installed and would be controlled by the user—passing the profile information to those servers it wants to. This would alleviate the need to complete multiple registration forms at various sites.

Federal Trade Commission

The concerns over privacy in the Web have led to hearings by the FTC involving advocacy groups, online marketers, and legislators. After several hearings on the subject of privacy the FTC recommended the Web industry practice self-regulation rather than having Congress take regulatory action.

European Data Protection Directive

Perhaps the greatest impact on the protection of online privacy for American web visitors and customers may not come from U.S. legislators at all but may instead come about because of a European initiative known as the "European Data Protection Directive." Under this new directive any country that trades personal information with the U.K., France, Germany, Spain, Italy, or any other of the ten

EU states will be required to comply with Europe's new strict standards for privacy protection. Under the directive European citizens are guaranteed:

- the right of have access to their data
- the right to have inaccurate data rectified
- the right to know where the data originated
- the right to recourse against unlawful processing
- the right to withhold permission to use their data in direct marketing campaigns

To enforce the directive, every EU country will have a privacy commissioner, to whom every individual will have the right to appeal should their rights be violated. EU states will not be allowed to send personal information to countries that do not maintain similar privacy laws—including the United States. This could mean that certain personal information gleaned from cookie, log, and CGI or Java registration forms by commercial U.S. websites from European individuals will have to comply with the European directive.

Glossary

Algorithm. A computational process that takes a value or set of values as input and produces an output value.

Analytical model. A process for analyzing a database or table, such as a graph, a decision tree, a neural network, or a cluster. A model may be descriptive or predictive.

Anomalous data. Dirty or spotty data that result from errors or that represent unusual events.

API. Application Program Interface. Some data mining tools provide APIs for using models in scoring new accounts or cases in production systems.

ASCII. Acronym for the American Standard Code for Information Interchange. The American National Standards Institute established this standard set of character codes for the transfer of text between systems.

Association. A rule or condition which describes how often events occur together. For example, if a person buys wine he will also buy cheese 15 percent of the time and French bread 20 percent of the time.

Back-propagation neural network. An architecture network design that uses an input, an output, and a hidden layer. During training, information is propagated back through the network and used to update the connection weights.

C5.0. A machine-learning algorithm that provides a set of rules that you can apply to a new unseen data set to predict which records will have a given outcome, it was developed by J. Ross Quinlan. C5.0 is the successor to the C4.5 and ID3 (Iterative Dichotomiser) algorithms.

CART. Classification and Regression Trees. A statistical algorithm technique used for segmentation of a database. It creates binary trees and segments in two-way splits and was developed by L. Briemen in 1984.

CBR. Case-Based Reasoning. A cyclic process of solving a new problem: when a problem is successfully solved, the experience is retained in order to solve similar problems in the future. When it fails, the reason for the failure is identified and remembered in order to avoid the same mistake in the future.

CHAID. Chi-Square Automatic Interaction Detection. A statistical algorithm that segments a data set by using chi-square tests to create multi-way splits. The chi-square test measures the statistical association between categorical variables. It was developed by J. A. Hartigan in 1975.

Churn. A term for customer attrition or for customers joining a client plan and then quitting within a short period of time.

CGI. Common Gateway Interface. A standard for external gateway programs to interface with a web server. It is executed in real-time and it generally outputs dynamic information from a database query.

Classification. The process of dividing a data set into mutually exclusive groups such that the members of each group are as "close" as possible to one another, and different groups are as "far" as possible, where distance is measured with respect to a variable you are trying to predict.

Clustering. The process of dividing a data set into a heterogeneous population into a number of more homogeneous subgroups or clusters. Unlike classification, clustering does not rely on predefined classes.

Collaborative filtering. A system that supports exploratory searching by providing users with information derived from the experiences of previous users. Collaborative filtering attempts to find information, products, and services of interest to their users, often using some scoring function.

Continuous value. Continuous value data has a value in an interval of real numbers. The value does not have to be an integer and is the opposite of discrete or categorical.

Cookies. Cookies are a standard mechanism that allows a website server to deliver an identification tag to a client browser, request that the client store the tag and, in certain circumstances, return the tag to the server. Cookies allow websites to maintain information on a particular user across HTTP connections.

Data mining. The iterative process of extracting hidden predictive patterns or profiles from large databases, using AI technologies as well as statistical and marketing techniques.

Data validation. The process of ensuring that all values in a database are consistent and correctly recorded.

Data warehouse. A decision support system for storing and delivering massive quantities of data that is nonvolatile, cumulative, integrated, time-variant, and subject oriented, used in support of management's decision-making process.

Decision tree. A graphical representation of the relationships between a dependent variable (output) and a set of independent variables (inputs). Usually in the form of a tree-shaped structure that represents a set of decisions. The tree may be binary or multibranch depending on the algorithm used to segment the data. Each node represents a test of decision.

Dependent variable. The field that you wish to analyze or predict, such as *Will Buy* or *Total Predicted Sales Amount*. The output or desired result from your data mining analysis.

Dimension. In a flat or relational database, each field in a record represents a dimension. In a multidimensional table, a dimension is a set of similar entities. For example, a multidimensional sales database might include the dimensions Product, Time, and City.

Expert system. A program that contains both declarative (facts) and procedural (actions) knowledge to emulate the reasoning processes of human experts in a particular domain.

Exploratory analysis. The use of graphical and descriptive statistical techniques to explore the hidden relationships and structure of a dataset.

Forms. A technique by which a user can input information on a web page and send it to the requesting site. There are innumerable uses for this technique for capturing customer information.

Fuzzy logic. A synonym for continuous logic, a deductive system predicated on the notion that truth is a multi-valued continuous quantity. A mathematical measurement of degree of membership, not necessarily 0 or 1.

Genetic algorithms. A set of techniques that use the concepts of natural evolution—processes such as genetic combination, mutation, and natural selection—to find the optimal solution to a problem.

HTML. Hypertext Markup Language.

HTTP. Hypertext Transfer Protocol. The communications protocol used to transport hypertext over the Internet and over private intranets.

Inductive data analysis. A data mining analysis that provides insights into trends, behaviors, or events that have already occurred and infers generalizations from examples in the data.

Kohonen neural network. See *Self-Organizing Map*.

Linear model. An analytical model that assumes linear relationships in the coefficients of the variables being studied.

Linear regression. A statistical technique used to find the best-fitting linear relationship between a target (dependent) variable and its predictors (independent variables).

Logistic regression. A linear regression that predicts the proportions of a categorical target variable, such as type of customer, in a population.

Machine learning. A branch of AI that deals with the design and application of learning algorithms.

Market basket analysis. A data mining analysis typically done by retailers who treat the purchase of a number of items (the shopping basket) as a single transaction with the intent of finding trends across large numbers of transactions and exploiting unique buying patterns.

MPP. Massively Parallel Processing. A computer configuration that is able to use CPUs simultaneously.

Multidimensional database. A database designed for on-line analytical processing. Structured as a multidimensional hypercube with one axis per dimension.

Nearest neighbor. A technique that classifies each record in a dataset based on a combination of the classes of the k record(s) most similar to it in a historical dataset (where k is greater than or equal to 1). Sometimes called a "k-nearest neighbor" technique.

Neural network. A nonlinear predictive model that learns through training and resembles a biological neural network in structure.

Nonlinear model. An analytical model that does not assume linear relationships in the coefficients of the variables being studied.

OLAP. Online Analytical Processing. Refers to array-oriented database applications that allow users to view, navigate through, manipulate, and analyze multidimensional databases.

Outlier. A data item whose value falls outside the bounds enclosing most of the other corresponding values in the sample. May indicate anomalous data. Should be examined carefully; may be significant.

Overfitting. Opposite of generalization, a tendency to assign importance to random variations in a data set.

Parallel processing. The coordinated use of multiple processors to perform computational tasks. Parallel processing can occur on a multiprocessor computer or on a network of workstations or PCs.

Prediction. A structure and process for predicting the values of specified variables in a dataset. A model resulting from data mining designed to predict future trends, behaviors, or events based on historical data.

Rule generated. The extraction of IF/THEN condition from data based on statistical significance.

Segmentation. The subdivision of a population according to variables which are good discriminators.

Self-organizing map. A neural network architecture that uses unsupervised learning for cluster analysis. It was developed by Teuvo Kohonen and is also known as a Kohonen network.

Sequencing. The analysis of a sequence of measurements made at specified time intervals. Time is usually the dominating dimension of the data.

SMP. Symmetric Multi-Processor. A multiprocessor hardware system design in which memory is shared among the processors.

SQL. Structured Query Language. A standard interactive and programming language for getting information from and updating a database. Although SQL is both an ANSI and an ISO standard, many database products support SQL with proprietary extensions to the standard language.

TCP/IP. Transmission Control Protocol/Internet Protocol. The set of communication protocols used by all computers on the Internet. While TCP/IP has always been used as the standard protocol for UNIX, versions of TCP/IP are now available for all major operating systems.

Visualization. The visual interpretation of complex relationships in multidimensional data.

Index

A

AC2, 106
access logs, 194–195, 210–211
Accrued, 6
Accrue Insight, 58
accuracy, 137–138
ACORN Consumer Classification
System, 157–158, 233–238
Acxiom, 229–232, 230–232
Adaptive Probabilistic Concept
Modeling (APCM), 250
address fields, 94
AdForce, 258–259
advertising
management software, 258–259
predicting clickthroughs of, 328
targeting, 74–77, 252–253
affluent families category, 233–234
agent logs, 194, 198
server configuration for, 199–200
agent software, 130, 277
Agentware Content Server, 250
AID, 103
algorithms. *See also* genetic algorithms (GAs); machine-learning
algorithms
association rule, 14–15
decision tree, 14–15
decision tree generation with,
102–104
defined, 355
determining most appropriate,
104–105
genetic, 107–114
K-nearest neighbor statistical,
310, 358
machine-learning, 63–64, 98–107
pattern recognition in, 83–84
segmentation with, 98–99,
104–105
Alice, 106
analysis
deductive, 84–85

drill up, 42
exploratory, 357
inductive, 85–86
link, 66–67
market basket, 310, 358
regression, 48
sensitivity, 140, 327
traffic, 6, 9
Analyst Notebook, 67
analytical models, 355. *See also*
models/modeling
Andromedia, 6
anomalous data, 355
anthuser field, 196
Apache server configuration,
199–200
APCM (Adaptive Probabilistic
Concept Modeling), 250
API (Application Program
Interface), 355
Applied Geographic Solutions,
228–229
Aptex, 9, 62, 249–250
Aquas Bazaar Analyzer, 58
Aria, 58–59
artificial intelligence (AI), 1, 83–86.
See also neural networks
case-based reasoning, 114–115
deductive analysis in, 84–85
fuzzy logic, 115–117
inductive analysis in, 85–86
OptiMark retailing system, 296
Art Technology Group (ATG),
248–249
ASCII, 355
association, 13–15
defined, 355
in e-mining, 310–318
rules/graphs, 14–15
when to use, 122
Astra, 59
SiteManager, 65
attributes, 45–46, 80
computing entropy of, 99–100

of cookies, 206–207
determining inclusion/exclusion
of, 132–133
discreting, 92–93, 133
identifying, 63–64
auctions, online, 282, 295
Autoclass, 44
Autonomy, 250

B

back-propagation neural networks,
10–11. *See also* neural networks
defined, 355
modeling with, 328–329
for nonlinear data, 144–145
optimizing with genetic algorithms, 334
structure and operation of, 88–90
training, 91–92
BackWeb, 129
balancing data, 97
banners
data collection on, 126
predicting clickthroughs of, 328
baselines, 121–123
Beyond Regression (Werbo), 88
biological-based business, 1
BrainMaker, 98
brand building sites, 124–125
brand loyalty
choice and, 36
measuring, 45–46
Briemen, L., 103
BroadVision One-To-One,
250–252
browsers, differentiating from buyers, 324–325
browsing, personalizing, 9
Business Miner, 106
business-to-business transactions
data providers on, 244
in e-retailing, 44
buttons, 127